Chocolates and Confections

atHome with
THE CULINARY INSTITUTE OF AMERICA

CHOCOLATES AND CONFECTIONS

Peter P. Greweling

THE CULINARY INSTITUTE OF AMERICA

WILEY

JOHN WILEY & SONS, INC.

THE CULINARY INSTITUTE OF AMERICA

President	Dr. Tim Ryan '77
Vice-President, Dean of Culinary Education	Mark Erickson '77
Director of Intellectual Property	Nathalie Fischer
Editorial Project Manager	Lisa Lahey '00
Editorial Assistant	Erin McDowell '09

Published by John Wiley & Sons, Inc., Hoboken, New Jersey

Published simultaneously in Canada

For general information on our other products and services or for technical support, please contact our Customer Care Department within the United States at (800) 762-2974, outside the United States at (317) 572-3993 or fax (317) 572-4002.

Wiley also publishes its books in a variety of electronic formats. Some content that appears in print may not be available in electronic books. For more information about Wiley products, visit our Web site at www.wiley.com.

Design by Vertigo Design NYC

Library of Congress Cataloging-in-Publication Data:

Greweling, Peter P.
  Chocolates and confections at home with the Culinary Institute of America / Peter P. Greweling.
    p. cm.
  Includes index.
  ISBN 978-0-470-18957-3 (cloth)
  1. Chocolate candy. 2. Confectionery. I. Culinary Institute of America. II. Title.
  TX791.G785 2009
  641.8'53—dc22
                        2008046668

Printed in China

10 9 8 7 6 5 4 3 2 1

Contents

Acknowledgments

I owe a debt of gratitude to many for the book you hold in your hands; as with any large undertaking, it is the result of many peoples' labor. As a group, I thank the student body of The Culinary Institute of America for providing me with a constant source of energy and inspiration through their own boundless enthusiasm, curiosity, and creativity. There are a number of students who have worked closely with me on this project, developing and testing recipes and making them accessible to readers. Amanda Meade, Samantha Ramirez, and Russell Karath probably all have enlarged arms from stirring and testing so many batches of fudge and nougat. I thank them for the afternoons they spent in the kitchen with me. Likewise, Joshua Rosen and Lindsay Humleker spent hours working to improve and perfect the recipes in this book. Karys Washburn was a cheerful, reliable, and valuable asset in both recipe development and photography sessions.

In the CIA's publishing department, I thank Lisa Lahey for providing guidance and keeping me on course, even when I was unsure of where I was going. Maggie Wheeler and Nathalie Fischer both played crucial roles in the development of this book.

I thank Ben Fink not only for creating the beautiful photographs in this book, but for making that process look so easy and being such a pleasure to work with.

And I thank my wife, Kyra, for once again abiding my writing process, which invariably involves papers and candies strewn about the house and many hours with my attention and energy focused elsewhere.

Equipment and Ingredients

A confection may loosely be defined as a sweet, but in a stricter sense, a true confection is an item that is preserved by its sugar content—a candy. Confection is also a term for a piece of work that displays excellent skill and craftsmanship, and with good reason. In many regards, confectionery or candy making is the most exacting of any of the culinary arts. That is not to say, however, that it cannot or should not be successfully practiced and enjoyed at home. In fact, like most branches of the culinary arts, the roots of confectionery lie with the homemaker taking the time to make something special for her family. Even in today's world, with time compressed as never before, and most people finding it hard to find time to even cook meals on a regular basis, home confectionery can still be a fun and satisfying pursuit. Whether you are making candies for your family, to serve to guests, or for holiday occasions, a range of home confectionery is within the reach of anyone with a kitchen and a few basic tools and ingredients.

Sugar as a Preservative

When sugar is present in a food in small quantities, that food is very susceptible to spoilage by a number of villains, including fermentation from yeast, bacterial spoilage, and the growth of molds. All of these organisms can, and do, utilize small quantities of sugar as a food source. (In the controlled settings of bread baking and wine or beer making, we take advantage of these organisms to break down sugar into alcohol and carbon dioxide. Without this fermentation there could be no bread, beer, or wine.)

When a food contains sugar in larger quantities, however, it becomes inhospitable for microorganisms. The reason for this lies in the attraction between sugar and water.

Sugars are hygroscopic; that is, they are attracted to water. All living things require water for their life processes. When simple organisms such as fungi or bacteria are put into contact with a food with a very high sugar content, the sugar actually draws water out of the organism, rendering it unable to function and to reproduce. The result is that the food is preserved by the sugar content.

People have realized for thousands of years that sugars could preserve foods. Originally, honey was used as a concentrated source of sugars to preserve fruit. Today's confections are much more likely to utilize cane or beet sugar and corn syrup than honey alone, but the fundamental concept remains the same: A true confection is a food that is preserved by sugar content.

Equipment for Home Candy Making

MAKING CANDIES IN A HOME KITCHEN requires little in the way of special equipment or conditions beyond what is found in any reasonably well-equipped home kitchen. The first concern is the environment itself.

When working with sugar or chocolate, the air temperature and humidity must be within certain guidelines. Ideally, the air temperature should be close to 68°F, and the humidity should be low. If these conditions are not available in your kitchen during certain times of the year, it will affect what types of candy you can make.

- If your kitchen is warm but not humid, you can still make all types of sugar confectionery like brittles, caramels, and fudge, but you will not be able to work with tempered chocolate to make truffles or other dipped centers.

- If you have humidity and heat in your kitchen, you are still able to make crystalline confectionery like fudge and fondants.

- In order to work with chocolate, you will need both a cool temperature of 66° to 70°F and low humidity of less than 50 percent. If necessary, a dehumidifier may be used in the kitchen to reduce humidity. The single most important factor in chocolate use is temperature. Strive for 68°F in the work area for optimum results.

Basic Kitchen Equipment

STOVE Any home stovetop used for food preparation can also be used for candy making. Most cooks prefer a gas flame to electric heat for cooking, but without a doubt, you can be successful with either heat source or with induction burners.

COUNTERS In a professional candy shop, stone surfaces of marble or granite are used to aid in the production of a wide variety of candies from fudge to caramel to hard candy, and to temper chocolate. In this book, I have eliminated the necessity of working on a stone surface, so any countertop with sufficient work space will serve perfectly well.

MICROWAVE OVEN A microwave oven is not mandatory for home candy making, but as with many other areas of culinary arts, it can be a useful time-saver in making candy. A microwave is often used for melting chocolate, softening butter, or warming ingredients for mixing. Anything performed by a microwave oven may also be accomplished using a more traditional method of heating. If you do use a microwave oven, remember that each model is different, so you must adjust the time accordingly.

REFRIGERATOR There are no special requirements for a home candy making refrigerator. In fact, a refrigerator is used very little in home candy production. Most of the finished products do not require, nor should they be subjected to, refrigeration, and chocolate should never be refrigerated in order to force it to set. Refrigeration is reserved mainly for storing perishable ingredients, and occasionally to speed up a nonchocolate setting process.

FOOD PROCESSOR Although not essential, occasionally a food processor will be useful in candy making for pureeing fruit or grinding nuts. Any food processor will work fine for these basic purposes, and nothing special is required of this piece of equipment.

MIXER A powerful mixer can be a great tool to speed and facilitate making candies in your home kitchen. A mixer will be useful to make fudge, aerate marshmallows and nougat, and stir ganache so that it sets properly for truffles. I recommend a 5-quart stand mixer that has separate paddle and whip attachments. Other types of mixers can also be used successfully, but a powerful machine is required for making nougat.

Cookware

SAUCEPANS Saucepans for candy making need not be different from those normally used in your home kitchen. In commercial candy shops, copper kettles are often used, but all of the recipes in this book are based on commonly available cookware. The most frequently used saucepans are 2-quart and 4-quart pans. These will satisfy nearly all of the requirements in this book. All cookware should be nonreactive, such as stainless steel, and should have a heavy bottom so that the heat is distributed evenly.

DOUBLE BOILERS When a double boiler is used in these recipes, a 4-quart saucepan should be filled with 1 inch of water in the bottom, and heated. Once hot, the flame should be lowered to keep the water from boiling. A heatproof bowl should fit snugly onto the saucepan, and should not be significantly larger than the saucepan.

BAKING PANS Two sizes of baking pans are used throughout this book: 9-inch square and 9 × 13 inches. Each of these pans is 2 inches deep, although that much depth is not mandatory. Nonstick pans are helpful, but the techniques used in these recipes make that feature less crucial.

SHEET PANS Either aluminum 12 × 16–inch pans or the more standard 10 × 15–inch pans may be used when sheet pans are used. Sheet pans may be used either with parchment paper or without.

BOWLS Stainless-steel bowls are the preferred mixing containers; a 3-quart size is the most useful for the majority of the recipes in this book. Occasionally, 5- or even 8-quart bowls may be helpful. In lieu of stainless steel, mixing bowls of ceramic, plastic, or glass may be used.

Hand Tools

All of the typical tools normally used in a kitchen are also useful in candy making—wooden spoons, whisks, rolling pins, and other common tools are standard equipment. In addition, the following items are basic essentials.

KNIVES A basic assortment of kitchen knives is all you need for candy making: A chef's knife, paring knife, and serrated slicing knife will be enough for almost any recipe in this book.

PALETTE KNIVES Sometimes called *cake spatulas*, one 8- or 10-inch offset palette knife and one 8- or 10-inch straight palette knife will be useful in a candy making kitchen. A bench scraper will also be useful.

RUBBER OR SILICONE SPATULAS Be sure these are heat resistant; the high temperatures of some of the candy recipes will melt an ordinary rubber spatula.

PASTRY BAGS A pastry bag is used in a few of the recipes. It may be either cloth and reusable, or plastic and disposable.

PARCHMENT PAPER Rolls or sheets of parchment paper will help to keep pans clean, speeding cleanup.

THERMOMETERS A good-quality thermometer for cooking sugar is probably the single most important piece of equipment for home candy making success. There are many good thermometers available, and any of them may work well for you. If I were to recommend one thermometer to use, it would be a good-quality digital thermometer.

> **GLASS TUBE THERMOMETERS** These have a long history of use for candy making and can still be used today. Be certain that these are immersed in the liquid deeply enough to provide an accurate reading. This minimum level will be marked with an arrow on most thermometers. Glass tube thermometers are available for high temperatures used in sugar cooking, and for lower temperatures for chocolate tempering.

> **DIGITAL PROBE THERMOMETERS** These are useful for both sugar cooking and for chocolate use; they are reasonably priced and are usually accurate. Be careful when using probe thermometers for cooking sugar that the probe is not touching the bottom of the saucepan; you will get a reading that is much higher than the actual temperature of the sugar.

> **DIAL THERMOMETERS** These can also be used for sugar cooking. Like the glass tubes, they require immersion up to a minimum level in order to provide an accurate reading.

> **INFRARED OR SURFACE THERMOMETERS** These can be used for maintaining the temperature of a bowl of chocolate, but they should not be used for sugar-cooking applications.

Measuring Tools

SCALE In professional formulas, all measurements are made in weight. Because this book is intended for the home candy maker, the recipes are given in both weight and volumetric measure, so although highly recommended for all ingredients, a scale is not an essential tool for home candy making. In this book, due to the different forms in which chocolate is sold (pistoles, chips, blocks, etc.), all chocolate measurements are expressed in weight. If a scale is not available, use the table on page 24 that lists volume measures for chocolate. A scale will, however, always provide a more accurate and consistent measurement for all ingredients than volumetric measurement, and small household digital scales are readily available for a reasonable cost.

MEASURING CUPS AND SPOONS Because these recipes are intended for home use, they are designed so that the ingredients may be measured in cups, tablespoons, and so on. Dry and liquid measuring cups and standard measuring spoons are all that is required to successfully make the recipes in this book.

Special Equipment

DIPPING FORKS These tools are made explicitly for dipping centers in chocolate. One round fork and one two-prong fork will be enough for most home candy cooks. These are available from candy making supply stores, Web sites, or at larger craft stores. Dipping forks can be improvised by bending back two tines on an inexpensive dinner fork to make a tool with the necessary space between the tines.

TRANSFER SHEETS Transfer sheets are plastic sheets that have been silk-screened with colored cocoa butter to create a pattern, logo, or picture. They are available from candy making specialty Web sites and supply stores and can be found with a wide variety of patterns and themes.

TEMPERING MACHINE Not a necessity, but a very convenient luxury. There are several chocolate tempering machines available intended for home use. They temper small quantities of chocolate and hold it at the correct temperature for use.

TOP ROW FROM LEFT: Bench scraper, ice pick, digital thermometer, and parchment paper.

CENTER ROW FROM LEFT: Dipping forks, palette knives, offset palette knives, and candy thermometer.

BOTTOM ROW FROM LEFT: Wooden spoon, silicone (heat-resistant) spatula, chocolate paddle, and pastry brush.

Ingredients

IF YOU DO ANY BAKING AT HOME, most of the ingredients used in home candy making are probably already in your pantry. Wholesome candy ingredients are familiar foods such as sugars, dairy products, eggs, and nuts. There are a few specialty items that will be helpful in some of the recipes, and these are readily available at candy making stores or from candy making Web sites. The only commonly used ingredient in this book that requires special attention to purchasing is chocolate. In fact, it is worthy of a chapter of its own, so for information on buying chocolate see Chapter 2.

Sweeteners

Sweeteners are the heart of candy making. Not only do they contribute flavor, but they make up the bulk of many candies, and they always help prevent spoilage. There are several sweeteners used in home candy making, each with its own flavor and characteristics.

SUGAR The word *sugar* may apply to any of a variety of sweeteners, but for the purpose of this book, sugar refers to sucrose, the sugar derived from either sugarcane or sugar beets. Sucrose is the gold standard sweetener when it comes to flavor, and is the sweetener to which all others are compared. When sugar is called for in a recipe in this book, use granulated white sugar, which may be measured either by weight or by volume.

Inclusions

The term *inclusions* in candy making refers to any type of added ingredient that is mixed into the mass of candy, and is spread throughout, but remains discrete from the rest of the candy. Inclusions are added to candies in order to provide textural contrast, visual appeal, and flavor complexity. The most important rule about inclusions to use in candy making is that they must be shelf stable. Perishable items such as fresh fruit do not make acceptable inclusions in candy because they would cause spoilage.

The most common inclusions found in candy are nuts, which provide a crisp textural contrast to many favorites such as fudge or soft caramels. Dried fruits are popular for their bright colors and vibrant flavors, and even pieces of other candy, such as peppermint hard candy, or marshmallow, can be used as inclusions in certain instances. Baked goods such as pretzels, crackers, or cookies may be used, but since they will absorb moisture and get soggy if improperly handled, they must only be used in very low moisture candies.

COARSE SUGAR Sugar is also available in a larger crystalline form, known as *coarse sugar* or *sanding sugar*. This type of sugar is used primarily for decoration on finished pieces, as its large crystal size makes it difficult to dissolve in recipes.

SUPERFINE SUGAR At the opposite end of the sugar spectrum from coarse sugar is superfine, or bar, sugar. This sugar is in crystalline form, but the crystals are very small and dissolve easily and quickly.

CONFECTIONERS' SUGAR Sometimes known as *powdered sugar*, confectioners' sugar is sugar that has been ground into a powder. Because pure powdered sugar would pick up moisture from the air and harden very quickly, manufacturers add a small amount of cornstarch to confectioners' sugar. This sugar is commonly available in 6X or 10X—the higher the number, the finer the sugar powder. The 10X confectioners' sugar is used in the recipes in this book.

BROWN SUGAR Brown sugar is fully refined sugar that has had molasses added back to it after refining. It is available in either light brown or dark brown, depending on the grade of the molasses that is added. In this book, only light brown sugar is used in the recipes.

TURBINADO SUGAR Sold under the trade name Sugar in the Raw, turbinado sugar is a less-refined sugar that actually leaves the molasses in the crystals rather than adding it back after the sugar has been refined.

CORN SYRUP Late in the nineteenth century, industry discovered how to convert cornstarch into a sweet syrup. The rest, as they say, is history. Corn syrup has become one of the most widespread food ingredients in America. When corn syrup is used in candy making, its purpose is to help prevent the sugar from crystallizing or graining. When corn syrup is called for in recipes in this book, light corn syrup should be used. Dark corn syrup has had refiner's syrup and caramel color added to it. Glucose syrup, a specialty type of corn syrup available to professionals, is not utilized in this book.

HONEY Honey is a natural sweetener made by honeybees. There are many different types of honey available, varying by the flower from which the bees gathered nectar. They range from very light in body and color, such as acacia honey, to very dark colored and strongly flavored, such as buckwheat honey. Anywhere honey is used in this book, commonly available wildflower or clover honey is the choice unless otherwise stated or desired.

MOLASSES Molasses is the syrup removed from sugar during refining. It is dark in color and rich in flavor. The color and flavor vary depending on the point at which it was removed from the sugar in the refining process. The darkest and strongest flavored molasses is called blackstrap. Golden molasses is slightly lighter in both color and flavor.

ARTIFICIAL SWEETENERS There are a wide variety of nonnutritive sweeteners available today. None of these sweeteners behaves like sugar, and they cannot be substituted for the sweeteners called for in candy making. Making candies with artificial sweeteners is a discipline unto itself and is not discussed in this book.

TOP ROW FROM LEFT: Turbinado sugar, superfine sugar, and sanding sugar.

SECOND ROW FROM LEFT: Dark brown sugar, light brown sugar, and confectioners' sugar.

THIRD ROW FROM LEFT: Light and dark corn syrup.

BOTTOM ROW FROM LEFT: Honey and molasses.

Water

Yes, water is an important ingredient in candy making, and controlling it is a large part of what confectionery is about. It is not an ingredient that requires special attention, though. Any potable tap or bottled water will suffice for making any of the candies in this book.

Dairy Products

Dairy products are an important ingredient in home candy making; ganache, fudge, caramels, and other candies all depend on dairy products for their function and flavor. While it is often best to use fresh dairy products, for some candy making applications a processed or dried product does a better job. Fresh dairy products are always the form to use, however, when making ganache for truffles.

FRESH LIQUID DAIRY PRODUCTS These include everything from skim milk all the way through heavy cream. The only difference between any of the various fresh dairy products is the percentage of fat that they contain. The U.S. Food and Drug Administration (FDA) defines these percentages, and a dairy product must fall within these guidelines in order to use a given legal name. For instance, heavy cream is defined as containing not less than 36 percent fat; if cream contains less fat, it cannot be legally called heavy cream. In the recipes contained in this book, all the cream is heavy cream and all the milk is whole milk unless otherwise stated. Because fresh dairy products are highly perishable, they must be stored properly and used within a short period of time.

PROCESSED DAIRY PRODUCTS These include evaporated milk and sweetened condensed milk, as well as lower fat and nonfat versions of these two products, which may be substituted in the recipes to save calories but will somewhat compromise the texture and flavor of the finished products. Evaporated milk is essentially whole milk that has had much of its water removed in the manufacturing process. Sweetened condensed milk is milk that has had much of its water removed and sugar added. The sugar in sweetened condensed milk makes it more shelf stable than evaporated milk. These products are ideal for making caramels and fudge because they do not require as extensive cooking as fresh dairy products do and are less likely to curdle in the process.

DRIED DAIRY PRODUCTS Dried milk and dried cream are simply the dairy product that has had all its water removed. These are of limited use in home candy making, but they are sometimes added to nougat to add flavor and richness without adding any additional moisture.

BUTTER Butter is an important ingredient in much home candy making; it provides flavor and a delicate, melt-in-the-mouth quality to any candy that contains it. Unsalted butter should always be used whenever possible for the recipes in this book. While salted butter may be substituted by reducing the salt elsewhere in the recipe, unsalted butter is generally a higher quality and is the first choice. Under no circumstances should margarine or shortening be substituted for butter in candy making recipes. To do so would severely diminish the quality of the finished product.

Eggs

Egg whites are often used in home candy making to aerate and lighten confections such as divinity, nougat, and sometimes marshmallows. The rules for using egg whites in candy making are the same as for making meringues: They must contain no fat or yolk, and the bowls and equipment must also be free of fat. Egg whites are available separated from yolks, fresh, frozen, or dried. The recipes in this book utilize only fresh egg whites. Frozen whites often do not respond well to the heat from cooked sugar syrups, and dried egg whites are not really necessary for the home candy maker. Large eggs should be used for the recipes in this book.

Binding Agents

Binding agents are used in making jellies, and occasionally in other products as well. When used in jellies, their primary function is to thicken a flavored syrup to the point that it will hold its shape and can be cut or portioned. There are four main types of binders used in confectionery, and they all are used in recipes in this book.

PECTIN Pectin is the binding agent that thickens jams, jellies, and preserves. It is extracted from fruit, usually apples or citrus rinds. In candy making, it makes a nearly perfect jelly because it has an appealing texture. Pectin requires a high sugar content and an acidic pH in order to bind. Because of these requirements, recipes made using pectin cannot be altered easily and should be followed closely to ensure success. The form of pectin used in the recipes in this book is liquid pectin, which is available in grocery stores under trade names such as Certo and Ball, as well as others.

GELATIN Gelatin is a binding agent made from animal collagen and is used in confectionery to make gummies. Because gelatin has a very chewy texture, it is not used as a binding agent unless that elasticity is desired. Gelatin must be hydrated in cold water before use, and it should not be exposed to high heat, which will damage the gelatin. In this book, gelatin is used as an aerator for marshmallows.

AGAR Derived from sea vegetables, agar is a binding agent more commonly used in Asian cuisines than in American kitchens. It is, nonetheless, a useful binding agent. The fruit that is used to make agar jellies does not need to be cooked, so agar jellies have a fresh flavor. The texture of agar jellies tends to be short; they crumble in the mouth rather than being chewy and elastic like gelatin. Agar is available in different forms. For candy making, however, powdered agar is best to use. Agar is available from online candy making suppliers (see Resources, page 289).

STARCH Cornstarch is a binder used when making the traditional candy Turkish Delight. While commercial candy makers use modified starch for jelly making, the Turkish Delight on page 185 honors tradition and uses ordinary cornstarch, as has been done for hundreds of years.

Nuts

Many varieties and forms of nuts are used in candy making. From whole toasted hazelnuts or pistachios to chopped pecans or sliced almonds to peanut butter or praline paste, nuts are indeed an important part of candy making. Nuts may be inclusions, like walnuts in maple fudge; they may make a filling, like Peanut Butter Bombs; or they may be made into dough, like marzipan.

The most important consideration in selecting nuts for use in candies is freshness. The oil in nuts is especially prone to rancidity, which will result in off-flavors. Nuts should be stored airtight in the refrigerator or freezer to protect from rancidity. Always taste nuts before using them to ensure that they are not rancid.

The most important factor in using nuts is toasting. Almost without exception, the flavor of nuts improves with proper toasting (see page 50 for instructions on toasting nuts). This is often done in the oven prior to use, and sometimes during cooking, as when making peanut brittle.

Nut Pastes

Nut pastes are a convenient way to use nuts in candy making when a smooth texture is the desired result. There are several forms of nut pastes, from peanut butter to more specialized forms such as praline paste. All nut pastes are high in oil and have the potential for rancidity, so they should always be used while fresh. Be sure to store all nut pastes properly, away from heat, light, and exposure to oxygen.

ALMOND PASTE Almond paste contains almonds, sugar, and bitter almond oil for fragrance. It is both sweet and aromatic and is used in making marzipan.

PRALINE PASTE Praline paste is a mixture of equal parts caramelized sugar and toasted hazelnuts that have been ground to a smooth paste.

NUT BUTTERS Nut butters are often made using cashews or almonds. These can be found in health food stores and generally contain no sugar. Some nut butters contain oil in addition to the oil in the nuts, but the best ones are made without any adjunct oil added.

PEANUT BUTTER The standard commercial smooth peanut butter is used in the recipes in this book.

Fruits

While fresh fruit is not suitable for use as an inclusion in candies due to its high water content and short shelf life, fruit that has been naturally preserved, either by drying or candying, is well suited to use in home confectionery.

DRIED FRUIT Excellent quality dried fruit is commonly available and makes a fine addition to many candies. The most frequently available dried fruits are cherries, cranberries, apricots, pears, and strawberries, in addition to the more traditional dates, currants, and raisins. All of these make interesting combinations with chocolate and nuts and have appropriate shelf lives, so they are well suited to candy making. Dried fruits are usually chopped and mixed into candy as an inclusion.

CLOCKWISE FROM TOP LEFT: Toasted peanuts, sliced toasted almonds, toasted cashews, dried apricots, dried cherries, dried cranberries, and pistachios.

CENTER TOP: Cocoa nibs.

CENTER BOTTOM: Dried pears.

CANDIED FRUIT To a great extent, candied fruit has fallen out of favor with American tastes. This is probably due mainly to the poor-quality candied fruit that floods the market. If, however, high-quality candied fruit is sought out, it can be a superb addition to the ingredients in a home candy maker's pantry.

Other Inclusions

Any type of dry, shelf-stable food product can be used in candy making as an inclusion. This includes seeds such as sesame or pumpkin, breakfast cereals, crackers, and other snack foods that can be mixed into a candy to provide flavor and textural contrast. The only caution is to avoid mixing dry ingredients that may absorb moisture, such as cereals, into a candy containing moisture, such as ganache. To do so is to invite not only a poor texture, but spoilage as well.

Flavoring Agents

Without various flavoring agents, most candy would have little to offer other than sweetness. Flavoring agents come in many forms, and the recipes in this book utilize nearly all of them.

SALT While salt is a minor ingredient in confectionery, it is an important flavor-enhancing agent. While there is arguably no difference in flavor between forms of salt, because of different crystal size there is a difference in the amount contained in a teaspoonful. The recipes in this book are designed to use common supermarket granulated salt crystals, either iodized or not. Using volumetric measures, such as teaspoons, with a different form of salt, such as kosher salt, will alter the flavor of the finished recipe.

VANILLA BEANS Vanilla beans are really the queen of all flavors. Rich, heady, and aromatic, they impart true vanilla flavor as no extract can. When they are called for in a recipe, vanilla beans should be split lengthwise down the entire length of the bean and the seeds scraped out of the bean. Both the seeds and the pod are then boiled with the batch in order to extract maximum flavor. The pods are removed after steeping, and the seeds remain in the batch. The pods may be rinsed, dried, and stored in a container of sugar to imbue the sugar with vanilla fragrance.

If cost is not an object, vanilla beans can be used anywhere vanilla extract is used, but they are generally reserved for candies where the rich vanilla flavor is the star. If vanilla beans are unavailable, substitute 1 tablespoon of extract for half a bean, but do not expect precisely the same flavor results.

EXTRACTS Extracts are flavors made by steeping the flavoring agent in an alcohol-based liquid, creating a strongly flavored liquid that can then be added to foods. The most common example is, of course, vanilla extract. Some flavors labeled as extracts may also contain manufactured flavors (see below); if you wish to avoid these, you must read the labels carefully.

MANUFACTURED FLAVORS This category includes artificial and so-called natural flavors. These are different from extracts and are very convenient to use. Manufactured flavors should generally be reserved for situations in which other flavors will not work well, such as in hard candy. These flavors vary considerably in strength, so following the manufacturer's advice on how much to use is wise. It is always easier to add more than to take it out once it has been added.

SPICES The spice cabinet should not be overlooked when flavoring homemade candies. Ground spices may be added to candies at various stages of cooking to provide unique flavors. Spices tend to burn at high temperatures, so they are not well suited to hard candies or brittles but are very much at home in ganache or fudge. Cream of tartar, sold as a spice, is actually an acidic ingredient added to aid in whipping egg whites and to help prevent the crystallization of sugar.

LIQUORS Because liquors are highly flavored liquids, they make ideal additions to candies and can provide unique flavors. They are often used to flavor ganache and can be added to many other types of candy as well. Because alcohol is highly flammable, always exercise care in handling, and never add it directly to a hot pan on the stovetop.

COFFEE AND TEA Coffee and tea are often used in candy making. Not only are they widely available and convenient to use, but they both go beautifully with chocolate. When tea is used in the recipes in this book, it is steeped into liquid and then strained. When coffee is used, it may be steeped or it may be made by reconstituting a small amount of instant coffee.

Coloring Agents

Home candy makers should generally avoid artificial colors; the color of most candies should come naturally from the foods contained in them. In some cases, however, use of food-approved colors is expected. Hard candies without color would still taste as good but would lose much of their visual appeal. Coloring agents should be added a little at a time until the desired shade is achieved.

Unless used for coloring chocolate, all of the coloring agents in this book are water based and may be in either paste or liquid form. For coloring chocolate, fat-based colors or colored cocoa butter must be used.

Specialty Ingredients

There are a few specialty ingredients used for some of the recipes in this book. All of these are available from the online retailers listed in the Resources (see page 289).

COCONUT FAT When used, coconut fat should be deodorized if possible. Nondeodorized coconut fat will impart a strong coconut smell to any recipe.

WAFER PAPER Wafer paper is used to seal and protect nougat such as Nougat Torrone (page 183). It is made from a starch, such as potato starch, and is white in color and neutral in flavor. When used on a nougat, it is intended to be consumed with the nougat as part of the candy.

INVERTASE Invertase is a naturally occurring enzyme extracted from yeast. It can be added to centers after cooking to cause them to soften after they are coated with chocolate. Cherry Cordials (page 147) are made using invertase in order to liquefy the center.

FRAPPE Frappe is a stable light foam that is mixed into certain types of candy to make them lighter in color and texture. Frappe in candy making is used the same way meringue is used in baking, and with good reason: Frappe is little more than a meringue that is very high in sugar. While it is not beyond the scope of home confectioners to make their own frappe, when frappe is required in a recipe in this book, commercially available marshmallow creme is used.

2

Chocolate, Chocolate, Chocolate!

Chocolate! Nearly everyone loves it, some folks claim to be addicted to it, and you almost never meet anyone who will flat-out tell you that they do not like chocolate. (If they do, they might be lying.) It can be a simple and delightful childhood treat, a rich and sophisticated adult taste experience, or a truly indulgent dessert. It may be light, sweet, and creamy; it can be dark, intense, and bitter. Like wine, chocolate may have decidedly fruity, earthy, spicy, or roasted flavor notes. It can be enjoyed on its own or made into a confection with many different fillings. But what exactly is chocolate?

Chocolate is fundamentally the seeds of the tree *Theobroma cacao*, roasted and finely ground. Of course, this is something of an understatement, akin to saying that wine is grape juice gone bad; there is much that goes into the agriculture, fermentation, and processing that makes chocolate the exquisite luxury that it is. These seeds are more commonly known as *cocoa beans*, and when they are fermented and roasted they develop the smell and flavor that we associate with chocolate. Cocoa beans have had a long history of importance to human beings; from the very beginning they have been considered special, valuable, and even sacred. (The name of the tree, *Theobroma*, means "food of the gods.") They have been used in rituals and ceremonies, reserved for the wealthy and powerful, and have even been used as currency.

What Is Chocolate Made Of?

COCOA BEANS contain a very high percentage of fat known as *cocoa butter*. When the beans are ground, that fat is released, giving chocolate its fluidity when melted and its rich mouthfeel. Most chocolate contains additional cocoa butter and some sugar. Milk solids are another ingredient frequently added to chocolate.

Flavors Added to Chocolate

Vanilla is the flavor most commonly added to chocolate. The best chocolate uses whole vanilla, while lesser chocolates use vanillin, a component of vanilla. Vanilla adds to the complexity of chocolate and provides balance for the bitter cacao. It is legally permissible for makers to add many other flavors to chocolate, as long as they are declared on the label and as long as they do not imitate the flavor of chocolate. All of the chocolate flavor in chocolate must come from the cocoa beans.

What About Lecithin?

Nearly every chocolate contains lecithin. Lecithin is added to chocolate to improve its viscosity; it makes chocolate more fluid when melted. Lecithin is present in chocolate in

TOP: Cocoa butter, milk powder, cocoa nibs, and sugar.

BOTTOM: Chopped dark chocolate, milk chocolate pistoles, and chopped white chocolate.

extremely small quantities, far less than 1 percent of the total ingredients. Adding more lecithin will not make the chocolate thinner. The lecithin in chocolate is extracted from soy, although generally even people with soy allergies have no problem tolerating the lecithin in chocolate.

Chocolate and Health

There is more and more published information suggesting that chocolate is not such a guilty pleasure after all; it may actually be good for you. It is a refreshing change to learn that something that we love may be healthy! As is often the case, there is both some truth and some exaggeration in these claims, and our perception may also be influenced by our tendency to hear what we want to hear.

The main documented health claim about chocolate is that it is high in antioxidants called *flavonoids*. These compounds help protect the body from many ills including heart disease and cancer, as well as helping to maintain good cardiovascular health in general. There is no question that cocoa beans are extraordinarily high in these antioxidants. That is the good news. The side of the story that does not receive quite as much publicity is that many of these compounds are unfortunately destroyed in processing. Every step involved in making chocolate from cocoa beans diminishes the quantity of flavonoids

present. But without fermentation, roasting, and the rest of the process, cocoa beans are quite unpalatable.

So what is the truth about chocolate and health? There is no question that chocolate contains flavonoids, but in order to maximize the benefits, you should consume high-percentage (see page 22) dark chocolate. Milk solids present in milk chocolate inhibit the absorption of flavonoids, and white chocolate, containing no cacao solids, has no flavonoid benefit. Of course, all chocolate has a high fat content, which will add significant calories to the diet, so it would be irresponsible to recommend eating a large quantity of chocolate daily in order to improve your health.

Health alone is probably not a reason to consume chocolate, but who needs an excuse? It is great to realize that eating a moderate amount of good-quality dark chocolate may be beneficial to not only your outlook, but to your body as well.

Cacao and Cocoa

The word *cocoa* is almost certainly an Anglicization of the word *cacao* (ka-KOW). Today, however, the words are not used interchangeably. The word cacao refers to the tree *Theobroma cacao* and the raw products that come directly from that tree, such as its fruit, the cacao pod, and the beans prior to fermentation. Once the beans have been fermented, the name of the products changes to cocoa, such as cocoa beans, cocoa powder, or cocoa butter. Fermentation is vital for development of chocolate flavor, but who knew that it could rearrange letter *A*s and *O*s?

FROM TOP: Dutch-process cocoa powder, natural-process cocoa powder, and cocoa butter.

FROM LEFT TO RIGHT: Cocoa beans, cocoa nibs, cocoa powder, and cocoa butter.

Legal Standards

THE FDA HAS standards of identity, or definitions, of what may and may not be in various forms of chocolate for it to be called chocolate. These standards protect the consumer and the chocolate trade in general by assuring some uniformity in products, so that if you buy bittersweet chocolate, you know you will always get a product with the same general ingredients.

CHOCOLATE LIQUOR Also known as unsweetened chocolate, chocolate liquor is pure ground cocoa beans with no sugar added. It may not contain milk solids and has a cocoa butter content of 50 to 60 percent. Chocolate liquor is added to candies such as fudge when a strong chocolate flavor is desired without any added sweetness.

SEMISWEET OR BITTERSWEET CHOCOLATE Although it sounds as though there should be a difference between the two, the government makes no distinction between semisweet and bittersweet chocolate. This chocolate is a minimum of 35 percent cacao, although most are much higher than this. If made in America, it may contain up to 12 percent milk solids and may contain butterfat, although the best-quality dark chocolate doesn't have either of these ingredients. This chocolate is the most frequently used type in the recipes of this book.

SWEET CHOCOLATE Sweet chocolate contains 15 to 34 percent cacao. It also may contain traces of milk solids and butterfat.

MILK CHOCOLATE Milk chocolate made in America may contain as little as 10 percent cacao, meaning that up to 90 percent of the chocolate can legally be sugar and milk solids. Good-quality milk chocolate typically contains in excess of 30 percent cacao, and many go much higher.

WHITE CHOCOLATE Until 2004, white chocolate was not a legally allowable name for labeling. The FDA now accepts the name, and the product is required to contain at least 20 percent cocoa butter, 14 percent milk solids, 3.5 percent butterfat, and not more than 55 percent sugar.

COCOA BUTTER Cocoa butter is the pure fat pressed from cocoa beans. It is usually deodorized and so is quite neutral in flavor and aroma.

COCOA POWDER Cocoa powder is essentially chocolate liquor that has had most of the cocoa butter pressed out of it. It is available with varying fat contents; some cocoa powder contains in excess of 22 percent fat, others less than 10 percent. Cocoa powder is often Dutch processed to neutralize some of its acidity (see "What Is Dutch Process?" on page 22).

COMPOUND COATING Compound coating is a chocolate substitute containing little or no cocoa butter. Coating does not require as meticulous tempering as chocolate does, but it does not have the excellent snap and mouthfeel of chocolate. Compound coating can be used for coating in any of the recipes in this book if you do not want to temper chocolate, but it should never be used in place of chocolate and mixed into a recipe.

What Is Dutch Process?

Dutch processing is the act of treating cacao with an alkali. It is an optional step in manufacturing chocolate or cocoa powder and must be declared on the label when it is employed. It is common practice to Dutch process cocoa powder, but few chocolates are Dutch processed. Dutch processing neutralizes acids in the cacao, and therefore will help to minimize sour flavors if they are present. Dutch processing also makes the cacao much darker in color. It does not truly contribute to chocolate flavor. Many purists insist that Dutch processing's sole purpose is to cover up inferior ingredients, but most of the best chocolate manufacturers produce Dutch-process cocoa powder. As with all things taste related, it is a subjective judgment.

Couverture

Couverture is a term used for European chocolates meeting standards similar to the American requirements for chocolate; they must be at least 35 percent cacao, and at least 31 percent fat. This term has no legal standing in American manufacturing.

Chocolate Labels

IT IS BECOMING A COMMON PRACTICE for chocolate labels to do more than just market and protect the product; labels also provide information about the chocolate inside. Fueling this trend is the public's increased level of awareness of and interest in chocolate. Let's look at what information might be on a label and what it really means to us.

PERCENTAGE Stating the cacao percentage is becoming nearly standard practice for chocolate sold on all levels, including supermarket chocolate bars. The number listed on a label tells you the total percentage of the chocolate liquor plus the cocoa butter in the chocolate. Another way to look at the percentage is the total of all ingredients that came from the cacao tree. If it came from *Theobroma cacao*, it is included in the stated percentage. If it did not come from the cacao tree, it is not included in the percentage.

In the case of dark chocolate, essentially the entire remainder of the chocolate is sugar. This means that if a chocolate is 60 percent cacao, it is 40 percent sugar. The higher the cacao percentage is in dark chocolate, the less sweet the chocolate will be because it contains less sugar. This is really the only thing that the percentage tells you about the chocolate. It does not indicate anything about quality or viscosity when melted; it only tells you about relative sweetness. Tasting many different chocolates can give you a general idea of what percentage you prefer, but there are enormous differences among different chocolates; even among those with the same percentage. In the case of milk chocolate, the percentage is still cacao versus total ingredients, but the remainder is a combination of milk solids and sugar, so the percentage tells you even less about the product within. In all cases, let your palate be your guide; taste and get to know each chocolate individually.

ORIGIN More and more manufacturers are indicating the geographic origin of the cocoa beans on their labels. This can be useful information once you have a general knowledge of what to expect of beans from different locations, as the chocolate will have the flavors common to that area. It can be interesting and fun to compare the flavor nuances of chocolates made from beans of different origins.

> **SINGLE ORIGIN OR BLENDED?** Until the early 1990s, all commercially available chocolate was made using a blend of beans from various parts of the world. Since then, there has been an emergence of single-origin chocolates, made of beans from one geographical location or even one plantation. Today, nearly every manufacturer makes single-origin chocolates, and they are available from just about any locale where cacao is grown. Venezuela, Madagascar, Cuba, Ecuador, Malaysia, Ghana—you name the location and if cacao is grown there, there is probably a single-origin chocolate featuring those beans. Marketers tout single-origin chocolates as being the finest quality simply because they are single origin. Others say that using a blend of beans from different parts of the world creates a more complex and satisfying chocolate. Regardless of your viewpoint, it is interesting to learn the flavor nuances that cocoa beans from each locale have to offer by tasting and comparing chocolate from different origins.

VARIETY Occasionally, chocolate labels will reveal the variety of cocoa bean used in making the chocolate. There are essentially three varieties of cocoa bean cultivated: Criollo, Forastero, and Trinitario. As a broad generalization, Criollo beans are considered the best quality and are most likely to be advertised on a label for that reason. However, excellent chocolate can be, and is, made from any or all varieties of cocoa bean.

What Chocolate Should I Use for the Recipes in This Book?

THERE ARE MANY EXCELLENT CHOCOLATES available from either local or online sources. For optimum results from the recipes in this book, the dark chocolate should be around 60 percent cacao and in the vicinity of 35 percent cocoa butter. If it is a European chocolate, it will be called couverture; if it is American, it will be bittersweet or semisweet chocolate. Milk chocolate should be close to 35 percent cacao, and white chocolate should be close to 30 percent cocoa butter. Other chocolates will work, but the results will be different.

No matter what, do not yield to the temptation to go the grocery store and buy a bag of chocolate chips to use in these recipes. Chocolate chips for baking are not well refined in manufacturing. They are usually very low in cocoa butter, so they are very thick when melted. Your results will suffer if you use chocolate chips meant for baking in the recipes in this book.

Great chocolate is not made only in Europe; there are fine chocolate makers all over the world. Excellent-quality American chocolate manufacturers include Guittard and Scharffen Berger, and their products are some of the best available anywhere. Excellent European makers that are fairly easy to find include Callebaut, Lindt, Valrhona, and Chocovic. The Venezuelan manufacturer El Rey makes superb chocolate. Higher-end grocery stores now frequently carry these chocolates in sizes suitable for home use.

The form the chocolate is in when you buy it makes little difference other than handling techniques. Pistoles are convenient small pieces that do not require chopping for melting or making ganache. Some blocks are marked in increments of weight, which is convenient if you do not use a scale (see Measuring Chocolate below), but ultimately, the form is not nearly as important as flavor and viscosity.

CLOCKWISE FROM TOP LEFT: white chocolate block, dark chocolate chips, chopped dark chocolate, milk chocolate pistoles, and dark chocolate block.

Measuring Chocolate

ALTHOUGH THE INGREDIENTS in all of the recipes in this book are listed with both weight and volume measurements, the chocolate should always be measured only by weight. This is because there simply is not an accurate way to measure chocolate other than weight. A cup of finely chopped chocolate weighs more than coarsely chopped chocolate, which weighs differently from pistoles or from melted chocolate. If you do not have a scale and need to make approximations of weight, the following conversions will help you.

WEIGHT	APPROXIMATE VOLUME
6 oz	1 cup pistoles or chopped chocolate, ½-inch pieces
8 oz	1⅓ cups pistoles or chopped chocolate, ½-inch pieces
10 oz	1 cup melted chocolate
8 oz	¾ cup melted chocolate

Tasting Chocolate

NO LABEL CAN TELL YOU what a chocolate tastes like. All the consumer information in the world and carefully crafted written descriptions will not tell you how a chocolate tastes. Ultimately, chocolate is a food, and the best evaluation of it is how it tastes to you. The range of flavor nuances created by different makers using different beans and different techniques is remarkable. Chocolate tasting has even become cause for a social event. You don't need to be a super taster, or even a wine connoisseur, to taste and appreciate the different flavors found in chocolate and learn which ones most appeal to you. With a little practice and some comparison, you will soon be able to pick out many of the nuances that can be found in good-quality chocolate.

"Tasting chocolate" is a bit of a misnomer. It really is evaluating chocolate, and it involves all of the senses.

- Look at the chocolate. It should be shiny and uniform in color and texture. Any signs of bloom (see "Bloom," page 26) mean that the chocolate has not been stored properly. This chocolate may still be viable for use but cannot be used to evaluate a chocolate fairly.

- The sound and the feel are next: Break a piece of the chocolate; it should have a decided snap to it, both in sound and in a crisp, brittle feel.

- Now to taste: Put a piece of the chocolate in your mouth and allow it to melt for a few moments. Note how quickly or slowly it begins to melt.

- Chew the chocolate a few times, but leave the pieces on your tongue. This will release both the cocoa butter and the volatile flavor compounds. You will likely notice that the flavor changes during the tasting. Chocolates might start with a cocoa flavor note, and then might exhibit spiciness, followed by a fruity finish; or perhaps you will detect floral notes or acidity. There are no wrong answers, and practicing is fun.

- As the chocolate melts, take note of its smoothness. Good-quality chocolate should exhibit no graininess whatsoever; it should melt to a smooth luxurious velvet. Is it thin and fluid, or is it thick, maybe even gummy? Notice if the flavor is long lasting or fleeting.

A few key points about tasting chocolate:

- Limit any tasting session to no more than five different chocolates. If you try to taste more than this, your palate will be dulled by overexposure.

- If you are tasting several chocolates, begin with the lightest or the lowest percentage chocolate, and taste consecutively toward the darkest or highest percentage.

- Be sure that all chocolates to be tasted *are at room temperature.*

- Cleanse your palate between each tasting with water.

- When comparing chocolates from different origins, try to get samples with the same cacao percentage so that they may be evaluated fairly.

Storing Chocolate

CHOCOLATE IS A VERY STABLE PRODUCT and has a long shelf life when properly stored. Under proper conditions, dark chocolate has a shelf life of twelve months, and milk or white chocolate will keep for six months. Some simple precautions will ensure that your chocolate is in pristine condition when you are ready to use it.

- Store chocolate at a cool room temperature (about 65°F). Do not refrigerate or freeze it. Chocolate does not require refrigeration; moreover, putting chocolate into the refrigerator or freezer will cause it to pick up moisture, which will ruin both the appearance and the viscosity of the chocolate.

- Store chocolate in airtight containers. Exposure to oxygen causes the quality of chocolate to deteriorate, so it should be wrapped tightly. For longer storage, a home vacuum sealer is an ideal way to protect your chocolate from oxygen exposure. In addition to preventing oxidation, sealing chocolate tightly will help to stop it from picking up foreign odors.

- Keep chocolate in the dark. Exposure to light also degrades chocolate, so it should always be stored away from light, particularly when the storage is longer term.

- Avoid humidity. Moisture is one of the factors most detrimental to the quality of chocolate. The storage area for chocolate should not be a humid area.

- Don't fear bloom. When you prepare to use your chocolate, it may have bloom on the surface, particularly if it has been used previously. This bloom is nothing more than cocoa butter on the surface of the chocolate, and it will disappear once the chocolate has been melted and tempered.

Bloom

When chocolate has been improperly handled, it forms a gray or white cast on the surface known as *bloom*. There are two types of bloom that occur on chocolate, each from a different cause.

- FAT BLOOM is caused by either improper tempering of chocolate or by exposure to high temperatures during storage. Fat bloom is cocoa butter that has come to the surface of the chocolate and set, resulting in gray streaks or spots on the surface of the chocolate.

- SUGAR BLOOM is caused by exposure to moisture, usually in the form of high humidity. This type of bloom is actually minute crystals of sugar that have formed on the surface of the chocolate after the moisture evaporates, resulting in a whitish film on the chocolate.

It is difficult to distinguish between the two types of bloom based on appearance, and neither type of bloom is harmful other than to the appearance and texture of the chocolate. Fat bloom can result in a soft or a grainy texture, but it will completely disappear once the chocolate is remelted and tempered properly. Sugar bloom will also disappear without adverse effect when the chocolate is remelted and tempered, as long as the moisture that caused it has evaporated before the chocolate is used. You can still enjoy any confections exhibiting bloom without concern, even though they do not have the polished appearance that you strive for.

3

Master Techniques

Master techniques are the foundation of home confectionery; they represent the skills that are used repeatedly in many different types of candy making. Anyone interested in making chocolates or candies in their home kitchen would be well advised to spend the time to understand and become accomplished in the techniques outlined in this chapter. These master techniques apply to not just one type of confection, but to a wide variety of candies and recipes. Learning these techniques will make it possible for you to follow all of the recipes and methods easily. Nothing in this chapter is beyond the grasp of anyone who loves food and has an interest in candy making. While not inherently difficult, these techniques are vital to the success of every home confectioner or chocolatier.

Because master techniques apply to such a range of confections, it should come as no surprise that the techniques relate to the building blocks of confectionery: sugar and chocolate. The steps applied to cooking sugar are not any more difficult than boiling any other liquid, but if you fail to follow them, you will likely wind up with a grainy, failed product. Chocolate too, although sensitive, is relatively simple to work with successfully. When the master techniques are not adhered to, though, you can expect chocolate that neither looks, feels, nor tastes like what we desire from chocolate. When the time comes to dip your creations in chocolate, proper setup and technique will help you to attain a great-looking product with relative ease and speed. Furthermore, using the garnishing techniques in this chapter, you will achieve a beautiful, professional appearance from everything you make. Take the time to learn these master techniques and you will be richly rewarded with sweet success!

Sugar Master Techniques

SUGAR IS THE DEFINING INGREDIENT of candy making. It provides sweetness, bulk, flavor, mouthfeel, and preservation to candies of every description. Even sophisticated chocolates that do not taste particularly sweet to us contain a fairly high percentage of

Is There a Doctor in the House?

For candy makers, one of the most important characteristics of sugar is that it tends to crystallize easily. If you are making pralines or fudge, crystallization at the proper time is the desired result. When you are cooking caramels or brittle, crystallization is the enemy. Controlling the crystallization of sugar is a large part of what candy making is about.

Any ingredient added to a batch of cooking sugar that helps to prevent it from crystallizing is called a *doctor*. There are two main types of doctors that home candy makers use: acids and syrups. The acids commonly added to sugar to prevent crystallization include cream of tartar, lemon juice, and vinegar. Adding a small amount of these ingredients to boiling sugar will not only help to prevent or control crystallization, but will also make the finished product softer, so they must be measured carefully and added when the recipe instructs. The syrups used as doctors include corn syrup (both light and dark), molasses, and honey. Maple syrup is not an effective doctor. Each of these ingredients contributes its own flavor and characteristics to a recipe, so they are not entirely interchangeable.

Proper use of doctors will help you to be successful any time you cook sugar.

sugar. Without sugar, there simply would not be such a thing as candy. In chocolates, the sugar is already contained in the chocolate itself, and we may add little or no additional sugar. In true candy making, such as hard candies or caramels, sugar is the principal ingredient and its sweetness is balanced by other flavors.

When cooking sugars for candy making, proper technique must be adhered to in order to prevent the recrystallization of the sugar (see "Is There a Doctor in the House?" on page 28).

Safety First

Caution: Sugar can give you one of the worst burns of anything in the kitchen. If hot sugar drips on your skin, it sticks in one place, burning deeper and deeper. When cooking and working with sugar for candy making, always be cautious of others in the area, and of how the sugar is handled. Simple basic precautions are all that is usually necessary to prevent painful accidents.

Keeping the handles of pans containing boiling sugar out of the way is a simple and effective way to avoid burns. Having a bowl of ice water nearby can prevent or minimize damage from the scorching hot sugar. If you get hot sugar on your skin, plunging it into ice water will cool the sugar instantaneously, avoiding a nasty burn.

While many parts of home confectionery are perfectly suited to children, handling hot sugar should always be left to adults.

Standard Sugar Cooking Technique

This is the standard technique that should be used when cooking sugar for any of various uses. This technique can be used to cook sugar to any temperature and stage, from a syrup all the way up through caramelization. It is important to remember that the temperature to which sugar is cooked greatly affects how the finished product will turn out; accuracy is critical. Undercooking sugar typically results in a soft product that may not hold its shape well. Overcooking sugar usually makes the finished product too firm and difficult to work with and eat.

1   Combine sugar, corn syrup (if using), and water in saucepan.

2   Bring to boil over high heat while stirring gently with a wooden spoon or rubber spatula.

3   Cover the saucepan with a lid and boil for 4 to 5 minutes over medium heat. This will allow the steam to dissolve and wash in the sugar crystals on the sides of the saucepan, helping to prevent crystallization.

4   Remove the lid from the saucepan and return the heat to high. Place a thermometer in the cooking sugar.

5   If there are sugar crystals remaining on the sides of the saucepan, wash them into the boiling syrup using a wet pastry brush.

6   Cook to the desired temperature without stirring. However, when the batch contains an ingredient that can burn easily, such as a dairy product, nuts, or a thickening agent like starch or pectin, it must be stirred constantly during cooking.

7   Use the cooked sugar as needed. The pan of sugar may be shocked in cold water to prevent carryover cooking.

Sugar Testing Techniques

The most accurate way to measure the temperature of cooking sugar syrup is to use a thermometer; there is little reason that a home confectioner would want to use any other method. Finger testing is a time-honored technique that can be used in place of, or in addition to, a thermometer: dipping fingers in ice water, quickly

Use a clean, wet pastry brush to wash any crystals from the sides of the pan back into the boiling syrup.

retrieving a sample of hot syrup from the boiling pot with your cold, damp fingers, and immediately placing your fingers, with the hot syrup, in the ice water before you burn them. While professionals frequently use their bare fingers and ice water to check the temperature of cooking sugar, this technique is best not attempted by nonprofessionals. A similar technique can be used at home using a teaspoon.

1   Place a small bowl of ice water next to the saucepan of cooking sugar.

2   As the sugar boils, spoon small samples of the syrup out of the saucepan and immerse the spoon holding the syrup in the ice water.

3   Allow the syrup to cool for several seconds, then remove the spoon from the water.

4   Take the cooled sample of syrup between your thumb and forefinger and squeeze it to evaluate the consistency.

5   The temperature of the cooking sugar corresponds with the stages of sugar cooking as illustrated in the photographs on the next page.

While this test is reasonably accurate in the hands of an experienced sugar cook, nothing beats the accuracy of a thermometer for achieving excellent results batch after batch. Perhaps the only time manually testing a batch of sugar is really useful is when cooking Soft Caramels (page 120). By spoon testing the cooking caramels, it is easier to be certain that the finished candies will have the right texture.

1 **THREAD STAGE:** The cooled syrup will form a thread between your fingers.

2 **SOFT BALL STAGE:** The cooled syrup will form a soft, malleable ball when rolled between your fingers.

3 **FIRM BALL STAGE:** The cooled syrup will form a hard ball that cannot be flattened easily between your fingers.

4 **SOFT CRACK STAGE:** The cooled syrup will form a flexible yet firm sheet between your fingers.

5 **HARD CRACK STAGE:** The cooled syrup will form a brittle sheet between your fingers and break cleanly.

6 **CARAMEL STAGE:** The sugar will be extremely brittle and exhibit the flavor, aroma, and brown color characteristic of caramel.

Dry Sugar Cooking Technique

The dry sugar cooking technique is used only when making caramel; it cannot be used to make any intermediate stages of sugar cookery such as soft ball, hard crack, and so on. In this technique, the sugar is placed without water in a saucepan on direct heat, and the crystals are melted rather than dissolved in water. The dry sugar technique is particularly well suited to smaller amounts of sugar.

1   Rub granulated sugar with lemon juice, if desired. A small amount of lemon juice will help to ensure a lump-free caramel. A few drops per cup of sugar are all that is required.

2   Preheat the saucepan. Preheating for several minutes will greatly speed the process.

3   Pour sugar into the pan and begin stirring immediately. Stirring is necessary in order for the sugar to heat uniformly and to reach its melting point all at once so that lumps are avoided.

4   Stir the sugar on the heat until all crystals have melted and the caramel is the desired color. The darker the caramel is, the stronger and more bitter the flavor will be.

1 The sugar begins to melt and turns light brown.

2 As the sugar continues melting, it turns amber.

3 A rich amber color provides caramel flavor.

Chocolate Master Techniques

CHOCOLATE is the most sensitive and complex of substances in a candy kitchen. Even so, it is not something to be feared. All that is required to work successfully with chocolate are a few basic guidelines and some fundamental techniques; no special scientific understanding is required. Once you have mastered these basics, you can work with and temper chocolate anytime you choose.

General Chocolate Handling Precautions

There are two factors that will destroy perfectly good chocolate faster than all others: water and excessive heat. A little bit of caution will help to prevent a lot of ruined chocolate.

- Water: It takes only a few drops of water to cause chocolate to thicken into an unusable paste. For this reason, whenever you work with chocolate, it is vital that all cutting boards, utensils, bowls, and anything else that will be in contact with the chocolate be perfectly dry. Do not underestimate this caution. Likewise, when melting chocolate over a water bath, take care not to allow steam to develop to the point where it will billow and come in contact with the chocolate. If chocolate does become contaminated with water, it is best reserved for other uses such as baking into products, where it will not greatly affect the final outcome.

- Heat: While a little heat is required for melting chocolate, too much heat will cause it to thicken and form granules, rendering it unsuitable for candy making. Milk and white chocolates are especially susceptible to damage, requiring even greater care and lower temperatures. When melting and working with chocolate always be careful not to allow dark chocolate to exceed 120°F, and do not go above 110°F for milk or white chocolate.

General Chocolate Handling Procedures

Whenever handling chocolate, there are several basic procedures to ensure your success. These should be followed whether using chocolate for tempering and dipping, making centers, or cooking with it.

1 Chop the chocolate to be melted. Chopping ensures that the chocolate will melt evenly at the lowest temperature possible. If the pieces of chocolate are large, they will not melt before the rest of the chocolate overheats. Chocolate may be chopped on a dry cutting board using a chef's knife, by rocking a serrated knife, or by using a multiprong ice pick such as those used in ice carving. Whatever the tool, the pieces should not be bigger than 1 inch per side. Of course, if the chocolate is in pistoles, it will not require further chopping before melting it.

Starting at one corner of the chocolate block, rock a serrated knife back and forth to chop the chocolate in small pieces.

Chop chocolate more quickly by pressing a multipronged ice pick straight down into the chocolate block, beginning at one corner and working inward.

2   Stir the chocolate frequently. When melting and working with chocolate, it must be stirred frequently to equalize the temperature and keep it from overheating. The best choice of implements for this is a wooden spoon, a rubber spatula, or a plastic paddle made specifically for chocolate. Whips should never be used to stir chocolate, as they will incorporate air, creating bubbles when the chocolate is used.

3   Melt over low heat. Always melt chocolate using low heat, and take care not to expose it to moisture. There are two basic techniques used for melting chocolate: microwave and water bath.

MICROWAVE TECHNIQUE Microwave ovens can be used successfully to melt chocolate, and they provide the extra benefit of not requiring water to be anywhere in the vicinity of the chocolate. When melting chocolate in a microwave, chop the chocolate (see page 33) and place it in a microwave-safe bowl. Pulse the chocolate in the oven for a few seconds at a time. The actual time varies with the oven, the type of chocolate, and the amount of chocolate in the bowl. In general, 10 to 45 seconds at a time is enough. Between each pulse of power, remove the chocolate from the oven and stir it to equalize the temperature. Continue this process until all the chocolate is entirely melted. Take care not to allow the temperature of any part of the chocolate to exceed 120°F for dark chocolate or 110°F for milk or white chocolate.

WATER BATH TECHNIQUE Water baths are the time-honored technique for melting chocolate. Chop the chocolate into small pieces and place it in a dry heatproof bowl. Place the bowl on top of an appropriately sized saucepan that contains an inch or two of water. At no time should the bottom of the bowl touch the surface of the water. Apply heat only to the bottom of the saucepan so that no direct heat from the burner can contact the edge of the bowl. As soon as steam appears from around the edges of the bowl, turn down the heat to prevent exposing the chocolate to excess heat or to moisture from the steam. Stir the chocolate nearly constantly as it melts to prevent localized overheating. The heat can be turned off, or the bowl removed from the heat, before the chocolate is completely melted, which allows the remainder to melt without building up too much heat.

Storing Chocolate After Use

Chocolate that has been melted but not used may be stored and remelted for future use indefinitely. The easiest way to handle melted chocolate that you want to store is to pour the melted chocolate onto parchment paper in a sheet pan. This will create a thin layer of chocolate. It does not matter if the chocolate is tempered or not. Allow the chocolate to sit at room temperature for several hours or overnight to fully set. Once the chocolate has fully set, you can break it up into pieces and store it as you would any other chocolate, whether used or fresh. (See page 25 for chocolate storage techniques.) Remember: Even if the chocolate you poured onto the pan was not tempered and is covered with bloom, there is nothing wrong with it! When you melt it again and temper it, the chocolate will look as perfect as the day it was made.

Utilizing Mistakes

No matter how careful you are, there will always be times that you accidentally overheat chocolate, get a little water into it, or have crumbs of something in it. This chocolate need not be thrown away, but it should not be used for dipping. The best use for slightly damaged chocolate is in recipes where the chocolate is mixed with other ingredients. Fudge is an ideal product in which to use less-than-perfect chocolate. Ganache can also accept slightly imperfect chocolate, but in severe cases, the chocolate should be reserved for baking or for chocolate mousse.

Tempering Chocolate

Many home candy makers are intimidated by the thought of tempering chocolate; they think it is complex or difficult. While the physics of chocolate tempering are indeed complex, we do not need to know much about these in order to be successful. In truth, tempering chocolate is very much like driving a car: Automobiles are complex machines with many moving and electronic parts that most people know nothing about. However, most of us think nothing of getting behind the wheel and driving. Tempering chocolate is much simpler than driving a car, and there is no danger of getting speeding tickets or having a fender bender while tempering chocolate. You *can* do it.

There are several professionally used techniques to temper chocolate by hand, and there are numerous tempering machines on the market suited to home candy making. For the home confectioner tempering by hand, there is little reason to temper chocolate using any method other than the seeding technique. It is fast, clean, and highly effective. With just a little practice and patience, you can use the seeding method to properly temper chocolate every time.

1   Weigh or measure the chocolate you will be tempering. As always, weight is the preferred method for measuring any ingredients; otherwise, use the chocolate conversion table on page 24.

2   Weigh or measure a second amount of chocolate equal to 25 percent of the original amount.

3   Fully melt the larger amount of chocolate using either a microwave or water bath (see pages 34 to 35). Remove the bowl of melted chocolate from the heat. The chocolate should be 120°F for dark chocolate or 110°F for milk or white chocolate.

What Is Tempering?

Tempering chocolate is the process of heating and cooling chocolate to ensure that it will set with a proper gloss and snap. Tempered chocolate will set quickly and will not show streaks or spots as it sets. Once set, properly tempered chocolate will harden and have the desired snap and shine. When chocolate is not tempered, it will take a long time to set and will have streaks on the surface. Once set, these streaks will turn gray and the chocolate will have a soft and grainy texture.

A thermometer can be helpful when tempering chocolate, but it is not mandatory. With a little practice, you can temper chocolate using only your wrist to gauge the temperature and a spoon to verify that it is setting properly.

Stir solid pieces of tempered chocolate into a bowl of melted chocolate to cool and seed it.

4   Add the smaller amount of unmelted chocolate to the melted chocolate. This is called the seed; it will cool the melted chocolate and cause it to set the way you want. You can use either pistoles or a single block as the seed; a single block has the advantage of easy removal once the chocolate is tempered.

5   Stir the melted chocolate gently and constantly until the temperature falls to 85°F for dark chocolate or 83°F for milk or white chocolate. This will take 15 to 20 minutes, and most or all of the seed should have melted by the end of this time.

6   Test the chocolate. Testing chocolate for temper is the only way to know for sure that chocolate is actually tempered. Following temperatures is a good guideline, but even with strict adherence to technique, no one can tell for sure whether chocolate is tempered without performing a test to see how it sets.

    •   Make sure the chocolate is below 90°F for dark or 87°F for milk or white chocolate.

    •   Dip a spoon in the chocolate, place the spoon on the work surface, and leave it undisturbed for 7 to 8 minutes in the working room at 68°F. Do not yield to the temptation to refrigerate the spoon! This will only give inaccurate results.

    •   After 8 minutes have passed, look closely at the chocolate on the spoon. If the chocolate has set so that it no longer looks wet, and the surface is uniform and without streaks, the chocolate is tempered.

    •   If the chocolate has not set or has set with a streaky appearance, the chocolate requires further seeding. (See step 8 of the tempering procedure.)

7   If the chocolate sets properly, gently warm it over a water bath not exceeding 89°F for dark chocolate or 86°F for milk or white chocolate.

8   If all the seed has melted but the chocolate is not setting quickly without streaks or spots, it must be seeded more. Add a few more pistoles or another small block to the bowl, and stir for another 3 to 4 minutes. After this time, test again (step 6), and proceed from there.

9   Remove any unmelted seeds from the melted chocolate.

10 Use the chocolate as desired while maintaining the proper working temperature (see Maintaining Chocolate Temperature, page 40).

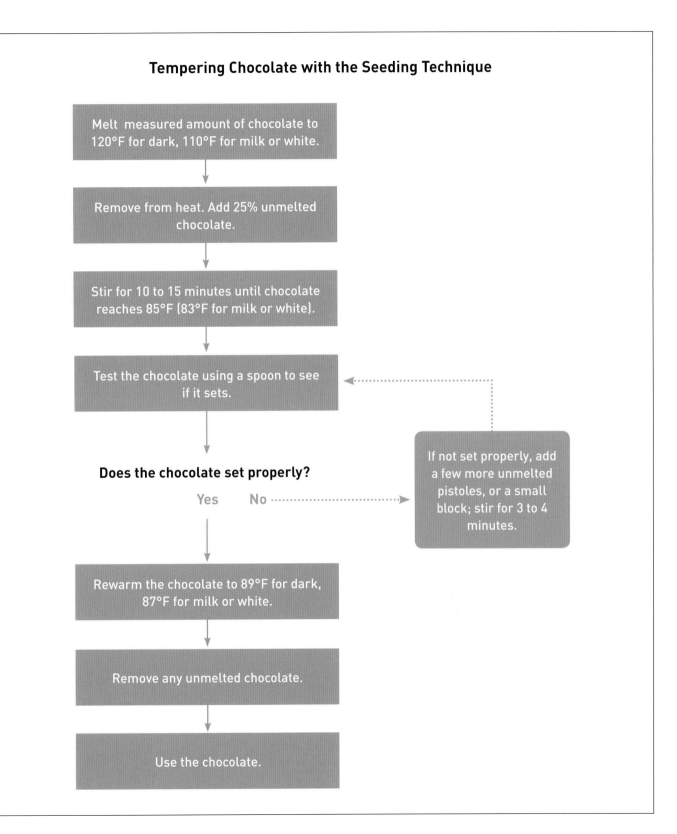

Tempering Chocolate with the Seeding Technique

Melt measured amount of chocolate to 120°F for dark, 110°F for milk or white.

↓

Remove from heat. Add 25% unmelted chocolate.

↓

Stir for 10 to 15 minutes until chocolate reaches 85°F (83°F for milk or white).

↓

Test the chocolate using a spoon to see if it sets.

↓

Does the chocolate set properly?

Yes   No ·······►

If not set properly, add a few more unmelted pistoles, or a small block; stir for 3 to 4 minutes.

↓ (Yes)

Rewarm the chocolate to 89°F for dark, 87°F for milk or white.

↓

Remove any unmelted chocolate.

↓

Use the chocolate.

Maintaining Chocolate Temperature

When you work with tempered chocolate, it is crucial to keep it at the proper temperature. If it cools too much, it will thicken and set. If it is too warm, it will no longer be tempered and will not set properly. Dark chocolate should be used at 86° to 90°F, milk chocolate at 84° to 87°F. There are several options for maintaining this crucial temperature:

- Some home candy makers use a heating pad to keep the bowl of chocolate warm.

- Some put the chocolate over a pot of water at the desired temperature.

- Some warm the chocolate in short bursts in a microwave.

- Others warm it briefly from time to time over a water bath or direct heat.

Regardless of which method you use, always take care to maintain your chocolate at these temperatures and you will be rewarded with a perfect set and shine.

How to *NOT* Temper Chocolate

When your schedule, your ambition, or your kitchen temperature makes it impractical or impossible for you to temper chocolate, you can still make chocolate-coated confections by using compound coating (see page 21). While this is not true chocolate, it is quick to work with, very forgiving of warm temperatures, and can be used as a coating on any product. Most coatings do not have the crisp snap of tempered chocolate, but when melted to the temperature the manufacturer recommends, they are ready for use without tempering and testing. They are particularly useful in hot weather, which is why they are frequently referred to as *summer coatings*. Any of the recipes in this book that require dipping in chocolate can be dipped in either tempered chocolate or melted coating.

Although coating is acceptable for the outside of chocolates, do not attempt to use it in place of chocolate in the recipes for centers.

FROM LEFT TO RIGHT: Incorrectly tempered chocolate with a spotty, grainy appearance; incorrectly tempered chocolate with streaks; and chocolate properly in temper.

Dipping Master Techniques

DIPPING CENTERS IN CHOCOLATE not only gives them a beautiful appearance and a crisp shell, it protects the centers from humidity and helps to maintain quality. Hand dipping chocolates is a technique that requires some precision and much practice to master. But, like all candy making, learning is much of the fun.

1   Place the center to be dipped upside down in the tempered chocolate.

2   Taking the dipping fork in hand, place the fork on the top of the center.

3   Push the center into the chocolate to submerge it, and with one swift *J* motion, invert it and lift it out of the chocolate.

4   Move the fork repeatedly up and down so that the bottom of the dipped center touches the surface of the chocolate. Do this six to eight times.

5   Clean the bottom of the dipped center on the edge of the bowl to remove the excess chocolate from the center. This will prevent a foot from forming when the center is put down.

6   When lifting the center out of the chocolate, try to allow the front of the dipped center to extend past the end of the fork. This will make it easier to put the finished piece down.

Garnishing Master Techniques

WHEN YOUR CENTERS are perfectly made and beautifully dipped, it is time to put the finishing touches on your products. Garnishing is a chance for you to individualize your work and give it your own personal flair. Garnishing may be a simple matter of making waves in the chocolate using a dipping fork, or it may involve intricate piping using a paper cone. No matter how they are applied, garnishes increase the visual appeal of your confections.

For right-handed work, set up your station to work from left to right with undipped centers, tempered chocolate for dipping, and a pan lined with parchment for the dipped centers. Left-handed workers may set the station to flow in the opposite direction. Rest the bowl of tempered chocolate in a pan or other container so that the bowl may be tilted toward you.

1 Place the rolled ganache center into the bowl of chocolate. Using a round dipping fork, push the center into the chocolate to submerge it, and with one swift *J* motion, invert it and lift it out of the chocolate. Move the fork repeatedly up and down so that the bottom of the dipped center touches the surface of the chocolate. Do this six to eight times.

2 Clean the bottom of the dipped center on the edge of the bowl to remove the excess chocolate from the center. This will prevent a foot from forming when the center is put down.

3 Gently roll the dipped truffle off of the loop and onto the prepared tray.

4 Allowing the front of the dipped center to extend past the end of the fork makes it easier to put the finished piece down.

HAND-DIPPING TRUFFLES To use the hand-dipping technique, with a small amount of chocolate in the palm of one hand, use the fingertips of the other hand to roll each truffle center in the chocolate until completely covered.

To remove excess chocolate, allow the truffle to roll across each of your fingertips on its way onto the prepared tray.

Making Waves

Using a dipping fork to make waves in the top surface of your chocolates is one of the simplest and most efficient ways to add visual appeal. While it is simple to do, timing is the key element in this technique. After dipping, wait for a minute or two until the chocolate begins to set very slightly. Place your dipping fork on the chocolate, flat on the top of the piece. Pick the fork up slowly, pulling a little of the chocolate up with it. As you pick up move the fork forward to create a wave pattern in the chocolate. When done at the correct moment, the wave is smooth and relatively well defined. If applied too early, the wave will be very subtle. If applied after the chocolate has set too much, the wave will look more like a scar. A little bit of practice will help you to know the right moment to make the wave.

As the chocolate begins to set, use a dipping fork to create a smooth, well-defined wave pattern on top.

Piping Filigree

Paper piping cones are frequently used to garnish finished chocolates. They can be used to create elaborate designs, apply simple dots of chocolate, or anything in between. When using a cone to apply garnish to finished chocolates, the centers are normally dipped and the chocolate is allowed to set before applying the decoration. Even though they are small, piped garnishes can bloom and diminish the appearance of your work if the chocolate is not tempered.

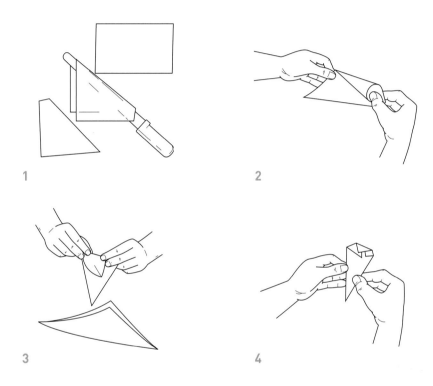

1 Cut a rectangle of parchment paper, fold the rectangle in half on the diagonal, and cut two triangles.

2 Hold the 90-degree angle of the triangle pointing toward you. Create a fine tip by rolling the corner at your right hand to meet the right angle, creating a point on the long flat end.

3 Wrap the last corner at your left around to meet the other two corners.

4 Fold the top inward to fix the cone in place. After rolling the cone you may adjust the size of the hole at the tip by cutting with a pair of scissors or a very sharp knife.

Using Transfer Sheets

Transfer sheets, available from chocolate specialty suppliers, have become a popular way to garnish chocolates. These sheets of flexible plastic have colored cocoa butter silk-screened on one side in a pattern, words, or a logo. When unset chocolate is placed on the transfer sheet, the colored cocoa butter from the sheet is transferred to the chocolate as it sets. When the chocolate sets, the plastic is peeled away, resulting in a shiny, smooth surface with the color and design of the transfer sheet on the chocolate.

While it is possible to turn the freshly dipped centers upside down onto the transfer sheets and allow them to harden, better results are usually obtained by cutting individual pieces of transfer sheet for each center and placing them on top of the freshly dipped pieces. It is best to leave the transfer sheets on overnight or to refrigerate your pieces briefly before releasing the plastic, to harden the chocolate fully and obtain the most brilliant shine.

Place individual pieces of transfer sheet on freshly dipped chocolates to create a smooth, shiny, decorative surface.

Allow the chocolate to harden fully, then carefully peel back the transfer sheet to reveal the design.

Other Garnishes

The most common examples of garnish are nuts, salt, sugar, sprinkles, and dried or candied fruit, but any type of dry item could be used. When applying this type of garnish, place it on the dipped confection before the chocolate has a chance to fully set. If the garnish is sizeable, such as a half or a whole nut, it can be applied as soon as the center is dipped. For smaller garnishes such as sanding sugar or salt, wait until the chocolate begins to set before you apply the garnish. Putting this type of garnish on too soon will cause it to sink into the chocolate so that it cannot be seen easily. In general, a garnish should give some hint of what is inside the chocolate shell.

Dipped truffles may be finished by rolling them in cocoa powder.

Making Chocolate Shavings

CHOCOLATE SHAVINGS are easy to make from a block of chocolate, using a chef's knife.

1   Place the block of chocolate, smooth side up, on a countertop, braced against a solid object to prevent it from sliding away from you.

2   Hold the handle of the knife in your right or left hand, as you would normally hold it. With the knife parallel to you, hold the top of the blade.

3   Using the heel of the knife blade, scrape across the chocolate block, away from you.

4   Do not handle chocolate shavings by hand; they will melt.

Toasting Nuts

ALMOST WITHOUT EXCEPTION, the flavor of nuts is improved by toasting. Any time that nuts are used in a recipe that does not cook them to a high temperature, they must be toasted before use. While small quantities of petite nuts, such as sliced almonds or pine nuts, may be toasted in a sauté pan on top of the stove, you will always achieve better results by spreading nuts on a sheet pan and toasting them in the oven prior to use. To roast nuts:

1   Preheat the oven to 350°F. (Set to 325°F when using convection.)

2   Spread the nuts in a single layer on a sheet pan and put in the oven.

3   Toast until the desired degree of color and flavor is developed, turning the nuts once or twice while in the oven to ensure even toasting. This takes 15 to 20 minutes.

Different nuts benefit from different degrees of toasting; hazelnuts are best toasted to a very golden color, and almonds are better more subtly toasted. Pecans are delicious as they just begin to darken in color, but easily become bitter if over toasted. Taste the nuts to decide when the flavor suits your preference. Pistachios are the exception to toasting; they will lose their appealing green color if they are toasted and so are usually left untoasted.

Nuts may be toasted ahead of time, but they will have the best flavor when freshly toasted. Toasted nuts will spoil from rancidity much more readily than untoasted, so prepare only what you will use and store any leftovers in the refrigerator or freezer.

Lining a Pan with Plastic Wrap

MANY OF THE CANDIES in this book are spread in standard baking pans to set. While this is convenient and effective, it can be difficult to remove the set candy from the pan without breaking the candy or scratching the nonstick surface of the pan. Lining the inside of the pans with plastic wrap before filling them will alleviate this problem and allow for easy release of the finished candy. Throughout this book, plastic wrap is used for this technique, although waxed paper is also an effective alternative, if desired.

1   Oil the inside of the pan lightly with oil or butter, or spray it with nonstick cooking spray.

2   Cut off a single piece of plastic that will be big enough to line the pan and leave some excess as well.

3   Place the plastic wrap in the pan. The oil will cause the plastic to adhere to the pan so it stays in place. Flatten the plastic so that most of the wrinkles are removed or minimized.

4   Push the plastic into the corners of the pan so that there are no air pockets under the wrap. This is especially important.

5   Do not drape the excess plastic over the top of the pan. Rather, allow the plastic to stay on the inside edge of the pan so that it can relax into the pan.

6   After the candy has set, remove it in one piece by lifting up the edges of the plastic and pulling the plastic and the candy out of the pan together.

When lining a pan with plastic wrap, first spray the pan, then press the plastic wrap firmly against all sides of the pan.

Packaging

HOME CANDY MAKERS do not often have to be concerned with packaging; their products are presented on platters and enjoyed while very fresh. There are times, however, when packaging your candies is desirable. Obviously, when you are giving your handmade chocolates as a gift, the packaging should reflect all of the care and work that went into producing them. If the candies are to be stored for a period of time before they are enjoyed, proper packaging will help ensure that they do not lose quality in that time.

There are many styles of packaging available to the home candy maker. You can find whatever style of packaging you want, from the frilly to the rustic to the modern and sleek. The best packaging protects the product and presents it in an attractive manner. Candies are scuffed or scratched easily, so they must not be allowed to move about freely within the package. The package also helps to protect from brief fluctuations in humidity and temperature that could otherwise ruin the appearance of chocolates. While it is not necessary that packaging for chocolates be airtight, it should be for hard candy, toffee, or brittle. For most home use, it is not necessary to protect chocolate from exposure to light, but for longer-term storage, light should be avoided, as it has a negative effect on chocolate. Whatever type of packaging you choose, keep in mind the two goals: protection and presentation.

CLOCKWISE FROM TOP LEFT: Wooden box, cardboard boxes, tins, colored foil for wrapping the candies, cardboard boxes with cellophane tops, tissue, and ribbon.

4

Truffles and Chocolates

This chapter will focus on using chocolate to make candies, for dipping, and for the most famous of all bonbons: the chocolate truffle. Chocolate truffles are named for their resemblance to the famous gastronomic fungus that grows mainly in France and northern Italy. Like their namesake, chocolate truffles are round, and they are also associated with fine dining and luxury. Chocolate truffles are often finished with a dusting of cocoa powder resembling the earth clinging to a freshly dug truffle.

We will also use tempered chocolate to make a range of barks and individual chocolate-dipped treats. To be successful with the recipes in this chapter, you will need to review the master technique of tempering chocolate (see page 36). Remember that if there is a little tempered chocolate left over when you are finished dipping all of the centers in a recipe, you can either store it for reuse another time, make Rochers (page 225) or T'ings (page 80), or simply dip a few items such as dried fruit or pretzels in it.

Truffles

CHOCOLATE TRUFFLES should always be a ganache center, round in shape. Because they are named for the fungus, which is round, it does not make sense to call a chocolate that is not round a truffle, regardless of the center used. They should be dipped in chocolate both to protect the ganache and to provide textural contrast. Truffles are perfect chocolates for the home confectioner to make: They are rich and indulgent, can be made in many flavor variations, and are always recognized and appreciated. There is a wide range of finishing techniques that can be employed with truffles, from the classic and simple cocoa powder dusting, to piping filigrees, to placing chopped nuts or other garnish on the tops of the finished truffles.

What's in it?

The center of a truffle is ganache (ga-NASH). Ganache is a mixture of heavy cream and chocolate and is widely used as a filling or glaze for cakes and pastries as well as for centers of chocolates. In spite of containing cream, these centers can and should be stored at room temperature and will remain fresh for more than a week (although they probably won't be around that long).

CREAM The cream in these recipes should be heavy cream, which has a high butterfat content. Using a lighter cream will adversely affect the way the ganache sets and handles.

CORN SYRUP Corn syrup is added to the ganache primarily to help keep it smooth and preserve the ganache (see Sugar as a Preservative, page 2). Corn syrup also sweetens the ganache slightly, which can be a benefit when using high-percentage chocolate.

FLAVORING INGREDIENTS These may be liquid flavors such as spirits, concentrated fruit juices, or purees; dry flavors such as spices; or extracts or manufactured flavors. Flavoring ingredients are an optional addition to ganache. There is nothing wrong with making ganache using just the best-quality cream and chocolate that you can find; flavors simply help us create variety.

BUTTER Butterfat is present in large quantities in heavy cream. Additional butter added to ganache gives the truffles more of a melt-in-your-mouth texture. Butter to be added to ganache should be unsalted and softened by warming slightly before adding it.

CHOCOLATE Chocolate is not only the principal flavor in truffle centers, it is the glue that holds the ganache together. It is the chocolate that makes the ganache firm enough to handle. Use only good-quality chocolate in your ganache, and you will be rewarded with luscious centers that are easily handled. If you try to use chocolate chips meant for baking, your ganache will not be firm enough to handle and will not have a good texture once set.

TEMPERED CHOCOLATE OR COMPOUND COATING The chocolate on the outside of the truffle gives it a crunch and textural contrast and protects the center from drying and becoming misshapen. Whenever practical, good-quality tempered chocolate should be used; it is well worth the extra cost. If conditions do not allow tempering chocolate, however, using a compound coating is an alternative. Coating is more forgiving of its environment and handling than chocolate is.

How it's made

Ganache is simple to make and not difficult to handle. The part of truffle making that requires the most skill is tempering the chocolate and dipping the truffles.

1 Combine the heavy cream and corn syrup in a small saucepan and bring to a boil. Bring just to a boil; do not boil for any length of time, or you will evaporate too much water from the cream, resulting in a ganache that is likely to separate (see "Separation Anxiety," page 57).

2 Remove from the heat and add the chocolate. Stir until the mixture is smooth. The heat of the cream in the saucepan will melt the chocolate and allow it to combine with the cream.

3 Check to be sure that all of the chocolate has melted. If there are unmelted chocolate pieces in the ganache, warm it gently over a water bath until they melt and the ganache becomes smooth.

4 Add the butter. Stir the softened butter into the ganache.

5 Add any liquid flavors. Stir in the flavor until the ganache is smooth.

6 Use parchment paper to line a 9 × 13–inch baking pan or other pan that will allow the ganache to spread in a thin, even layer, and then pour in the ganache. Cover with plastic wrap and refrigerate for 1 hour or more to allow the ganache to firm. The ganache may remain refrigerated overnight if desired.

1

2

3

1 With the pot off the heat, add the chocolate pieces to the boiled cream.

2 Stir until all of the chocolate is completely melted and the mixture is smooth and homogeneous.

3 Pour the ganache into a pan and allow it to spread into a thin, even layer before covering with plastic wrap.

Separation Anxiety

Ganache is an emulsion; that is, it contains both fat and water in a homogeneous mixture. Because fat and water do not mix easily, any emulsion can separate, which simply means that the fat portion and the water portion do not remain homogeneous. When this happens to ganache, it takes on a grainy appearance and has a thin consistency. If your ganache doesn't look smooth and thick, it has probably separated. If it is allowed to set while separated, it will have a grainy, fatty mouthfeel. Fortunately, there is a simple two-step procedure that will restore any separated ganache.

1 Warm the ganache over a water bath until it is 95° to 100°F and whisk it vigorously. This procedure will repair nearly every case of separated ganache, making the ganache ready for use. If it does not come back together in a thick, smooth mixture within 2 minutes while whisking, however, you should move to step 2.

2 Add a small amount of room-temperature liquid while whisking the ganache vigorously. Add the liquid a little at a time while whisking until the ganache is smooth again. Either milk or a liquor will work well. Heavy cream should be avoided because it contains too much fat to be effective. This step should require only a small amount of liquid, usually not more than 1 to 2 tablespoons for the recipes in this book. Always use as little liquid as possible to restore the ganache.

FROM LEFT TO RIGHT: Emulsified ganache and separated ganache.

How it's formed

1   Place the chilled ganache in a bowl and mix it. If using a mixer, this will only take about 30 seconds. If mixing by hand, it will take a minute or two. Mixing the ganache helps it to set firm enough to handle.

2   Allow the ganache to rest for 5 minutes. During this time, the ganache will harden slightly, making handling easier.

3   Scoop balls of ganache using a #100 scoop or a teaspoon. These will not be perfectly round yet, but should be the size that you want the truffles to be. Place the balls on a parchment paper–lined sheet pan as you scoop them.

4   Roll the ganache scoops into balls by hand. Work in the same order in which you scooped the ganache. Handle it lightly, and if necessary, wipe any melted ganache off your hands with a dry paper towel. Place on a clean parchment-lined pan.

Using a scoop or a teaspoon, scoop the ganache onto a prepared sheet pan, then gently roll the ganache scoops into balls by hand.

How it's finished

1   Temper the chocolate for dipping (see page 36). The exact amount is not important, as long as you have enough for dipping the truffles. If there is extra left over, you can store it or make other chocolates with it before it sets.

2   Dip the centers in the tempered chocolate. You can use a fork for dipping, or use your hands (see Dipping Master Techniques, page 42). Try to keep the chocolate from setting while you are dipping by keeping it warm (see Maintaining Chocolate Temperature, page 40). In professional settings, truffles are usually dipped twice in chocolate, but once is sufficient for home use, unless you prefer a thicker chocolate shell.

3   Garnish as desired. You can use any of numerous finishing techniques for truffles. Using a different technique for each variety creates a unique identity for each piece.

How else can I use it?

Ganache is ubiquitous in desserts and candy making. For the home chocolatier, ganache can be piped into shapes other than round truffles, and it is often used as a filling in chocolate molds (see Chapter 9). If you have extra ganache and do not have the time to make chocolates from it, it makes a great topping when warmed and poured over ice cream.

How it's stored

Finished truffles should be stored at a cool room temperature (66° to 68°F) and protected from light and humidity. They will have a shelf life of up to two weeks. Of course, this is the optimum condition and is not always possible. Truffles can be refrigerated if they are wrapped tightly and removed from the refrigerator and allowed to return to room temperature before unwrapping. If long-term storage is the goal, they can be frozen using this technique as well, but the chocolate shell may suffer damage from freezing either in the form of cracks or bloom on the surface. If these conditions occur, the truffles are still good to eat, but their visual appeal is reduced.

Bark and T'ings

BARK is a sheet of tempered chocolate on which any of various nuts, dried or candied fruits, or candy is sprinkled. T'ings are similar but are made as individual disks. In Switzerland they are known as *knackerli*, and in France as *mendiants*, where the colors of the fruits and nuts used signify the different colors of robes worn in monastic orders. Both bark and t'ings are simple to make and can be a way to utilize tempered chocolate left over after dipping a batch of centers.

What's in it?

TEMPERED CHOCOLATE The chocolate is so important here that I strongly recommend using tempered chocolate of the highest quality. Milk, dark, or white chocolate, or a combination, can be used to make these products. If conditions or time do not permit the use of tempered chocolate, compound coating may be used, but the quality of the finished product will suffer.

GARNISH The garnish on bark or t'ings is nearly limitless. The only requirement is that it is a shelf-stable product that does not contain too much moisture, so fresh fruit cannot be used unless the finished pieces will be used within several hours. Some examples of commonly used toppings include chopped toasted nuts and dried fruit. Hard candy is often used, especially in peppermint bark; toffee or croquant can also be used, as can any dry item such as seeds, cereals, crackers, or pretzels.

How it's made

1 Temper the chocolate. Chocolate used for bark or t'ings must be tempered in order to have the proper shine and snap when broken (see Tempering Chocolate, page 36).

2 Spread or pipe the chocolate. When making bark, the chocolate should be spread in a layer just under ¼ inch thick on a parchment paper–lined sheet pan. Different chocolates may be marbled or layered, as in Peppermint Bark, where white and dark chocolate are layered. When making t'ings, the tempered chocolate is piped or spooned in quarter dollar–size disks on parchment paper.

3 Place the garnish on the chocolate before it sets. Timing is key here: The chocolate must not have been allowed to set, or the garnish will not adhere to the chocolate. The garnish may be sprinkled randomly on a sheet of bark, or placed more precisely on individual t'ings.

4 Allow the chocolate to set. Chocolate should always set at proper working room temperature (about 68°F), rather than be forced to set in a refrigerator. Remember that tempered chocolate sets quickly, but it continues to harden and develop proper snap for twenty-four or more hours after it first sets. Bark can then be broken in pieces to serve; t'ings are made as individual pieces.

How it's stored

These chocolates can be made well ahead of the time they are to be used; they do not spoil because they contain no moisture. Like any chocolate, these products are best stored at room temperature, protected from extremes of temperature, light, and humidity. When stored under these conditions, they have a shelf life of months.

1 Spread the dark chocolate in an even layer over the white chocolate after it has nearly set.

2 Apply an even sprinkling of the topping to the bark before the chocolate sets.

3 As the chocolate begins to set, garnish the t'ings with fruit and nut pieces.

Meltaways

MELTAWAYS are made by combining chocolate with coconut fat and a flavoring. The coconut fat lowers the melting point of the chocolate, giving them their characteristic rapid melt-in-your-mouth appeal. In fact, they melt so quickly that they actually draw heat from your palate, leaving a cool sensation in your mouth. The most commonly used flavors in meltaways are mint and peanut butter, but other dry or oil flavors may be used to create variety. Meltaways may be dipped in chocolate, but more often they are finished simply with a dusting of confectioners' sugar, cocoa powder, or a combination of the two.

What's in it?

The list of ingredients for meltaways is simple: chocolate, coconut fat, and flavoring. Do not try to substitute another oil for the coconut fat if you want the true meltaway sensation; other fats will not supply the same effect.

CHOCOLATE Dark, milk, or white chocolate may be used to make meltaways, although dark or milk chocolate is most commonly used. The most important thing to remember about the chocolate for meltaways is that it must be tempered in order for the meltaways to set properly.

COCONUT FAT It is the coconut fat that results in the namesake mouthfeel of these candies. If you use coconut fat from a health food store, it will work properly, but it will lend a strong coconut fragrance to the meltaways. Deodorized coconut fat is available from home candy making supply Web sites, and should be used when the coconut aroma is not desired.

FLAVORING Mint is commonly used; when mint is combined with the mouth-cooling effect from the meltaways, the result is extraordinary. Meltaway recipes in this book also include peanut butter and green tea. Any oil-based flavoring such as orange oil, or dry flavor such as a spice, can be used successfully to make meltaways. Do not attempt to use flavorings containing water, such as extracts, as they will thicken the mixture.

How it's made

Mixing up meltaways is nearly as simple as combining all of the measured ingredients. The only caveats are that the chocolate must be tempered and the other ingredients must not be hot enough to take the chocolate out of temper.

1   Temper the chocolate. See page 36. Always test the chocolate to verify that it is properly tempered.

2   Melt the coconut fat. The fat may be melted over a water bath or in a microwave. Make sure the fat is not above 85°F when it is added to the chocolate. Cool the fat after melting if necessary.

3 Combine the tempered chocolate, coconut fat, and flavoring. They may be mixed together by hand using a rubber spatula or a paddle.

4 Stir by hand for 3 minutes. The additional stirring helps to ensure that the entire mixture is tempered before it is poured into a pan to set.

5 Pour into a prepared pan. The pan for meltaways should be lined with plastic wrap (see page 51) to facilitate unmolding.

6 Allow to set fully at room temperature. It usually takes about an hour at room temperature for the meltaways to set. If possible, avoid letting them set overnight, as they will become more brittle and be difficult to cut.

How it's finished

1 Dust with sifted confectioners' sugar or cocoa powder and remove from the pan. The dry ingredient will make the meltaways easier to handle.

2 Cut into individual bite-sized pieces using a chef's knife. Any thin-bladed sharp knife will cut meltaways well.

3 Roll each piece in the confectioners' sugar or cocoa powder. Shake off the excess powder.

How it's stored

Meltaways are not easily damaged by humidity, but heat will quickly reduce them to a pool of melted-aways. The optimum storage conditions are as for any chocolate: sealed in an airtight container and stored at a cool room temperature. If these conditions are not available, refrigeration is acceptable, but take care to protect meltaways from damage due to moisture.

Chocolate-Dipped Anything

THE NAME SAYS IT ALL: There are not many limits on what you might want to dip in chocolate, although handling and storage differ depending on what the center is.

This is an ideal way to utilize chocolate left over after dipping centers from another recipe, and it can provide a variety of colors, flavors, and textures to a selection of chocolates that you are offering. Dried fruit, pretzels, and strawberries are traditional, but tradition is made to be broken; put together your own chocolate-dipped vision.

What's in it?

A CENTER Any type of dried fruit is well suited to dipping in chocolate. The rich flavor and texture is a perfect match for a crisp chocolate shell. Dried apricots are ideal dipped in dark chocolate, pears are superb dipped in dark or milk chocolate, and pineapple pairs well with milk chocolate. The crisp texture and salty flavor of pretzels is also a welcome complement to chocolate. Fresh fruit is also good when dipped in chocolate; whole strawberries are the most commonly seen examples. Their two-bite size, tart flavor, and convenient stem handle make them ideal for dipping. Be careful of moisture from cut fruit, such as fresh melon or pears; it will contaminate the chocolate, making it unacceptable for dipping other centers. When fresh fruit is dipped in chocolate, it should be enjoyed within a day of dipping.

TEMPERED CHOCOLATE Without question, tempered chocolate is the preferred ingredient here, but a compound coating can work well, too. Milk, dark, or white chocolate, or a combination, may be used for creating dipped centers.

When the white chocolate first coat has set, dip each strawberry into the dark chocolate, leaving a portion of the white chocolate visible.

How it's made

1   Prepare the centers. The centers to be dipped should be dry and at a cool room temperature. When dipping fruit in chocolate, allow it to warm to room temperature rather than dipping it while it is ice-cold from the refrigerator. If cutting fruit for dipping, dry the cut pieces with a paper towel to remove excess moisture from the surface of the fruit.

2   Temper the chocolate or melt the coating. Dipping centers in untempered chocolate will result in bloom and chocolate that is not sufficiently crisp. If using a compound coating, follow the manufacturer's guidelines for temperature.

3   Dip the centers. The centers may be entirely enrobed in the chocolate by dipping with a fork (see page 42), or partially coated by holding one end of the center and dipping up to the desired level in the chocolate.

4   Allow the chocolate to set. Placing the dipped centers on parchment paper to set keeps them clean and ensures that they will not stick to the surface. This step should always be performed at room temperature to obtain the best shine and snap from the chocolate.

How it's stored

If you have dipped fresh fruit and will not be using it for several hours, storing under refrigeration may be necessary to preserve the fruit. In all other cases, however, these should be stored at a cool room temperature and protected from heat, humidity, and light. The shelf life will be as long as that for the original center: many weeks for dry centers under ideal conditions.

What if

What if my ganache for truffles looks grainy and oily?

The ganache has separated. It is easy to repair: Warm it up over a water bath to 95°F or slightly higher and whisk it. This will repair most separated ganache.

If this does not repair the ganache, pour a little milk or spirit into the ganache slowly while whisking. In most cases, it will require only a tablespoon or so of the liquid to repair the ganache.

What if my ganache for truffles is too soft to handle?

You may be using a chocolate that is too low in cocoa butter. Make sure you are using a good-quality chocolate and not chips meant for baking.

Allow the ganache to chill in the refrigerator a little longer and try again.

Mix the ganache a little more in a mixer or by hand. This stimulates setting.

What if my ganache for truffles is too stiff to mix?

Your chocolate probably has a very high cocoa butter content. Allow the ganache to sit at room temperature for 30 minutes, and then try mixing it.

What if my chocolate is not setting?

Assuming the room is at the correct temperature (68°F), the chocolate is not tempered. It needs to be seeded a little bit more (see page 36).

What if my chocolate in the bowl is setting quickly?

The chocolate needs to be maintained at a temperature where it will not set yet remain in temper. Warm the chocolate very gently, not exceeding 90°F for dark chocolate and not exceeding 87°F for milk or white chocolate. You will need to do this periodically as you work with the chocolate (see page 40).

What if my chocolate has set, but it has streaks and bloom on the surface?

The chocolate was not properly tempered and so it bloomed. There is no reason not to eat the products, but they do not have the desired appearance. You can temper more chocolate and dip them again if you do not mind a thick chocolate shell.

What if I do not have proper storage for chocolate and must refrigerate my products?

Seal the products in an airtight container and refrigerate them until several hours before you intend to use them. Remove them from the refrigerator, but leave them sealed until they have reached room temperature. This technique will help to minimize damage from condensation on the surface of the chocolate.

Black Forest Truffles (page 67), Sesame-Ginger Truffles (page 70), Dark Chocolate Liqueur Truffles (page 71), Coffee Truffles (page 72), and Honey-Lavender Truffles (page 75)

Black Forest Truffles

The Old World combination of chocolate, cream, and cherries is brought together in a new way in this truffle. Chocolate shavings echo the traditional Black Forest cake garnish.

SKILL LEVEL

4 oz (½ cup) **Heavy cream**

½ oz (1 tbsp) **Light corn syrup**

12 oz (2 cups) **White chocolate, pistoles or chopped in ½-inch pieces**

½ oz (1 tbsp) **Butter, unsalted, soft**

1 oz (2 tbsp) **Kirsch**

1 oz (3 tbsp) **Dried cherries, finely chopped**

10 oz (1⅔ cups) **Dark chocolate or dark compound coating, chopped in ½-inch pieces, for dipping**

2 oz (⅓ cup) **Dark chocolate shavings** (see page 50)

---

1 Line a 9 × 13–inch baking pan with parchment paper.

2 Combine the cream and corn syrup in a 2-quart saucepan and bring to a boil.

3 Remove from the heat. Add the chopped white chocolate or pistoles and butter to the cream and stir until smooth and homogeneous.

4 Stir in the kirsch and the cherries.

5 Pour the finished ganache into the baking pan to make a thin layer and cover with plastic wrap. Refrigerate for 1 hour or more until the ganache is firm.

6 Put the ganache in a mixer bowl and mix on medium speed using a paddle attachment for 30 seconds. Or stir vigorously in a mixing bowl by hand, using a spatula.

7 Allow the ganache to rest at room temperature for 5 minutes. Line a sheet pan with parchment paper.

8 Using a #100 scoop or a teaspoon, scoop out balls of ganache and place on the sheet pan at room temperature.

9 When all of the ganache has been scooped, roll each portion by hand into a round ball.

10 Melt and temper the chocolate for dipping using the procedure on page 36. If using compound coating, follow the heating instructions on the package.

11 Dip the ganache centers in the tempered chocolate or compound coating using one of the techniques illustrated on pages 44 and 45.

12 After dipping, but before the chocolate sets, roll the truffles in the chocolate shavings.

Keys to Success

○ Make sure the ganache has enough time to firm in the refrigerator. An hour is a good guideline, but it is okay to leave it longer, even overnight if desired.

○ Resting the ganache after mixing allows it to harden slightly, which makes scooping much easier.

○ Dipping the truffles twice creates a thicker chocolate shell, but dipping once provides a faster alternative.

○ Spread the chocolate shavings on a sheet pan to make rolling the truffles easier.

Chocolate Truffles

MAKES 60 PIECES

While truffles can be made in a wide variety of flavors, simply using top-quality chocolate and fresh cream without any other flavors is perhaps the purest form. Other spices or flavorings may be used in these recipes to create your own variations.

SKILL LEVEL

Dark Chocolate Truffles

8 oz (1 cup) **Heavy cream**

1½ oz (2 tbsp) **Light corn syrup**

½ oz (1 tbsp) **Butter, unsalted, soft**

14 oz (2⅓ cups) **Dark chocolate, pistoles or chopped in ½-inch pieces**

12 oz (2 cups) **Dark chocolate or dark compound coating, chopped in ½-inch pieces, for dipping**

Milk or White Chocolate Truffles

4 oz (½ cup) **Heavy cream**

1½ oz (2 tbsp) **Light corn syrup**

½ oz (1 tbsp) **Butter, unsalted, soft**

12 oz (2 cups) **Milk or white chocolate, pistoles or chopped in ½-inch pieces**

12 oz (2 cups) **Milk or white chocolate or white compound coating, chopped in ½-inch pieces, for dipping**

1 Line a 9 × 13–inch baking pan with parchment paper.

2 Combine the cream and corn syrup in a 2-quart saucepan and bring to a boil.

3 Remove from the heat. Add the butter and chopped chocolate or pistoles to the cream and stir until smooth and homogeneous.

4 Pour the finished ganache into the baking pan to make a thin layer and cover with plastic wrap. Refrigerate for 1 hour or more until the ganache is firm.

5 Put the ganache in a mixer bowl and mix on medium speed using a paddle attachment for 30 seconds. Or stir vigorously in a mixing bowl by hand, using a spatula.

6 Allow the ganache to rest at room temperature for 5 minutes. Line a sheet pan with parchment paper.

7 Using a #100 scoop or a teaspoon, scoop out balls of ganache and place on the sheet pan at room temperature.

8 When all of the ganache has been scooped, roll each portion by hand into a round ball.

9 Melt and temper the chocolate for dipping using the procedure on page 36. If using compound coating, follow the heating instructions on the package.

10 Dip the ganache centers in the tempered chocolate or compound coating using one of the dipping techniques illustrated on pages 44 and 45. Garnish as desired (see page 49).

Keys to Success

○ Make sure the ganache has enough time to firm in the refrigerator. An hour is a good guideline, but it is okay to leave it longer, even overnight if desired.

○ Resting the ganache after mixing allows it to harden slightly, which makes scooping much easier.

○ Dipping the truffles twice creates a thicker chocolate shell, but dipping once provides a faster alternative.

○ Basic truffles can be garnished by any method desired, or left ungilded for simple perfection.

Sesame-Ginger Truffles

MAKES 48 PIECES

The nontraditional combination of sesame and chocolate is brought to life with the addition of ginger. Fresh ginger gives the best results.

SKILL LEVEL

4 oz (½ cup) **Heavy cream**

1½ oz (2 tbsp) **Light corn syrup**

1 oz (¼ cup) **Ginger, peeled and grated**

1 oz (2 tbsp) **Tahini**

8 oz (1⅓ cups) **Dark chocolate, pistoles or chopped in ½-inch pieces**

1 tsp Toasted sesame oil

½ oz (2 tbsp) **Chopped crystallized ginger** (optional)

12 oz (2 cups) **Dark chocolate or dark compound coating, chopped in ½-inch pieces, for dipping**

Toasted sesame seeds or finely chopped crystallized ginger, for garnish (optional), **as needed**

---

1 Line a 9 × 13–inch baking pan with parchment paper.

2 Combine the cream, corn syrup, and grated ginger in a 2-quart saucepan and bring to a boil.

3 Remove from the heat. Add the tahini and chopped dark chocolate or pistoles to the cream and stir until smooth and homogeneous.

4 Stir in the sesame oil.

5 Strain the ganache through a fine-mesh strainer.

6 Stir the crystallized ginger into the ganache, if desired.

7 Pour the finished ganache into the baking pan to make a thin layer and cover with plastic wrap. Refrigerate for 1 hour or more until the ganache is firm.

8 Put the ganache in a mixer bowl and mix on medium speed using a paddle attachment for 30 seconds. Or stir vigorously in a mixing bowl by hand, using a spatula.

9 Allow the ganache to rest at room temperature for 5 minutes. Line a sheet pan with parchment paper.

10 Using a #100 scoop or a teaspoon, scoop out balls of ganache and place on the sheet pan at room temperature.

11 When all of the ganache has been scooped, roll each portion by hand into a round ball.

12 Melt and temper the chocolate for dipping using the procedure on page 36. If using compound coating, follow the heating instructions on the package.

13 Dip the ganache centers in the tempered chocolate or compound coating using one of the techniques illustrated on pages 44 and 45.

14 After dipping, but before the chocolate sets fully, garnish with toasted sesame seeds or finely chopped crystallized ginger as desired.

Keys to Success

○ Make sure the ganache has enough time to firm in the refrigerator. An hour is a good guideline, but it is okay to leave it longer, even overnight if desired.

○ Resting the ganache after mixing allows it to harden slightly, which makes scooping much easier.

Dark Chocolate Liqueur Truffles

MAKES 60 PIECES

Liqueurs are an easy way to add a range of flavors to your truffles. This standard
recipe uses dark chocolate and pairs well with stronger spirits like brandy or rum.

SKILL LEVEL

8 oz (1 cup) **Heavy cream**

1½ oz (2 tbsp) **Light corn syrup**

1 oz (2 tbsp) **Butter, unsalted, soft**

14 oz (2⅓ cups) **Dark chocolate, pistoles or chopped in ½-inch pieces**

2 oz (¼ cup) **Liqueur or spirit**

12 oz (2 cups) **Dark chocolate or dark compound coating, chopped in ½-inch pieces, for dipping**

Garnish (see Keys to Success), **as needed**

---

1 Line a 9 × 13–inch baking pan with parchment paper.

2 Combine the cream and corn syrup in a 2-quart saucepan and bring to a boil.

3 Remove from the heat. Add the butter and chopped dark chocolate or pistoles to the cream and stir until smooth and homogeneous. Stir in the liqueur.

4 Pour the finished ganache into the baking pan to make a thin layer and cover with plastic wrap. Refrigerate for 1 hour or more until the ganache is firm.

5 Put the ganache in a mixer bowl and mix on medium speed using a paddle attachment for 30 seconds. Or stir vigorously in a mixing bowl by hand, using a spatula.

6 Allow the ganache to rest at room temperature for 5 minutes. Line a sheet pan with parchment paper.

7 Using a #100 scoop or a teaspoon, scoop out balls of ganache and place on the sheet pan at room temperature.

8 When all of the ganache has been scooped, roll each portion by hand into a round ball.

9 Melt and temper the chocolate for dipping using the procedure on page 36. If using compound coating, follow the heating instructions on the package.

10 Dip the ganache centers in the tempered chocolate or compound coating using one of the techniques illustrated on pages 44 and 45.

11 After dipping, but before the chocolate sets fully, garnish as desired.

Keys to Success

- Make sure the ganache has enough time to firm in the refrigerator. An hour is a good guideline, but it is okay to leave it longer, even overnight if desired.

- Resting the ganache after mixing allows it to harden slightly, which makes scooping much easier.

- Dipping the truffles twice creates a thicker chocolate shell, but dipping once provides a faster alternative.

- Suggested garnishes: Roll in cocoa powder, texture with a fork, apply chopped nuts, or pipe tempered chocolate on each piece.

Coffee Truffles

Coffee and chocolate are naturals together, each seeming to intensify the flavor of the other. These truffles use instant coffee crystals in the ganache to make a rich, creamy treat. The amount of coffee can be altered to taste.

SKILL LEVEL

8 oz (1 cup) Heavy cream

1½ oz (2 tbsp) Light corn syrup

1 tbsp Instant coffee granules

½ oz (1 tbsp) Butter, unsalted, soft

14 oz (2⅓ cups) Dark chocolate, pistoles or chopped in ½-inch pieces

12 oz (2 cups) Dark chocolate or dark compound coating, chopped in ½-inch pieces, for dipping

2 tsp Instant coffee granules, for garnish

1 Line a 9 × 13–inch baking pan with parchment paper.

2 Combine the cream and corn syrup in a 2-quart saucepan and bring to a boil.

3 Remove from the heat. Add the instant coffee granules and stir to dissolve.

4 Add the butter and chopped chocolate or pistoles to the cream and stir until smooth and homogeneous.

5 Pour the finished ganache into the baking pan to make a thin layer and cover with plastic wrap. Refrigerate for 1 hour or more until the ganache is firm.

6 Put the ganache in a mixer bowl and mix on medium speed using a paddle attachment for 30 seconds. Or stir vigorously in a mixing bowl by hand, using a spatula.

7 Allow the ganache to rest at room temperature for 5 minutes. Line a sheet pan with parchment paper.

8 Using a #100 scoop or a teaspoon, scoop out balls of ganache and place on the sheet pan at room temperature.

9 When all of the ganache has been scooped, roll each portion by hand into a round ball.

10 Melt and temper the chocolate for dipping using the procedure on page 36. If using compound coating, follow the heating instructions on the package.

11 Dip the ganache centers in the tempered chocolate or compound coating using one of the techniques illustrated on pages 44 and 45.

12 After dipping, but before the chocolate sets fully, put a pinch of instant coffee on top of each piece.

Keys to Success

- Make sure the ganache has enough time to firm in the refrigerator. An hour is a good guideline, but it is okay to leave it longer, even overnight if desired.

- Resting the ganache after mixing allows it to harden slightly, which makes scooping much easier.

- Dipping the truffles twice creates a thicker chocolate shell, but dipping once provides a faster alternative.

- Putting the instant coffee for garnish in a shaker makes it easier to apply.

Gianduja Truffles

Gianduja (pronounced jhan-DOO-ya) is a mixture of toasted hazelnuts in chocolate.
Praline paste gives these truffles a pronounced roasted, nutty, caramel flavor.

SKILL LEVEL

4 oz (½ cup) **Heavy cream**

1½ oz (2 tbsp) **Light corn syrup**

5 oz (½ cup) **Praline paste, well stirred**

8 oz (1⅓ cups) **Dark chocolate, pistoles or chopped in ½-inch pieces**

12 oz (2 cups) **Dark chocolate or dark compound coating, chopped in ½-inch pieces, for dipping**

2 oz (¼ cup) **Chopped toasted blanched hazelnuts, for garnish** (see page 50)

1 Line a 9 × 13–inch baking pan with parchment paper.

2 Combine the cream and corn syrup in a small saucepan and bring to a boil.

3 Remove from the heat. Add the praline paste and chopped dark chocolate or pistoles to the cream and stir until smooth and homogeneous.

4 Pour the finished ganache into the baking pan to make a thin layer and cover with plastic wrap. Refrigerate for 1 hour or more until the ganache is firm.

5 Put the ganache in a mixer bowl and mix on medium speed using a paddle attachment for 30 seconds. Or stir vigorously in a mixing bowl by hand, using a spatula.

6 Allow the ganache to rest at room temperature for 5 minutes. Line a sheet pan with parchment paper.

7 Using a #100 scoop or a teaspoon, scoop out balls of ganache and place on the sheet pan at room temperature.

8 When all of the ganache has been scooped, roll each portion by hand into a round ball.

9 Melt and temper the chocolate for dipping using the procedure on page 36. If using compound coating, follow the heating instructions on the package.

10 Dip the ganache centers in the tempered chocolate or compound coating using one of the techniques illustrated on pages 44 and 45.

11 After dipping, but before the chocolate sets fully, garnish each truffle with a pinch of chopped toasted hazelnuts on top. As an alternative garnish, roll the truffles in chopped nuts after the final coat.

Keys to Success

○ When using praline paste, be sure to stir it well to obtain a uniform consistency.

○ Make sure the ganache has enough time to firm in the refrigerator. An hour is a good guideline, but it is okay to leave it longer, even overnight if desired.

○ Resting the ganache after mixing allows it to harden slightly, which makes scooping much easier.

○ Dipping the truffles twice creates a thicker chocolate shell, but dipping once provides a faster alternative.

Coconut-Lime Truffles

MAKES 48 PIECES

The tropical flavors of coconut and lime combine with white chocolate to make a surprising and unconventional truffle.

SKILL LEVEL

2 oz (¼ cup) **Heavy cream**

2 oz (¼ cup) **Cream of coconut**

½ oz (1 tbsp) **Light corn syrup**

1 **Lime, grated zest and juice**

12 oz (2 cups) **White chocolate, pistoles or chopped in ½-inch pieces**

12 oz (2 cups) **White chocolate or white compound coating, chopped in ½-inch pieces, for dipping**

2 oz (½ cup) **Sweetened shredded coconut, lightly toasted, for garnish**

1. Line a 9 × 13–inch baking pan with parchment paper.

2. Combine the cream, cream of coconut, corn syrup, and lime zest in a 2-quart saucepan and bring to a boil.

3. Remove from the heat. Add the chopped white chocolate or pistoles and stir until smooth and homogeneous. Stir in the lime juice.

4. Pour the finished ganache into the baking pan to make a thin layer and cover with plastic wrap. Refrigerate for 1 hour or more until the ganache is firm.

5. Put the ganache in a mixer bowl and mix on medium speed using a paddle attachment for 30 seconds. Or stir vigorously in a mixing bowl by hand, using a spatula.

6. Allow the ganache to rest at room temperature for 5 minutes. Line a sheet pan with parchment paper.

7. Using a #100 scoop or a teaspoon, scoop out balls of ganache and place on the sheet pan at room temperature.

8. When all of the ganache has been scooped, roll each portion by hand into a round ball.

9. Melt and temper the chocolate for dipping using the procedure on page 36. If using compound coating, follow the heating instructions on the package.

10. Dip the ganache centers in the tempered chocolate or compound coating using one of the techniques illustrated on pages 44 and 45.

11. After the second coat of chocolate, roll the truffles in the coconut to cover them fully.

Keys to Success

- Make sure the ganache has enough time to firm in the refrigerator. An hour is a good guideline, but it is okay to leave it longer, even overnight if desired.

- Resting the ganache after mixing allows it to harden slightly, which makes scooping much easier.

- Dipping the truffles twice creates a thicker chocolate shell, but dipping once provides a faster alternative.

- Make sure your toasted coconut has cooled completely before rolling the truffles in it.

Honey-Lavender Truffles

MAKES 48 PIECES

The warm Mediterranean flavors of honey and lavender combine with milk chocolate in these truffles to create a floral summery flavor. Dried lavender flower garnish makes them especially aromatic.

SKILL LEVEL

4 oz (½ cup) **Heavy cream**

1 tbsp Dried lavender flowers

2 oz (3 tbsp) **Honey**

12 oz (2 cups) **Milk chocolate, pistoles or chopped in ½-inch pieces**

12 oz (2 cups) **Milk or white chocolate or compound coating, chopped in ½-inch pieces, for dipping**

About 1 tbsp Dried lavender flowers, for garnish

1 Line a 9 × 13–inch baking pan with parchment paper.

2 Combine the cream and lavender flowers in a 2-quart saucepan. Heat nearly to a boil. Remove from the heat, cover, and allow to steep for 5 minutes.

3 Strain the cream into a clean 2-quart saucepan using a fine-mesh strainer. Press down well on the lavender to extract all the liquid possible.

4 Add the honey to the flavored cream and bring to a boil.

5 Remove from the heat. Add the chopped milk chocolate or pistoles to the cream and stir until smooth and homogeneous.

6 Pour the finished ganache into the baking pan to make a thin layer and cover with plastic wrap. Refrigerate for 1 hour or more until the ganache is firm.

7 Put the ganache in a mixer bowl and mix on medium speed using a paddle attachment for 30 seconds. Or stir vigorously in a mixing bowl by hand, using a spatula.

8 Allow the ganache to rest at room temperature for 5 minutes. Line a sheet pan with parchment paper.

9 Using a #100 scoop or a teaspoon, scoop out balls of ganache and place on the sheet pan at room temperature.

10 When all of the ganache has been scooped, roll each portion by hand into a round ball.

11 Melt and temper the chocolate for dipping using the procedure on page 36. If using compound coating, follow the heating instructions on the package.

12 Dip the ganache centers in the tempered chocolate or compound coating using using one of the techniques illustrated on pages 44 and 45.

13 Garnish each truffle with 3 dried lavender flowers after dipping but before the chocolate fully sets.

Keys to Success

○ Be certain to press all of the moisture from the steeped lavender flowers.

○ Make sure the ganache has enough time to firm in the refrigerator. An hour is a good guideline, but it is okay to leave it longer, even overnight if desired.

○ Resting the ganache after mixing allows it to harden slightly, which makes scooping much easier.

○ Dipping the truffles twice creates a thicker chocolate shell, but dipping once provides a faster alternative.

Green Tea Truffles

Macha green tea not only flavors this ganache, but also provides its distinctive green color. Different green teas have different flavor nuances; try different teas and vary the amount to find your own cup of tea.

SKILL LEVEL

4 oz (½ cup) **Heavy cream**

2 tsp **Macha green tea powder**

1½ oz (2 tbsp) **Light corn syrup**

12 oz (2 cups) **White chocolate, pistoles or chopped in ½-inch pieces**

½ oz (1 tbsp) **Butter, unsalted, soft**

12 oz (2 cups) **White chocolate or white compound coating, chopped in ½-inch pieces, for dipping**

1 tsp **Macha green tea powder, for garnish**

---

1 Line a 9 × 13–inch baking pan with parchment paper.

2 Combine the cream, green tea, and corn syrup in a 2-quart saucepan and bring to a boil.

3 Remove from the heat. Add the chopped white chocolate or pistoles and butter to the cream and stir until smooth and homogeneous.

4 Pour the finished ganache into the baking pan to make a thin layer and cover with plastic wrap. Refrigerate for 1 hour or more until the ganache is firm.

5 Put the ganache in a mixer bowl and mix on medium speed using a paddle attachment for 30 seconds. Or stir vigorously in a mixing bowl by hand, using a spatula.

6 Allow the ganache to rest at room temperature for 5 minutes.

7 Using a #100 scoop or a teaspoon, scoop out balls of ganache and place on a pan with parchment paper at room temperature.

8 When all of the ganache has been scooped, roll up each portion into a round ball by hand.

9 Melt and temper the white chocolate for dipping using the procedure on page 36. If using compound coating, follow the heating instructions on the package.

10 Dip the ganache centers in the tempered white chocolate or white compound coating using one of the techniques illustrated on pages 44 and 45.

11 After dipping, but before the chocolate sets, sprinkle green tea on top of each truffle.

Keys to Success

○ Make sure the ganache has enough time to firm in the refrigerator. An hour is a good guideline, but it is okay to leave it longer, even overnight if desired.

○ Resting the ganache after mixing allows it to harden slightly, which makes scooping much easier.

○ Dipping the truffles twice creates a thicker chocolate shell, but dipping once provides a faster alternative.

○ Putting the green tea for garnish in a shaker makes it easier to apply.

Green Tea Truffles and Orange Truffles
(page 79)

Milk or White Chocolate Liqueur Truffles

MAKES 55 PIECES

Milk chocolate pairs well with less intense liqueurs like Irish Cream or amaretto, while white chocolate is at home with fruit liqueurs such as limoncello or Chambord.

SKILL LEVEL

4 oz (½ cup) **Heavy cream**

½ oz (1 tbsp) **Light corn syrup**

½ oz (1 tbsp) **Butter, unsalted, soft**

15 oz (2½ cups) **Milk or white chocolate, pistoles or chopped in ½-inch pieces**

1 oz (2 tbsp) **Liqueur or spirit**

10 oz (1⅔ cups) **Milk or white chocolate or compound coating, chopped in ½-inch pieces, for dipping**

Garnish, as needed

---

1 Line a 9 × 13–inch baking pan with parchment paper.

2 Combine the cream and corn syrup in a 2-quart saucepan and bring to a boil.

3 Remove from the heat. Add the butter and chopped milk or white chocolate or pistoles to the cream and stir until smooth and homogeneous.

4 Stir the liqueur into the ganache.

5 Pour the finished ganache into the baking pan to make a thin layer and cover with plastic wrap. Refrigerate for 1 hour or more until the ganache is firm.

6 Put the ganache in a mixer bowl and mix on medium speed using a paddle attachment for 30 seconds. Or stir vigorously in a mixing bowl by hand, using a spatula.

7 Allow the ganache to rest at room temperature for 5 minutes. Line a sheet pan with parchment paper.

8 Using a #100 scoop or a teaspoon, scoop out balls of ganache and place on the sheet pan at room temperature.

9 When all of the ganache has been scooped, roll each portion by hand into a round ball.

10 Melt and temper the chocolate for dipping using the procedure on page 36. If using compound coating, follow the heating instructions on the package.

11 Dip the ganache centers in the tempered chocolate or compound coating using one of the techniques illustrated on pages 44 and 45.

12 Garnish as desired.

Keys to Success

○ Make sure the ganache has enough time to firm in the refrigerator. An hour is a good guideline, but it is okay to leave it longer, even overnight if desired.

○ Resting the ganache after mixing allows it to harden slightly, which makes scooping much easier.

○ Dipping the truffles twice creates a thicker chocolate shell, but dipping once provides a faster alternative.

○ Suggested garnishes: Texture with a fork, apply chopped nuts, or apply dried fruit.

Orange Truffles

Citrus and chocolate is always a welcome combination. The bright flavor of oranges brings a vibrant appeal to these little gems, while the dark chocolate shell adds elegance.

SKILL LEVEL

4 oz (½ cup) **Heavy cream**

½ oz (1 tbsp) **Light corn syrup**

½ oz (1 tbsp) **Butter, unsalted, soft**

18 oz (3 cups) **White chocolate, pistoles or chopped in ½-inch pieces**

1 oz (2 tbsp) **Orange juice concentrate**

1 oz (2 tbsp) **Orange liqueur**

12 oz (2 cups) **White chocolate or compound coating, chopped in ½-inch pieces, for dipping**

Grated zest of 1 orange, for garnish

1 oz (2 tbsp) **Coarse sugar, for garnish**

---

1   Line a 9 × 13–inch baking pan with parchment paper.

2   Combine the cream and corn syrup in a 2-quart saucepan and bring to a boil.

3   Remove from the heat. Add the butter and chopped white chocolate or pistoles to the cream and stir until smooth and homogeneous.

4   Stir the orange juice concentrate and the liqueur into the ganache.

5   Pour the finished ganache into the baking pan to make a thin layer and cover with plastic wrap. Refrigerate for 1 hour or more until the ganache is firm.

6   Put the ganache in a mixer bowl and mix on medium speed using a paddle attachment for 30 seconds. Or stir vigorously in a mixing bowl by hand, using a spatula.

7   Allow the ganache to rest at room temperature for 5 minutes. Line a sheet pan with parchment paper.

8   Using a #100 scoop or a teaspoon, scoop out balls of ganache and place on the sheet pan at room temperature.

9   When all of the ganache has been scooped, roll each portion by hand into a round ball.

10   Melt and temper the white chocolate for dipping using the procedure on page 36. If using compound coating, follow the heating instructions on the package.

11   Dip the ganache centers in the tempered chocolate or compound coating using one of the techniques illustrated on pages 44 and 45.

12   Mix the orange zest and coarse sugar and sprinkle on top of each truffle after dipping but before the chocolate sets fully.

Keys to Success

○ Make sure the ganache has enough time to firm in the refrigerator. An hour is a good guideline, but it is okay to leave it longer, even overnight if desired.

○ Resting the ganache after mixing allows it to harden slightly, which makes scooping much easier.

○ Dipping the truffles twice creates a thicker chocolate shell, but dipping once provides a faster alternative.

T'ings

T'ings are the perfect way to take advantage of tempered chocolate left over after finishing other chocolates. There is no real need to measure, just spoon any leftover chocolate in bite-size pools and place the garnish of your choice on the tops; the possibilities are endless. They are so good that you will soon be tempering chocolate just to make t'ings.

SKILL LEVEL

4 oz (⅜ cup) Milk, dark, or white chocolate, tempered, or compound coating, melted

1 oz (¼ cup) Chopped nuts or dried or candied fruit, for topping

---

1 Line a sheet pan with parchment paper.

2 Using a teaspoon, drop the tempered chocolate in half dollar–size pieces onto the sheet pan.

3 Place the desired garnishes on the pools of chocolate before they begin to set.

4 Allow the t'ings to set fully before releasing from the paper.

SUGGESTED COMBINATIONS

White chocolate with dried cherries and pistachios

Milk chocolate with macadamias and candied pineapple

Dark chocolate with toasted hazelnuts and dried apricots

Keys to Success

○ If you think you might have leftover tempered chocolate, prepare the toppings for the t'ings ahead of time.

○ Make certain that the toppings are at room temperature before putting them on the chocolate; very hot or very cold toppings will not give good results.

○ Be sure to put the toppings on the t'ings before the chocolate sets.

Peanut Butter, Mint, and Green Tea Meltaways

Mint Meltaways

MAKES 81 PIECES

They are called meltaways for a reason: When coconut fat is mixed with chocolate, the result is a mixture that melts very quickly in the mouth. Add flavoring to it, and you have a singular sensation. No need to dip these in chocolate—just dust with powdered sugar or cocoa powder and they are ready to savor.

SKILL LEVEL

12 oz (2 cups) Dark chocolate, pistoles or chopped in ½-inch pieces, melted, tempered

4 oz (½ cup) Coconut fat, melted, at 85°F

⅛ tsp Mint oil

4 oz (1 cup) Confectioners' sugar

1 Line a 9-inch square baking pan with plastic wrap (see page 51).

2 Mix together the tempered chocolate, coconut fat, and mint oil. Stir for 3 minutes.

3 Pour into the baking pan. Allow to set at room temperature for 1 hour or until firm.

4 Dust the surface of the meltaways with sifted confectioners' sugar.

5 Remove from the pan by pulling the plastic wrap up and out. Remove the plastic from the slab of meltaways.

6 Cut into 1-inch squares, or the desired sizes.

7 Toss lightly in sifted confectioners' sugar. Shake off excess.

GREEN TEA MELTAWAYS Use 1 lb/2⅔ cups white chocolate, pistoles or chopped in ½-inch pieces, melted, tempered; 4 oz/½ cup melted coconut fat at 85°F; and 2 tbsp Macha green tea.

PEANUT BUTTER MELTAWAYS Use 12 oz/2 cups milk chocolate, pistoles or chopped in ½-inch pieces, melted, tempered; 2 oz/¼ cup melted coconut fat at 85°F; and 4½ oz/½ cup peanut butter at 85°F.

PRALINE MELTAWAYS Use 1 lb/2⅔ cups dark chocolate, pistoles or chopped in ½-inch pieces, melted, tempered; 2 oz/¼ cup melted coconut fat at 85°F; and 2 oz/¼ cup praline paste.

Keys to Success

○ Temper the chocolate using the method on page 36. If the chocolate is not tempered, the meltaways will not set properly.

○ Use deodorized coconut fat. If you use nondeodorized fat, they will set and melt properly but will have a strong coconut flavor.

○ Cut the meltaways when they are firm, but do not refrigerate and do not wait overnight before cutting, or they will be too brittle to cut cleanly.

Chocolate-Dipped Anything

MAKES ABOUT 25 PIECES

Fresh and dried fruit are both ideal for dipping in chocolate. Fresh fruit should be enjoyed within hours of dipping, while dried fruit will keep for weeks. Pretzels, crackers, and virtually any other dry food may also be dipped in chocolate to create quick, easy confections. Both the weight and volume given for the product for dipping are approximate, and will vary depending on the centers being dipped.

SKILL LEVEL

1 lb (2 cups) **Products for dipping**
8 oz (¾ cup) **Milk, dark, or white chocolate, melted, tempered, or compound coating, melted**

---

1 Line a sheet pan with parchment paper.

2 Using one of the dipping techniques on pages 42 and 43, dip the centers partially or completely in the tempered chocolate.

3 Lay the dipped pieces on the sheet pan. Allow the chocolate to set at room temperature.

Keys to Success

○ The exact measurements of the centers to dip will vary greatly depending on what they are.

○ Keep your chocolate in temper while dipping (see Maintaining Chocolate Temperature, page 40).

○ Allowing the chocolate to set at room temperature will result in the best appearance of the chocolate.

○ Fresh foods such as fruit should be enjoyed the same day, while dry foods such as pretzels or dried fruit can be stored for weeks at room temperature.

OPPOSITE: Chocolate-dipped dried fruit and pretzels

Peppermint Bark

Peppermint bark is the perfect homemade chocolate for the holidays. Festive, quick to make, and delicious, it will quickly become part of your holiday tradition. The amount and type of candy on the top may be varied to suit your taste.

SKILL LEVEL

8 oz (1½ cups) **Candy canes** (crushed)

⅛ **tsp Peppermint oil**

8 oz (¾ cup) **Dark chocolate, tempered, or dark compound coating, melted**

8 oz (¾ cup) **White chocolate, tempered, or white compound coating, melted**

---

1 Line a 10 × 15–inch sheet pan with parchment paper.

2 Place the candy canes in a heavy plastic bag. Crush lightly with a rolling pin.

3 Mix the mint oil into the dark chocolate.

4 Pour the white chocolate on the sheet pan. Spread with an offset palette knife to an even thickness. Let set at room temperature.

5 When the white chocolate has set, spread the dark chocolate on top of the white in an even layer. This should be done immediately, or no more than 1 hour after the white chocolate has set.

6 Sprinkle the crushed candy canes uniformly on the surface of the dark chocolate before it sets.

7 Allow to set at room temperature for 1 hour or longer.

8 Break in pieces to serve.

Keys to Success

○ Spread the layer of dark chocolate as soon as possible after the white chocolate has set. This will ensure that the layers stick together.

○ Sprinkle the crushed candy on the dark chocolate before the chocolate has even thought about setting so that it adheres.

○ The candy cane will get sticky if exposed to moisture, so always store the bark away from humidity.

Bark

There is virtually no limit to the combinations of chocolate and toppings that can be used to make bark; if you like it, it goes! Dried fruit and toasted nuts are the most common combinations, but seeds, cereal, and candies are all suitable candidates. Mix and match to make you own signature chocolates.

SKILL LEVEL

1 lb (1½ cups) **Milk, dark, or white chocolate, tempered, or compound coating, melted**

4 oz (1 cup) **Chopped toppings** (see Keys to Success)

1 Line a 10 × 15–inch sheet pan with parchment paper.

2 Pour the tempered chocolate or melted coating on the sheet pan. Spread with an offset palette knife to an even thickness.

3 Before the chocolate begins to set, sprinkle the chopped toppings on top of the chocolate.

4 Allow the chocolate to set fully, about 1 hour.

5 Break the bark in random pieces 2 to 3 inches across.

Keys to Success

○ Be certain that your chocolate is tempered (see page 36) or that your coating is at the right temperature according to the manufacturer's instructions.

○ Tempered chocolate sets quickly, so put the toppings on as soon as the chocolate has been spread to ensure that they adhere properly.

○ Suggested toppings: dried apricots and toasted hazelnuts, dried cherries and toasted almonds, coconut and candied pineapple, pretzel pieces and peanuts, chopped crystallized ginger and toasted sesame seeds.

5

Brittles, Toffees, and Taffies

This chapter explores many of the popular candies based on cooked sugar. While the candies in this chapter are of many different textures, colors, and flavors—from hard candy, brittles, and toffee to soft caramels and taffy—they all share some common traits. All are made by cooking sugar mixtures to precise temperatures, and in all of these confections, the sugar remains uncrystallized in the finished product, resulting in either a crisp, glassy texture or a soft, chewy one. The differences in the products are the result of slightly differing ingredients, cooking temperatures, and handling techniques.

Success with these items depends on the Sugar Master Techniques (see pages 28 to 32). Of particular importance when cooking these candies are the temperature to which they are cooked and proper cleaning of the pan during cooking. The temperature to which a batch is cooked controls how firm the finished product will be; overcooking taffy by just a few degrees will turn what should have been a soft, tender candy into a hard nugget that will challenge your teeth, and undercooking hard candy will result in a candy that sticks to your teeth rather than breaking crisply. Because of the importance of sugar cooking temperature, an accurate thermometer is vital to success with these recipes.

In addition to proper temperature, correct cooking technique must also be observed. Improper skimming or cleaning during cooking can recrystallize the sugar, turning your hard candy from bright, brilliant glass into a crumbly, sandy slab.

Nothing about the candies in this chapter is terribly difficult—they just require attention to proper cooking technique and temperature. It is recommended that you review the sugar cooking techniques on pages 29 to 32 before trying the recipes in this chapter for the first time.

Caution

Cooked sugar can give you one of the worst burns in a kitchen—always exercise extreme caution when working with it. Wearing clean leather or canvas gloves while handling the batches is a reasonable caution for those who are not experienced with the techniques involved. Whether or not you wear gloves, having a large bowl of ice water handy can prevent a minor burn from turning into a major one. If you spill hot sugar on your hand while molding hard candies, you can quickly immerse it in the ice water and avert the burn. While children can and should be involved in many aspects of home candy making, working with batches of hot cooked sugar is best left to adults with steady hands.

Cleaning Sugar-Boiling Pans

Few kitchen chores can seem more daunting than cleaning pans that have been used to boil sugar or cook caramel; the hard sugar or caramel coats the inside of the pan and is unyielding to even vigorously applied scrub pads. Soaking and scrubbing eventually do the trick, but only after a great deal of time and effort. Fortunately, cleaning is a very simple matter of filling the offending pan with water and boiling it for a few minutes. The boiling water will quickly dissolve the sugar in the pan, leaving you with a very simple cleanup.

Hard Candies

HARD CANDIES are the most fundamental of the confections in this chapter, consisting of little more than sugar, corn syrup, water, and flavor. What gives them their crisp appeal is that the water is all but removed during cooking, resulting in the glassy, hard candy that is so well known. As simple as it is, hard candy may be treated in a variety of ways, from simply pouring it onto a slab and cutting it, to molding it, to dipping apples or other fruit in it. For more elaborate hard candy techniques such as candy canes, warming apparatus and practice are required, but molding, slabbing, and dipping are all well within the reach of the home confectioner.

What's in it?

Hard candies are nothing more than a sugar syrup cooked until almost all of the water has evaporated. When this syrup cools to room temperature it becomes a crisp, brittle glass made of sugar. These are the ingredients you will need to make hard candies in your kitchen:

WATER Water is necessary to dissolve the sugar in the candy. Essentially all of the water will be removed during cooking.

SUGAR (CANE OR BEET) Ordinary sugar is the primary ingredient in hard candies. It provides both the bulk of the product and the sweet flavor expected from these confections.

CORN SYRUP Corn syrup is almost universally used when making hard candies because it helps to prevent the sugar from recrystallizing and thus losing its glassy appearance and smooth texture.

COLOR Color is commonly added to hard candy. It should be added late in the cooking process to allow the color to disperse throughout the entire batch. Any water-soluble food color may be used to color hard candies.

FLAVORING Flavorings in hard candies must be very concentrated manufactured flavors, so as to provide flavor without adding excessive water that would soften the candy. Most manufactured flavors are adversely affected by extreme heat, so they should be added only after cooking, just before pouring or forming the candy.

ACIDS When making fruit-flavored candies, an acid such as citric acid is commonly added to the batch after cooking to provide a tart balance to the sweet flavor and make a more realistic fruit candy. They are not used to complement nonfruit flavors such as mint. Acids must be added after cooking is completed or they will soften the candies excessively.

How it's made

Hard candies are one of the simplest types of candy to cook at home. Caution: Always take great care whenever cooking sugar because of the potential for severe burns.

1   Combine sugar and water in a saucepan. Stir over high heat until the mixture boils.

2   Add the corn syrup. Do not stir after this point.

3   Add color. Add the color at around 280°F.

4   Boil to 315°F. Accuracy is important! Use a good thermometer.

5   Remove from heat and shock in cold water. This prevents carryover cooking, which will brown the sugar and give it a caramel flavor.

6   Allow sugar to cool undisturbed for 5 minutes. During this time, any bubbles in the hot sugar will dissipate, and the sugar will begin to thicken slightly as it cools, making it easier to handle.

7   Add the flavor and acid, if using. Stir gently with a spoon or spatula to incorporate.

How it's formed

1   Carefully pour the cooked batch into a lightly oiled pan and allow the slab to cool to a firm but malleable consistency.

2   Use a sharp pair of scissors to cut the hard candy into bite-sized pieces.

using candy molds

Using molds to make hard candies is very easy and requires only the desired molds suitable for use with sugar. There are different types of molds available that can be used with hard candy; metal molds, either heavy cast molds or lighter stamped molds, are the most common variety, and the most durable. These molds may be modern, but antique metal candy molds are also available. Some molds are designed to be used with sticks to create lollipops, and others are intended for use without sticks (see "Clear Toys," page 95). Special silicone molds may also be found for use with hard candy. These molds are designed to tolerate the high heat of cooked sugar and have the advantages of flexibility and not requiring oiling. Rubber or plastic molds should be used with hard candy only if they are designed specifically for that purpose.

1   Clean, dry, and lightly oil molds to prevent the sugar from sticking. Vegetable oil is suitable for this purpose. Note that silicone molds do not require oil.

2   Pour the thickened sugar into the prepared molds. Pour slowly to control the sugar.

3   Insert sticks if desired. If making lollipops, insert sticks as the sugar begins to cool.

4   Allow the candy to cool. The hot sugar must cool entirely before it can be released from the molds, which can take a surprisingly long time, especially with larger molds. Refrigeration can speed the process, but the molds should never be refrigerated so much that the candy itself gets chilled, or it will be damaged by moisture when it is removed from the mold.

5   Release from the molds. Once the molded candy has cooled to room temperature, it can be released from the mold.

6   Wrap immediately to prevent damage from exposure to moisture in the air.

Slowly pour the thickened sugar into molds; to create lollipops, insert sticks as the sugar begins to cool.

How else can I use it?

Cooked hard candy can also be used to coat various types of fresh or dried fruit, nuts, or other types of centers. In this technique, the candy batch is cooked, shocked, and cooled as usual. The centers are then dipped, creating a crisp candy coating on the outside. The sugar may be colored and flavored, or it may be simply left natural.

1   Prepare the centers. Fruit is the most commonly used center for dipping in hard candy sugar. Small pieces such as kumquats, strawberries, or grapes work well, as do larger fruits such as apples. Nuts or marzipan shapes may also be dipped. When dipping a strawberry, the stem and hull provide a convenient handle by which to hold it. When dipping an apple, kumquat, or other fruit that has no such stem, a toothpick or other stick can be used to hold the fruit for dipping.

2   Dip the prepared centers in the hot sugar. Should the sugar cool off too much and become too thick, it can be rewarmed by gently stirring over direct heat. Excessive rewarming and stirring, however, can cause the sugar to recrystallize, at which point there is little that can be done to correct it.

3   Place dipped fruit on a lightly oiled surface or parchment paper to cool. Allow the dipped creations to cool completely so that the sugar will be crisp and not be sticky.

4   Use as soon as possible. Candy-coated fruit makes a delightful treat and supplies brilliant colors to a tray of candies, but due to the moisture in the fruit, it has a short life. Fruit should be dipped as close as possible to the time it will be enjoyed, should never be refrigerated, and should always be protected from humidity.

Dipping fresh fruit in cooked sugar gives the fruit a beautiful, crisp candy coating. It should always be enjoyed within hours of dipping.

How it's stored

Moisture is the enemy of sugar in general, and of hard candy especially. Hard candies can be stored indefinitely, but they should always be stored tightly sealed. All hard candies are vulnerable to damage from humidity and must be wrapped or packaged immediately to protect them from exposure to moisture, which will make them sticky and waxy. They must also be protected from heat, but refrigeration is never advised, as it will contribute to damage from moisture. Hard candy should be wrapped in plastic immediately upon cooling and stored at room temperature in plastic bags. Placing a desiccant such as silica gel in the bag will help to absorb moisture and contribute to a longer shelf life.

Clear Toys

Hard candy today is found in many colors and a wide range of flavors, but generally only in a few basic shapes. This is entirely the opposite of the way hard candy was sold in the nineteenth century. "Clear toys" were boiled sugar molded into various shapes or characters, without the stick that lollipops have. Clear toys are sometimes referred to as *barley sugar* or *barley pops* because domestic barley sugar was frequently used in their production rather than imported cane sugar, which at that time was more expensive. Food colors were not yet available, and flavors were limited and expensive, so clear toys are traditionally left the natural light amber color that they develop during cooking, with the slight hint of lightly caramelized sugar being the only flavor.

In the 1800s, clear toy molds were made of cast metal by a company called Thomas Mills and Brother and were available in hundreds of shapes, from battleships and trains to camels and a frog on a bicycle. These molds bear a number on the outside that corresponds to the original Thomas Mills catalog. The original molds have amazing detail that translates on each candy that comes out of them. More recent molds are often aluminum and do not have the detail of the originals; modern clear toy molds may be made of aluminum or silicone and can be found in a range of quality. The original clear toy molds have become desirable as collectibles, so they are expensive when found in good condition.

With the more common availability of cane sugar and the advent of corn syrup in the nineteenth century, these ingredients were boiled together to produce clear toys that had previously been made using barley sugar.

Most food historians credit German immigrants with bringing the tradition of clear toys to America, and they are still made in regions where these immigrants settled, such as Lancaster County, Pennsylvania. Today, several candy makers make traditional clear toys, many using the original Thomas Mills molds from the 1800s. Some use colors and flavors to give the candy a more modern appeal, some follow a more traditional approach, forgoing color and manufactured flavors, and some even incorporate barley sugar for its unique flavor, slight color, and historical accuracy.

Clear toys are simple for the home confectioner to make; all that is required is sugar, corn syrup, water, a thermometer, and the molds, along with a basic knowledge of sugar cooking technique. They can easily become a simple and delicious homemade holiday tradition that celebrates simpler times.

Brittle

PEANUT BRITTLE is a truly American candy. Although nuts cooked with various sweeteners have appeared worldwide throughout recorded history, peanut brittle as we know it today probably dates to the nineteenth century, when corn syrup first became available.

What's in it?

Like hard candy, brittle contains sugar and corn syrup. Unlike hard candy, though, brittle has the addition of nuts, butter, salt, and baking soda, and the flavor of brittle is developed from the roasting nuts and caramelizing sugar, rather than from the addition of flavors as in hard candy.

WATER Water is necessary to dissolve the sugar in the brittle. Essentially all of the water will be removed during cooking.

SUGAR (CANE OR BEET) Ordinary sugar is the primary ingredient in brittle and provides both the bulk of the candy and the sweet flavor.

CORN SYRUP Corn syrup in brittle helps to prevent the sugar from recrystallizing and contributes to the brown color and roasted flavor.

NUTS Peanuts are the most common variety, but others may be used as well. The nuts to be used in brittle must be untoasted, as they will roast during the cooking process. The nuts provide flavor, texture, and color.

SALT Salt is added to brittle purely to bring out the flavor of the toasted nuts and to provide a flavor contrast to the sweet brittle.

VANILLA EXTRACT Vanilla extract is added to round out the flavor.

BUTTER Butter contributes flavor and a shorter texture to brittle, resulting in a more delicate bite.

BAKING SODA Baking soda aerates brittle, making for a more delicate crunch than just nuts imbedded in caramel. Baking soda also contributes to the golden brown color and the caramel flavor (see "Why It Works," page 98).

How it's made

When making brittle, the sugars are cooked with the nuts, and after the proper temperature is reached, salt, butter, baking soda, and vanilla extract are stirred in off the heat. Once these ingredients are incorporated, the brittle is spread as thin as desired on a marble surface or in an oiled pan and allowed to cool to room temperature, when it can be broken into the desired pieces.

1   Combine the sugar, corn syrup, and water and bring to a boil. Stop stirring once the batch reaches a boil.

2   Add the nuts at 220°F. Do not add them sooner, or they will absorb water and become soggy.

3   Stir constantly while continuing cooking. Nuts can scorch if they are not stirred during cooking.

4   Cook to 315°F. This will make the candy crisp and develop the proper color.

5   Remove from the heat and stir in the salt, butter, and vanilla extract.

6   Add the baking soda. Stir well to ensure even incorporation.

7   Pour onto an oiled surface or parchment paper and spread with an offset palette knife. An oiled pan, parchment paper, or stone countertop will all work equally well for spreading brittle. Work quickly—the brittle hardens rapidly!

How it's formed

Allow the brittle to cool, then break into desired pieces. Once completely cooled, the brittle can be broken easily into conveniently sized pieces.

Brittle hardens very quickly, so work rapidly to spread it to cool on parchment paper or an oiled surface.

How it's stored

Like other candy items, peanut brittle has a great shelf life as long as it is protected from humidity; it should be sealed in an airtight container as soon as possible after it cools to prevent it from absorbing moisture and becoming sticky. A desiccant such as silica gel in the container will help to prevent it from becoming sticky.

Toffee

TOFFEES go by several names, the best known of which are English toffee and butter-crunch. Regardless of the name you use, toffee is a crisp candy with a rich caramel flavor. It may have nut inclusions or be left without, and it may be coated in chocolate or ungilded.

Why It Works

Maillard Browning in Brittles, Toffees, and Caramels

Candies like brittles, toffees, and especially soft caramels have a caramel flavor and color, and yet the sugar itself never caramelizes: Why do they look and taste like caramel?

The answer is in a complex series of reactions between proteins and sugars called the *Maillard reaction* or *Maillard browning*. In all of these candies, there are proteins present during cooking, either from various dairy products, as in caramels and toffees, or from nuts, as in brittles. These proteins react with certain sugars and result in the roasted color and flavor vital to these favorite candies. Maillard browning not only applies to confectionery, but it is responsible for the flavors of many of our favorite foods and beverages. Chocolate flavor is developed during roasting of the beans as a result of the Maillard reaction; coffee flavor, too, is a direct result of this phenomenon, as are the color and flavor of brown or stout beers and ales. In fact, most "caramelized" products such as bread crust and browned meats are a result of these complex reactions.

The next time you enjoy some delicious soft caramels, also enjoy the knowledge that they are not "caramels" at all, but are actually delicious "Maillards"!

Baking Soda in Caramel

Baking soda is often added to the sugar when making peanut brittle or cara-mel-coated popcorn. It is best known as a leavener added to baked goods, where it reacts with acidic ingredients and produces carbon dioxide gas, lightening them. What is the purpose of baking soda in candies, and how does it work?

Just like in baked goods, when baking soda is added to hot sugar it generates carbon dioxide in the form of thousands of tiny bubbles. When you add baking soda to a cooked brittle mixture, the first thing you notice is that the batch turns milky opaque. This is because of all of the gas being created. These tiny gas bubbles get trapped in the cooked sugar as it cools, resulting in a more delicate bite than it would have without them, just as in a baked good. The difference is in the reaction itself: Unlike in baked goods, the baking soda in cooked sugar does not require an acidic ingredient to form gas. When it is exposed to temperatures around 150°F or higher, the baking soda spontaneously and rapidly releases gas, resulting in a lightened candy.

The second function of baking soda in candies is in flavor development. When you add baking soda, the sugar immediately begins to turn golden brown. The increased pH fosters this reaction resulting in not only brown color, but increased caramel flavor.

So why add baking soda to brittles? For more caramel color, increased flavor, and a more delicate mouthfeel.

What's in it?

SUGAR All toffees contain sugar. It provides sweetness and bulk to the candy.

WATER Water in toffee allows the sugar to dissolve during cooking. Water may be added directly or may be added in the form of milk or other dairy products that are mostly water.

CORN SYRUP (OPTIONAL) Not all toffees contain corn syrup. When it is used, its purpose is to prevent the recrystallization of the sugar. Toffees that do not contain corn syrup are more likely to crystallize during cooking and handling.

DAIRY PRODUCT Fresh dairy products such as milk or cream may be used in toffees; processed dairy products such as evaporated milk may also be used. Fresh butter is also a common ingredient in toffee. Dairy products all contribute to the brown color and roasted flavor expected from toffees.

BUTTER Butter makes toffee more tender and short textured. High-butter toffees (buttercrunch) are more tender, while lower butter toffees have a texture more similar to hard candies.

FLAVORING Toffee's flavor is produced mainly by browning the milk product during cooking, but flavoring adjuncts are commonly added as well. Vanilla extract and salt are the most common flavors added to toffees and serve to balance and complete the flavor, but other flavors such as coffee extract may also be used.

NUTS (OPTIONAL) Used as inclusions, nuts provide flavor and textural contrast to toffee.

How it's made

Like hard candy and brittle, toffee is a sugar candy cooked to a high temperature. Unlike brittle and hard candy, however, toffee contains dairy products, which provide its caramel color and flavor through cooking. Different dairy products may be used in making toffee, including fresh dairy products such as milk, cream, or butter, or processed dairy products such as evaporated or sweetened condensed milk. Toffee made using higher fat dairy products has a crisp and delicate texture, while toffee made using lower fat ingredients has more of a hard candy texture. Because of the dairy products in toffee, it must be stirred constantly during cooking to prevent scorching.

1   Combine all ingredients except for the inclusions and the flavors.

2   Stir while cooking. Toffee is prone to boiling over during cooking, so care must be taken to regulate the temperature. Constant stirring is vital to prevent scorching. The temperature to which it is cooked is critical. Undercooking toffee will make a sticky product rather than a properly crisp one; overcooking will result in an excessively dark color and bitter flavor.

3   Add the remaining ingredients. Flavorings and inclusions are added after cooking.

1 Use an offset palette knife to spread the cooked toffee in a thin layer on the parchment paper.

2 When the toffee layer has cooled to room temperature, spread a layer of tempered chocolate on top.

3 Before the chocolate begins to set, sprinkle the surface with chopped nuts.

How it's formed

1   Spread the toffee in the desired container. Once the toffee is cooked, the candy can be spread out on parchment paper or poured into a buttered pan and allowed to cool. If desired, toasted nuts may be pressed into the toffee before it cools and hardens.

2   Allow to cool to room temperature.

3   Once cooled to room temperature, toffee may be coated with tempered chocolate. This is both for flavor and to protect it from moisture. Nuts might then be applied before the chocolate sets completely.

4   Cooled toffee can be broken into pieces.

5   Toffee should be sealed in airtight packages to protect it from moisture. This is, if it is not consumed immediately (hard to resist!).

How it's stored

Toffee must be protected from humidity, so it is stored in airtight containers at room temperature.

Taffy

THE TERM *taffy* refers to any of a number of chewy candies that may be made using molasses, peanut butter, honey, chocolate, or manufactured flavors. Many types of taffy are pulled in order to incorporate air and lighten their texture and color; others are not pulled but are left to cool, resulting in a denser, chewier candy. Molasses taffy is probably the oldest type, dating at least to colonial America. Saltwater taffy is the most celebrated member of the family, found at seashores and resorts across the country. Saltwater taffy also provides the most opportunity for creative license, as it can be colored, flavored, and combined as desired.

What's in it?

SUGAR Sweetness and bulk are the functions of sugar in taffy.

CORN SYRUP Corn syrup helps to prevent recrystallization of the sugar and contributes to the chewy texture of taffy.

OTHER SUGARS Optional sugars include honey and molasses, added for their unique flavor contributions.

DAIRY PRODUCT Fresh or processed milk provides flavor and richness to taffy.

SALT Salt in taffy brings out the flavors of the candy.

FRAPPE (OPTIONAL) Frappe is essentially a meringue, and it is used to lighten the texture of the taffy; it helps to aerate the taffy.

FLAVORING Flavor in taffy may come from an extract such as vanilla or peppermint, a manufactured flavor, a food ingredient such as peanut butter or chocolate, or may come from one or more of the sweeteners such as honey or molasses. This wide range of possibilities helps to illustrate how many varieties of taffy exist.

COLOR Color is usually added to saltwater taffy to suggest the flavor it contains. Color is not customarily added to other varieties of taffy.

How it's made

Making taffy is very much like making the other candies in this chapter: Careful cooking of the batch will result in the proper texture of the candy. Overcooking will make the taffy too hard, and undercooking will make a taffy that doesn't have the characteristic chew.

1   Combine all ingredients except the flavor, color, and frappe (if using these ingredients) and stir while cooking, which will prevent the batch from scorching. Carefully watch the temperature of the batch so as not to overcook it.

2   Pour the cooked batch into an oiled baking pan. This will facilitate rapid cooling of the batch to prevent crystallization and allow you to move on to the next step more quickly.

3   If using them, place the frappe, flavor, and colors on the batch. These are added after cooking so that they are not damaged by the heat of cooking.

4   Turn the batch over periodically as it cools. This ensures even cooling and incorporates the optional ingredients.

5   Pull the taffy to lighten it. The batch should cool completely before pulling. The lighter a taffy is desired, the more it should be pulled.

 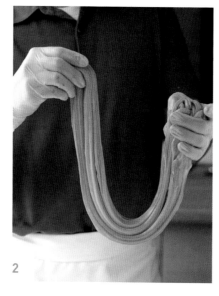 

1 Place the coloring, flavoring, and frappe on the batch after cooking so that they are not damaged by heat.

2 When the batch has cooled completely, place a hand at each end and pull the taffy to lighten it. Repeat until the batch reaches the desired lightness.

3 Use a pair of clean, sharp scissors to cut the ropes of taffy into pieces for wrapping.

How it's formed

Taffy may be shaped any way desired, but it is often seen in short logs (saltwater taffy), flat paddles, or long strips. The batch is pulled and shaped into the desired shapes and cut using oiled scissors.

How it's stored

All taffy must be wrapped immediately after forming to prevent it from slowly flowing back into one single sticky mass. Wrappers may be simple pieces of waxed paper, parchment paper, or specially made candy wrappers. Pulled taffies, while delicious fresh, will develop a better texture after resting for a day.

Soft Caramels

SOFT CARAMELS are among the most popular of all confections, and in any box of assorted chocolates they are very likely to be the first to disappear. The name *caramels* is not entirely accurate, as the brown color and roasted flavor are not at all due to the caramelization of sugar, but to the browning of the milk solids contained in them (see "Why It Works," page 98).

What's in it?

SUGAR Sugar provides sweetness and bulk to the candy.

CORN SYRUP The purpose of corn syrup is to prevent the recrystallization of the sugar and to contribute to the chewy texture of the candy. Soft caramels normally contain a high proportion of corn syrup, nearly equal to that of sugar.

DAIRY PRODUCT While fresh dairy products such as milk or cream may be used in caramels, processed dairy products such as evaporated milk or sweetened condensed milk are more common due to their lower water content and their greatly reduced cooking time. Regardless of the dairy product used, it provides the milk solids that give caramels their characteristic color and flavor, and it helps the candy hold its shape when being cut after it is cooked.

BUTTER Butter provides flavor and a shorter texture to caramels.

SALT Salt is an optional ingredient; it can be added to improve the flavor of the candy.

FLAVORING Vanilla extract and salt are the most common flavors added to caramels, but other flavoring agents such as extracts, fruit purees, or spices may also be added.

How it's made

Caramels are fundamentally simple to make; sugars and dairy products are cooked to remove water and develop color and flavor, while being stirred constantly to prevent scorching. The most crucial step in cooking soft caramels is the temperature to which they are cooked: Undercooking leads to very soft candies; overcooking results in caramels that are too hard to comfortably bite.

1   Combine the milk product, sugar, corn syrup, salt, and flavorings and stir while boiling. Unlike candies that do not contain milk, soft caramels must be stirred constantly while cooking to prevent scorching. Caramels have a decided tendency to boil over during cooking, so the heat must be carefully moderated to prevent spills.

2   Add butter. The butter is usually added part way through the cooking process.

3   Cook to final temperature. The temperature to which the caramels are cooked determines the consistency and is critical to the caramels. The consistency of the batch can be verified by testing in ice water (see Sugar Testing Techniques, page 30).

1 Pour the batch into a lightly oiled pan to cool.

2 Using an oiled chef's knife, slice the cooled slab into strips and then into squares.

How it's formed

Almost without exception, soft caramels are poured into a pan or frame and allowed to cool. Once cooled, they can be cut with a knife.

How else can I use it?

Soft caramel is the classic coating for caramel apples. The recipe requires no changes to make your own caramel apples or other caramel-dipped products. These delicious jewels can be further gilded by rolling them in toasted nuts or by allowing the soft caramel to cool and then dipping them in chocolate.

How it's stored

Like all of the candies in this chapter, soft caramels are susceptible to damage from moisture, so they must be protected from humidity. Cut caramels should either be individually wrapped immediately or else dipped in chocolate to insulate them from moisture.

What if

What if my candies turn opaque and brittle during working?

They have crystallized! The most likely cause is too much agitation during working. Unfortunately, there is little that can be done to fix this problem. Try again, and try not to agitate too much as it cools.

What if my candies are too soft?

They were not cooked to a high enough temperature. Sometimes as little as two degrees can cause a noticeable difference in the products. Calibrate your thermometer and cook another batch.

What if my candies are excessively browned?

They were cooked to too high a temperature, or cooked too slowly. Cook a new batch, cooking quickly and to a lower temperature.

What if my candies get sticky?

They have absorbed moisture from the air. Protect finished candies from humidity as soon as possible after cooking.

What if my caramels, toffee, brittles, or taffy have dark spots in the candy?

They were scorched during cooking. Stir gently and constantly with a heat-resistant rubber spatula during cooking. Cook in a heavy-bottomed saucepan.

Hard Candy

MAKES APPROXIMATELY 150 INDIVIDUAL HARD CANDIES

This basic recipe can be used in many different ways: poured into molds, poured into pools with a stick for lollipops, put in a pan and cut before it completely cools, or dipped into to make candied apples or candy-dipped fruits, to name just a few.

SKILL LEVEL

1½ lb (3 cups) **Sugar**

10 oz (¾ cup) **Light corn syrup**

4 oz (½ cup) **Water**

Color (see Keys to Success), **as desired**

Flavoring (see Keys to Success), **as desired**

---

1 Combine the sugar, corn syrup, and water in a 2-quart saucepan. Stir while bringing to a boil.

2 Cover the saucepan and boil for 4 minutes. Remove the cover, insert a thermometer, and cook without stirring until the temperature reaches 310°F.

3 Remove from the heat and shock the saucepan in ice water for 20 seconds to prevent carryover cooking.

4 Allow the cooked sugar to sit undisturbed for 5 minutes to cool and for bubbles to subside.

5 Gently mix in the color and flavoring until the batch is uniform in color.

6 Pour the candy into an oiled 9-inch square pan and allow to cool until the candy is firm yet still pliable.

7 Turn the slab of candy out of the pan and cut it into 1-inch strips using shears. Cut the 1-inch strips into 1-inch pieces to make 1-inch square individual hard candies. If necessary, the candy can be gently warmed in a 200°F oven to maintain pliability.

8 Allow the candy to cool fully, and store at room temperature in an airtight container.

FREE-FORM LOLLIPOPS *Pour the cooled candy onto a piece of oiled aluminum foil that has been flattened on a countertop. Pour disks the desired size, and push a lollipop stick into the sugar before it hardens.*

MOLDED HARD CANDIES OR LOLLIPOPS *After the candy has cooked and been allowed to cool for 5 minutes, pour it into molds made for hard candies or lollipops. Push a lollipop stick into the sugar before it hardens. Unmold when the candy has cooled.*

Keys to Success

○ Be careful to cook the sugar accurately. If the candy is cooked to too high a temperature, it will have a caramel color and flavor; if cooked too low, it will stick to your teeth rather than breaking cleanly.

○ Exercise extreme caution when cooking sugar for hard candy, as it can cause severe burns (see "Caution," page 90).

○ Paste colors are preferred, but liquid colors may be used as well.

○ Flavorings vary greatly in strength, and so the amounts will vary. If using fruit flavors, the addition of ½ tsp citric acid after cooking will enhance the flavor.

○ Do not stir the sugar during the cooling stage.

Lollipops

Candy-Coated Fruits

Candy-dipped fruits are the perfect combination of fresh fruit and hard candy. They have a crisp outer shell of sugar and the season's best fruit within—the perfect way to impress your guests at the end of a meal. They should never be refrigerated and must be used within hours of making.

SKILL LEVEL

Up to 80 pieces **Fresh fruit, with skin** (see Keys to Success)

1½ lb (3 cups) **Sugar**

10 oz (¾ cup) **Light corn syrup**

4 oz (½ cup) **Water**

---

1 Clean and dry the fruit. Insert a toothpick into each piece to make them easier to handle. Lightly oil a sheet pan, or line it with parchment paper, to hold the dipped pieces.

2 Combine the sugar, corn syrup, and water in a 2-quart saucepan. Stir while bringing to a boil.

3 Cover the saucepan and boil for 4 minutes. Remove the cover, insert a thermometer, and cook without stirring until the temperature reaches 310°F.

4 Remove from the heat and shock the saucepan in ice water for 20 seconds to prevent carryover cooking.

5 Allow the cooked sugar to sit undisturbed for 5 minutes to cool and for bubbles to subside.

6 Dip the fruits one at a time in the hot sugar to coat the outside of the fruit with candy.

7 Allow the excess candy to drip off the fruit, and put on the prepared pan to cool and harden.

8 Once the fruit has cooled, remove the toothpicks.

9 Store at room temperature in a dry area and use within several hours, or the sugar will begin to dissolve.

Keys to Success

○ The fruit must have a skin or its moisture will quickly destroy the sugar coating. Using pieces of cut fruit such as melon or pineapple will not work unless they are served immediately.

○ Suggested fruits: strawberries, kumquats, grapes, clementine sections.

○ Be careful to cook the sugar accurately. If the candy is cooked to too high a temperature, it will have a caramel color and flavor; if cooked too low, it will stick to your teeth rather than breaking cleanly.

○ Exercise extreme caution when cooking sugar for hard candy, as it can cause severe burns (see "Caution," page 90).

○ Do not stir the sugar during the cooling stage.

Candy-Coated Apples

Apples coated with crisp red cinnamon hard candy are like a little slice of a New England autumn day on a stick. If protected from humidity, they hold up surprising well for a day or two. The excess candy can be poured into molds or cut into pieces (see page 92).

SKILL LEVEL
■ □ □

12 Apples

12 sticks

2 lb (4 cups) **Sugar**

12 oz (1 cup) **Light corn syrup**

8 oz (1 cup) **Water**

Red coloring (see Keys to Success), **as needed**

Cinnamon flavor, **as needed**

---

1 Clean and dry the apples. Insert a stick into the stem end of each apple. Lightly oil a sheet pan, or line it with parchment paper, to hold the dipped apples.

2 Combine the sugar, corn syrup, and water in a 2-quart saucepan. Stir while bringing to a boil.

3 Cover the saucepan and boil for 4 minutes. Remove the cover, insert a thermometer, and cook without stirring until the temperature reaches 310°F.

4 Remove from the heat and shock the saucepan in ice water for 20 seconds to prevent carryover cooking.

5 Gently stir the color and flavor into the hot sugar.

6 Allow the cooked sugar to sit undisturbed for 5 minutes to cool and for bubbles to subside.

7 Dip the apples one at a time in the hot sugar to coat the outside of the fruit with candy.

8 Allow the excess candy to drip off the apple, and put on the prepared pan with the stick facing up to cool and harden.

9 Store at room temperature in a dry area and use within several hours, or the sugar will begin to dissolve.

Keys to Success

o If using supermarket apples, you must wash off the wax for the candy to adhere.

o Be careful to cook the sugar accurately. If the candy is cooked to too high a temperature, it will have a caramel color and flavor; if cooked too low, it will stick to your teeth rather than breaking cleanly.

o Exercise extreme caution when cooking sugar for hard candy, as it can cause severe burns (see "Caution," page 90).

o Do not stir the sugar during the cooling stage.

o If the sugar is too hot during dipping, it will make a very thin candy coating; allow it to cool enough first. If it is too cool, it will make a very thick coating and should be reheated first.

o Paste color is preferred, but liquid color may also be used.

Peanut Brittle

MAKES ONE 10 × 15-INCH SHEET

Peanut brittle is second only to fudge in the realm of homemade American candies. It is best made in the cold months, when the air does not carry as much moisture. Peanut brittle makes an ideal holiday treat.

SKILL LEVEL

1 lb (2 cups) **Sugar**

4 oz (½ cup) **Water**

12 oz (1 cup) **Light corn syrup**

1 lb (3 cups) **Unsalted blanched raw whole peanuts**

1 tsp **Salt**

1 oz (2 tbsp) **Butter, unsalted, soft**

1½ tsp **Vanilla extract**

1½ tsp **Baking soda**

1 Lightly oil a 10 × 15–inch sheet pan, or line it with parchment paper. Lightly oil an offset palette knife.

2 Combine the sugar, water, and corn syrup in a 4-quart saucepan. Bring to a boil, stirring constantly with a heat-resistant rubber spatula. Cover and boil for 4 minutes.

3 Remove the cover, insert a thermometer, and cook without stirring to 240°F.

4 Add the peanuts and cook while stirring to 320°F, or until the batch is light brown.

5 Remove from the heat; mix in the salt, butter, vanilla, and baking soda thoroughly.

6 Pour onto the prepared pan and spread to the edges using the oiled palette knife.

7 Allow to cool to room temperature. Break into the desired size pieces. Store sealed in an airtight container.

COCOA NIBS BRITTLE *Replace the peanuts with 4 oz/1 cup cocoa nibs.*

PECAN BRITTLE *Replace the peanuts with an equal amount of coarsely chopped pecans.*

SESAME BRITTLE *Replace the peanuts with 8 oz/1½ cups sesame seeds.*

Keys to Success

- If you use a rubber spatula, be certain that it is heat-resistant.
- Prevent scorching by stirring constantly and gently once the peanuts have been added.
- The batch will brown more when the baking soda is added, so it should be only very lightly browned when removed from the heat.

OPPOSITE: Peanut Brittle and Pecan Buttercrunch (page 107)

Pecan Buttercrunch

MAKES ONE 10 × 15–INCH SHEET

Thin and crisp, with a delicate bite, buttercrunch is near perfection. It is easy and quick to make—but just as quick to disappear. It makes a perfect holiday gift, and no selection of chocolates would be complete without it.

SKILL LEVEL

8 oz (1 cup) **Sugar**

8 oz (16 tablespoons; 2 sticks) **Butter, unsalted, melted**

2 oz (¼ cup) **Water**

½ tsp Salt

½ oz (1 tbsp) **Vanilla extract**

12 oz (1¼ cups) **Dark chocolate, melted, tempered, or dark compound coating, melted**

8 oz (2 cups) **Chopped salted toasted pecans**

1. Lightly butter a 10 × 15–inch sheet pan, or line it with parchment paper.

2. Combine the sugar, butter, water, salt, and vanilla extract in a 2-quart saucepan. Bring to a boil, stirring constantly with a heat-resistant rubber spatula.

3. Insert a thermometer and continue stirring while cooking until the thermometer reads 300°F and the buttercrunch is light golden brown.

4. Pour onto the prepared pan and spread quickly to the edges of the pan with an offset palette knife.

5. Allow to cool completely to room temperature.

6. Wipe the top of the buttercrunch with a dry paper towel to remove any oil.

7. Spread half of the chocolate on the top of the buttercrunch and top with half of the chopped salted pecans before the chocolate has begun to set. Allow the chocolate to set.

8. Carefully turn the buttercrunch out of the pan onto the back of another sheet pan. Spread with the remaining chocolate. Sprinkle the remaining pecans on the chocolate before it has set.

9. Allow the chocolate to set fully. Break the buttercrunch into the desired size pieces to serve.

10. Store at room temperature sealed in an airtight container.

MACADAMIA-COFFEE TOFFEE Mix together 2 tsp of instant coffee granules and 2 tsp of water. Add to the batch when the temperature reaches 290°F. Substitute milk chocolate for the dark chocolate and replace the pecans with toasted salted macadamia nuts.

Keys to Success

- Keep the bottom of the pan from scorching by stirring with a heat-resistant rubber spatula.

- Cook over moderately high heat; when cooked too slowly, the batch will crystallize during cooking.

- Spread in the sheet pan quickly; buttercrunch begins to set very quickly.

- Wiping the buttercrunch with a dry towel removes any oil and helps the chocolate layer to adhere.

- Make sure the buttercrunch has fully cooled to room temperature before spreading the chocolate on it.

English Toffee

English toffee is a venerable classic that is slightly harder than buttercrunch. The chocolate coating provides not only flavor and a way to adhere toasted nuts, but also protects the toffee from picking up moisture from the air.

SKILL LEVEL

4 oz (½ cup) **Water**

1 lb (2 cups) **Sugar**

2 oz (¼ cup) **Light brown sugar, packed**

6 oz (½ cup) **Sweetened condensed milk**

6 oz (½ cup) **Light corn syrup**

4 oz (8 tbsp) **Butter, unsalted, soft**

½ tsp **Salt**

2 tsp **Vanilla extract**

1 lb (2⅔ cups) **Milk chocolate, melted, tempered, or milk compound coating, melted**

8 oz (3 cups) **Crushed or chopped salted toasted almonds**

---

1 Lightly butter a 10 × 15–inch sheet pan, or line it with parchment paper.

2 Combine the water, sugar, brown sugar, condensed milk, corn syrup, and butter in a 4-quart saucepan. Bring to a boil, stirring constantly with a heat-resistant rubber spatula.

3 Insert a thermometer, turn the heat to medium, and stir constantly while cooking to 290°F.

4 Remove from the heat. Add the salt and vanilla extract.

5 Pour onto the prepared pan and spread quickly to the edges of the pan with an offset palette knife. Allow to cool completely to room temperature, 1 hour or longer.

6 Spread half of the chocolate on the top of the toffee. Sprinkle half of the almonds on the chocolate before it sets. Allow the chocolate to set.

7 Carefully turn the toffee out of the pan onto the back of another sheet pan. Spread with the remaining chocolate.

Sprinkle the remaining almonds on the chocolate before it has set.

8 When the chocolate has set, break into the desired size pieces for serving.

9 Store at room temperature in an airtight container.

Keys to Success

○ Stir constantly using a heat-resistant rubber spatula to keep the bottom of the saucepan from scorching.

○ Moderate the heat to prevent scorching.

○ Be certain that the toffee has completely cooled to room temperature before coating with chocolate.

○ Sprinkle the nuts on the chocolate before the chocolate has even begun to think about setting.

Chocolate Taffy

Stretch your chocolate into a long-lasting chewy treat. Not only is this recipe delicious, but it is a good way to use up chocolate left over from other projects.

SKILL LEVEL

8 oz (1 cup) **Sugar**

15 oz (1¼ cups) **Light corn syrup**

2 oz (¼ cup) **Water**

10 oz (¾ cup) **Sweetened condensed milk**

½ tsp **Salt**

6 oz (⅔ cup) **Melted unsweetened chocolate**

1 tsp **Vanilla extract**

---

1 Lightly oil a 9 × 13–inch baking pan.

2 Combine the sugar, corn syrup, water, and condensed milk in a 4-quart saucepan. Bring to a boil, stirring constantly with a heat-resistant rubber spatula.

3 Insert a thermometer and continue cooking while stirring until the temperature reaches 240°F.

4 Remove from the heat and stir in the salt, chocolate, and vanilla extract. Pour the batch into the prepared pan. Allow to cool nearly to room temperature, about 45 minutes.

5 Pick up the taffy from the pan and begin to stretch it between your hands, folding it back over on itself. Continue pulling the taffy until it lightens in color, about 10 minutes.

6 Stretch ropes of taffy about ¾ inch in diameter. Cut off pieces 1½ inches long using oiled shears, and wrap each piece individually in cellophane or waxed paper.

Keys to Success

○ Stir the batch constantly as it cooks to prevent scorching.

○ Cooking to 240°F will produce a medium-firm texture. If you like the taffy more tender, cook only to 238°F; for very firm taffy, cook to 242°F.

○ Taffy that is pulled more will have a slightly shorter and lighter texture, while taffy not pulled as much will have a chewier texture.

○ The taffy may be shaped into any size and shape, but it must be wrapped immediately to prevent it from joining back into one large mass.

Molasses Taffy

MAKES 125 PIECES

Molasses taffy is surely the predecessor to salt water taffy and was the
focal point for nineteenth-century taffy pulls, which became social events
for young people of the day. The tradition may seem quaint by today's
standards, but the taffy is still rich, chewy, and full of character.

SKILL LEVEL

12 oz (1 cup) **Molasses**

24 oz (2 cups) **Light corn syrup**

8 oz (1 cup) **Sugar**

2 oz (4 tbsp) **Butter, unsalted, soft**

1 tsp **Salt**

2 tsp **Vanilla extract**

1   Lightly oil a 9 × 13–inch baking pan.

2   Combine the molasses, corn syrup, sugar, and butter in a
    4-quart saucepan. Bring to a boil, stirring constantly with a
    heat-resistant rubber spatula.

3   Insert a thermometer and continue stirring while cooking
    until the temperature reaches 252°F.

4   Remove from the heat and stir in the salt and vanilla extract.
    Pour the batch into the prepared pan. Allow to cool nearly
    to room temperature, about 45 minutes.

5   Pick up the taffy from the pan and begin to stretch it
    between your hands, folding it back over on itself. Continue
    pulling the taffy until it gets very light in color, about 10
    minutes.

6   Stretch ropes of taffy about ¾ inch in diameter. Cut off
    pieces 1½ inches long using oiled shears, and wrap each
    piece individually in cellophane or waxed paper.

Keys to Success

- Stir the batch constantly as it cooks to prevent scorching.

- Cooking to 252°F will produce a medium-firm texture. If you
  like the taffy more tender, cook only to 250°F; for very firm taffy,
  cook to 254°F.

- Taffy that is pulled more will have a slightly shorter and
  lighter texture, while taffy not pulled as much will have a
  chewier texture.

- The taffy may be shaped into any size and shape, but it must be
  wrapped immediately to prevent it from joining back into one
  large mass.

Saltwater Taffy

MAKES 125 PIECES

The name for saltwater taffy has been attributed to a curmudgeonly candy storeowner whose shop was flooded. Regardless of its origin, saltwater taffy is the classic seashore candy, and pulling and wrapping taffy is an activity that the whole family can get their hands into.

SKILL LEVEL

12 oz (1½ cups) **Sugar**

18 oz (1½ cups) **Light corn syrup**

2 oz (¼ cup) **Water**

3 oz (¼ cup) **Sweetened condensed milk**

¼ tsp **Salt**

1 oz (¼ cup) **Marshmallow creme**

½ tsp **Flavoring** (see Keys to Success)

Color, as desired

---

1 Lightly oil a 9 × 13–inch baking pan.

2 Combine the sugar, corn syrup, water, and condensed milk in a 4-quart saucepan. Bring to a boil, stirring constantly with a heat-resistant rubber spatula.

3 Insert a thermometer and continue stirring while cooking until the temperature reaches 245°F.

4 Remove from the heat and stir in the salt. Pour the batch into the prepared pan. Place the marshmallow creme on top of the cooling batch and allow to cool nearly to room temperature, about 45 minutes.

5 Pick up the taffy from the pan and begin to stretch it between your hands, folding it back over on itself and incorporating the marshmallow creme. Put the taffy on a clean work surface and add the flavoring and color as desired.

6 Continue pulling the taffy until it gets very light in color, about 20 minutes.

7 Stretch ropes of taffy about ¾ inch in diameter. Cut off pieces 1½ inches long using oiled shears, and wrap each piece individually in cellophane or waxed paper.

VARIATIONS Multiple flavors and colors may be created from a single cooked batch. Simply divide the batch during pulling and add different flavors and colors to each piece. Recombine if desired to make stripes, bull's-eyes, and so on.

Keys to Success

○ Stir the batch constantly as it cooks to prevent scorching.

○ Cooking to 240°F will produce a medium-firm texture. If you like the taffy more tender, cook only to 238°F; for very firm taffy, cook to 242°F.

○ Any manufactured liquid flavor is suitable to taffy, including extracts, oils, and other flavoring compounds.

○ The taffy may be shaped into any size and shape desired, but it must be wrapped immediately to prevent it from joining back into one large mass.

Peanut Butter Taffy

All of the rich flavor and golden color of this taffy come from the peanut butter with just
a hint of molasses. Like other taffies, if you cook it just a little higher, it will be firmer
and chewier, or you can make it more tender by cooking a couple of degrees less.

SKILL LEVEL

12 oz (1 cup) **Light corn syrup**

4 oz (⅓ cup) **Molasses**

8 oz (1 cup) **Sugar**

10 oz (¾ cup) **Sweetened condensed milk**

1 tsp **Salt**

9 oz (1 cup) **Peanut butter**

1 tsp **Vanilla extract**

---

1 Lightly oil a 9 × 13–inch baking pan.

2 Combine the corn syrup, molasses, sugar, and condensed
milk in a 4-quart saucepan. Bring to a boil, stirring constantly with a heat-resistant rubber spatula.

3 Insert a thermometer and continue stirring while cooking
until the temperature reaches 240°F.

4 Remove from the heat and stir in the salt, peanut butter, and
vanilla extract. Pour the batch into the prepared pan. Allow
to cool nearly to room temperature, about 45 minutes.

5 Pick up the taffy from the pan and begin to stretch it
between your hands, folding it back over on itself. Continue
pulling the taffy until it gets very light in color, about 10
minutes.

6 Stretch ropes of taffy about ¾ inch in diameter. Cut off
pieces 1½ inches long using oiled shears, and wrap each
piece individually in cellophane or waxed paper.

Keys to Success

○ Cooking to 240°F will produce a medium-firm texture. If you
like the taffy more tender, cook only to 238°F; for very firm taffy,
cook to 242°F.

○ Any manufactured liquid flavor is suitable to taffy, including
extracts, oils, and other flavoring compounds.

○ Taffy that is pulled more will have a slightly shorter and
lighter texture, while taffy not pulled as much will have a
chewier texture.

○ The taffy may be shaped into any size and shape desired, but it
must be wrapped immediately to prevent it from joining back
into one large mass.

Soft Caramels

Soft caramels may be the most popular chocolate in any box; they always seem to be the first to disappear. These caramels may be flavored many different ways and can be dipped in chocolate or wrapped without dipping.

SKILL LEVEL

4 oz (½ cup) **Water**

1 lb (2 cups) **Sugar**

1 **Vanilla bean, split and seeds scraped**

1 can (14 oz) **Sweetened condensed milk**

12 oz (1 cup) **Light corn syrup**

6 oz (12 tbsp, 1½ sticks) **Butter, unsalted, soft**

1 tsp **Salt**

---

1 Lightly butter a 9 × 13–inch baking pan.

2 Combine the water, sugar, vanilla bean, condensed milk, corn syrup, and butter in a heavy-bottomed 4-quart saucepan. Bring to a boil, stirring constantly with a heat-resistant rubber spatula.

3 Continue stirring while cooking until the batch reaches 245°F. This is a good estimation of the required temperature. When the thermometer reads 240°F, begin testing the caramel using the spoon technique outlined on page 30. The cooled piece on the spoon should be firm but not hard when the caramel is properly cooked.

4 Remove from the heat and stir in the salt. Pour into the prepared pan and remove the vanilla bean using a fork.

5 Allow to cool completely to room temperature, at least 2 hours.

6 Remove the sheet of caramels from the pan. Cut into the desired size pieces using a sharp chef's knife.

7 The pieces may be dipped in tempered chocolate or compound coating, or may be wrapped individually in cellophane or waxed paper if they are not going to be used within a day or two.

CARAMELS WITH NUTS Mix 12 oz/2½ cups chopped toasted nuts into the caramels after they are cooked but before pouring them into the pan.

CHOCOLATE CARAMELS Add 6 oz/1 cup dark chocolate, chopped in ½-inch pieces, or dark chocolate pistoles to the mixture at the beginning of cooking.

COFFEE CARAMELS Add 1 tbsp instant coffee granules to the mixture at the beginning of cooking.

FRUIT CARAMELS Add 8 oz/1 cup fruit puree (raspberry, mango, and apricot work nicely) to the batch when it reaches 240°F. Continue cooking to 245°F.

SPICE CARAMELS Add 2 tsp of desired ground spice (such as cinnamon, anise, or ginger) to the batch at the beginning of cooking.

Keys to Success

○ Caramels tend to foam during cooking. Use a larger than normal saucepan to prevent boiling over.

- Caramels scorch easily. Stir constantly during cooking with a heat-resistant rubber spatula, and moderate the heat to prevent scorching.

- A few degrees can make a big difference in the finished product: Undercooked caramels will be too soft and will not hold their shape; overcooked caramels will be too hard to bite.

Caramel Apples

No one can resist caramel apples. Lately this simple treat has been elevated to a true indulgence with the addition of a layer of chocolate, nuts, and in some cases, a hefty price tag. They will never be better than when you make them fresh in your own kitchen.

SKILL LEVEL

12–18 **Apples**

12–18 **sticks**

4 oz (½ cup) **Water**

1 lb (2 cups) **Sugar**

1 can (14 oz) **Sweetened condensed milk**

12 oz (1 cup) **Light corn syrup**

6 oz (12 tbsp, 1½ sticks) **Butter, unsalted, soft**

1 tsp **Salt**

2 tsp **Vanilla extract**

1   Clean and dry the apples. Insert a stick into the stem end of each apple. Line a sheet pan with parchment paper.

2   Combine the water, sugar, condensed milk, corn syrup, and butter in a heavy-bottomed 4-quart saucepan. Bring to a boil, stirring constantly with a heat-resistant rubber spatula.

3   Continue stirring while cooking until the batch reaches 245°F. This is a good estimation of the required temperature. When the thermometer reads 240°F, begin testing the caramels using the spoon technique outlined on page 30. The cooled piece on the spoon should be firm but not hard when the caramel is properly cooked.

4   Stir in the salt and vanilla extract.

5   Pour the caramel into a 2-quart saucepan or other narrow, deep, heatproof container.

6   Dip the prepared apples in the hot caramel. Allow the excess caramel to drain off and place on the prepared pan. Allow to cool fully, about 20 minutes. Any excess caramel can be poured onto parchment paper or into a buttered pan, allowed to cool, and cut and wrapped.

CARAMEL APPLES WITH NUTS *Before the caramel has cooled completely, roll the dipped apple in chopped toasted walnuts or pecans.*

CHOCOLATE-COATED CARAMEL APPLES *After the caramel has cooled entirely to room temperature, melt and temper 2 lb/5⅓ cups milk chocolate, chopped into ½-inch pieces, and dip the apples. Roll in chopped toasted nuts before the chocolate sets fully, if desired.*

Keys to Success

○ If using supermarket apples, wash off the wax for the caramel to adhere.

○ Caramels tend to foam during cooking. Use a larger than normal saucepan to prevent boiling over.

○ A few degrees can make a big difference in the finished product: Undercooked caramel will be too soft, and overcooked caramel will be too hard to bite.

○ If the caramel gets too thick during dipping, rewarm it by stirring it over low heat or in the microwave.

6

Fudge, Fondant, and Pralines

The candies in this chapter include some of the most traditional and well-known homemade candies—fudge and pralines—as well as some not commonly made at home, such as fondant and cordials. Although the latter are not usually thought of as homemade products, there is little in the way of special techniques or ingredients required to make them, and they can make excellent additions to any home confectioner's repertoire.

As in the previous chapter, all of the candies here are sugar based. What links these confections together, though, is that the sugar in these candies is in a crystalline state, resulting in the characteristic short texture of fudge rather than the chewy texture of caramels. The keys to success in these formulas are cooking to the proper temperature, causing crystallization at the right time, and forming small sugar crystals that will result in a smooth texture rather than a grainy one.

Fudge

FUDGE is without question the quintessential homemade candy; it has been made in home kitchens for over 100 years. Mention fudge, and most of us immediately think of chocolate, but chocolate is not the defining ingredient in fudge; it can be made using a wide variety of flavoring ingredients. The precise origin of fudge is not entirely clear, but it is believed to have originated from a batch of caramels gone awry—"fudged," if you will! This seems surprising at first glance, because caramels and fudge have such different textures that they seem to be completely unrelated. The ingredients, cooking temperatures, and techniques for making fudge and caramel, however, are nearly identical. It is only after cooking that fudge is stirred rapidly to cause it to crystallize, giving it its short texture, whereas caramels are allowed to cool undisturbed to prevent the sugar from crystallizing, resulting in their chewy texture.

What's in it?

Fudge contains virtually the same ingredients as soft caramels, although usually not in precisely the same proportions. Because crystallization of the sugar is the desired result when making fudge, it usually contains less corn syrup, which hinders crystallization, than do caramels. In addition, fudge often has inclusions such as nuts, dried fruit, and marshmallows that are added for textural and flavor contrast.

SUGAR Fudge is a sugar-based confection, so it comes as no surprise that it contains a high percentage of sugar. Cane or beet sugar (sucrose) is the sugar that crystallizes, providing the characteristic texture of the candy.

CORN SYRUP Although we want our fudge to crystallize, fudge contains corn syrup to help slow down and control that crystallization. Without the "doctoring" effect of corn syrup, most batches of fudge would end up as rock-hard, sugary boulders before we could get them into pans! In addition to allowing extra time to work with fudge, corn syrup helps create smaller crystals of sugar, leading to a smooth texture rather than a grainy one.

DAIRY PRODUCT Good-quality fudge always contains dairy products, either fresh or processed. The dairy product provides flavor, both from the product itself and from Maillard browning (page 98), creating a caramel-like flavor. Dairy products also contain fat, which makes a richer, more satisfying candy. The advantage of processed products such as sweetened condensed milk or evaporated milk is that they contain more of the desired milk solids and less water, which must be evaporated during cooking. When made with fresh dairy products, fudge will take much longer to cook to remove the extra water.

FLAVORING Although fudge can be flavored with manufactured flavors, it is much more common for it to get its flavor from foods like chocolate or peanut butter. Most often the flavoring is added after cooking, when stirring begins. Many of the flavoring ingredients in fudge contain fat as well as sugar, so each fudge recipe is carefully balanced for that flavor. Substituting flavoring ingredients in fudge recipes seldom gives desirable results unless other elements of the recipe are also changed.

FRAPPE Frappe is an optional ingredient sometimes used when making fudge. Frappe is essentially a meringue and is used to lighten the texture of the fudge. Fudge made using frappe is typically softer and smoother than one made without it.

INCLUSIONS There are few limits to the types and varieties of inclusions that can be used to bolster the appeal of fudge. From nuts and seeds to dried or candied fruit, or to candies such as hard candy or marshmallows, the combinations are limitless. The only real requirement for an inclusion is that it must not be a perishable item like fresh fruit. Adding inclusions that are not shelf stable will cause fudge to spoil rapidly. So choose any of the nonperishable products that you want and add them to your fudge recipe to create your own unique treat!

How it's made

Making fudge is a simple matter of cooking the batch to the correct temperature, allowing it to cool undisturbed, and then stirring it vigorously until it takes on a creamy appearance. In professional candy shops, the batch is cooled on a thick stone tabletop and the stirring is replaced by agitation (repeated turning) on the marble. At home, usually the batch is cooled in a baking pan and crystallization is accomplished by vigorous stirring in a bowl with a spoon. The true art to fudge making is the amount of stirring: too little, and your fudge will have a sugary texture; too much, and the fudge will harden in the bowl rather than in the pan.

1   Combine the sugar, corn syrup, and dairy products and stir while cooking. Use moderate heat to prevent scorching or boiling over.

2   Cook to the specified temperature. The temperature is crucial. Use an accurate thermometer.

3   Remove from the heat and pour into a baking pan to cool. Pouring into a pan cools the batch faster.

4   Allow the batch to cool without stirring. Fudge recipes should specify a length of time to cool or a desired temperature.

5   Transfer the cooked batch to a bowl and add flavoring and inclusions. These are nearly always added after cooking so as not to damage them.

6   Stir until creamy. This takes some experience to get right, but 3 to 5 minutes of vigorous stirring with a wooden spoon is usually adequate.

7   Pour into a prepared pan. Buttered baking pans are commonly used for fudge.

8   Allow to harden. Fudge usually sets within 30 minutes of spreading into the pan.

9   Slice and serve. Like most homemade products, fudge is at its best when served fresh.

1 Pour the cooked batch out of the pan and allow it to cool.

2 Stir vigorously with a wooden spoon until creamy.

3 Pour into a buttered pan, spread in an even layer, and allow the fudge to set.

How it's formed

buttered pans

Once the fudge has been stirred to the proper consistency, it can be poured into a baking pan that has been buttered or lined with parchment paper and spread to create an even layer. If desired, a garnish such as nuts can be sprinkled on the top after spreading but before the fudge hardens. This is the most common and simplest technique for home confectioners; it allows you to cut uniform pieces after the fudge hardens.

free-form fudge

It is not mandatory to use a pan for containing fudge. Home candy makers can emulate the technique used by fudge shops by piling up the thickened batch into a loaf on a counter and allowing it to harden before slicing. The slices then resemble half-moons of delicious homemade fudge—perfect for immediate enjoyment.

How it's stored

Unlike its cousin soft caramels, fudge will not pick up moisture from the air, but rather will tend to dry out if left unprotected from the atmosphere. When properly made and stored, fudge has a shelf life of several weeks—longer than most home candy makers need to be concerned with. The key is to wrap the fudge to prevent drying. Unlike caramels or brittles, fudge to be stored for more than a few days will benefit from refrigeration.

History of Fudge

The French most likely gave us chocolate truffles; gianduja probably originated in Italy; and marzipan's roots may well extend back to the Middle East. But fudge is an undeniably American candy of a relatively young age. While its exact origin has been obscured by the passage of time, most historians and confectioners agree that fudge arose from a botched batch of another type of candy, the most likely candidate being caramels. Fudge and caramels both contain virtually the same ingredients, and both are cooked to nearly the same temperature. The great difference in texture and appearance between the two is that the sugar in caramels is not crystallized, whereas the sugar in fudge is in a crystalline state.

The way to crystallize the sugar is simple: Stir the caramels too much after they are cooked. So some well-meaning cook who was a little too vigorous with the wooden spoon inadvertently created one of the world's most popular candies!

The first reliable documentation of fudge being made intentionally indicates that it was made and sold by women enrolled at Vassar College in Poughkeepsie, New York in 1888. These students may not have been the original creators of the candy, but they were certainly among the first. Did the Vassar students also give fudge its name? Again, no one can be sure, but it certainly seems plausible. Dictionaries of the time defined "fudge" as a noun meaning "nonsense" or a verb meaning to "fake it." Either one seems fitting for a candy that turned out as it did quite by accident.

Fondant

FONDANT is a crystallized sugar mixture used by bakers, pastry chefs, and candy makers as icing, glaze, and as the foundation of candies. Home candy makers seldom make their own fondant from scratch, more commonly buying it from candy making supply stores. Making fondant, however, is no more difficult to make at home than fudge. In fact, the techniques used to make fondant are nearly identical to fudge making. The real difference between the two is the ingredients: Fondant is simply fudge without the dairy product or flavoring. In other words, fondant is nothing but sugar, corn syrup, and water cooked together and then allowed to cool before being stirred to a creamy consistency either by hand or machine. It is common practice when making fondant to seal it tightly in an airtight container and allow it to rest at room temperature overnight before using it, a process called ripening.

Crystallization

The sugar that we use every day is sucrose, a sugar extracted and refined from sugarcane or sugar beets. One of the prominent characteristics of sucrose is that it readily forms crystals. Indeed, the common form of sugar available is already in crystal form; those tiny crystals are each made up of thousands of sugar molecules. When we put sugar into water, the crystals dissolve and the individual sucrose molecules mix freely with the water. When there is a high concentration of sugar dissolved in a small amount of water, as in a cooked batch of fudge, the sugar is likely to re-form into crystals and settle to the bottom of the container. This is what happens when we make rock candy: The sugar molecules reassociate on the sticks that hang in the syrup and form large sugar crystals. When making fudge or fondant, the stirring motion also causes the sugar to crystallize, but this time in many very small crystals.

The chemistry and physics of crystallization may be a bit beyond most of us, but the concept is simple enough and can be illustrated by thinking of sugar molecules as squares. In a heavy sugar syrup, there are many sugar molecules dissolved in little water. Because of that, the sugar molecules are in close proximity to each other. As long as they are not disturbed, the sugar molecules are less likely to join together to form crystals. Once they are stirred into motion, however, the molecules collide and join together to form crystals. The addition of corn syrup, which has long chains of sugar molecules, acts to prevent or slow the crystallization of sugar by getting in the way of the sugar molecules and preventing them from joining together into crystals.

When you make fondant or fudge, stirring the cooked batch sets the sugar molecules in motion, causing the crystallization that results in the proper texture for the candy. These candies contain just enough corn syrup to slow, but not prevent, the desired crystallization.

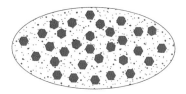

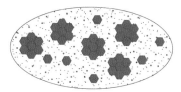

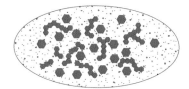

1

2

3

1 Many sugar molecules are dissolved in little water.

2 When heavy sugar syrup is agitated, sugar molecules collide and join together to form crystals.

3 Corn syrup added to sugar syrup prevents or slows crystallization by getting in the way of the sugar molecules, stopping them from joining together into crystals.

How it's made

In candy making, fondant is most commonly used to make mint or other flavor patties, and for making cherry cordials. The technique for using fondant to make candy is slightly different from the technique for using fondant as a glaze or icing. When using fondant as a glaze for pastries, it must be heated to no more than 110°F to preserve its shine. When using fondant in candy making, however, it is important to heat the fondant to a much higher temperature, as much as 170°F, for it to set firm enough to handle.

1   Place fondant in a stainless-steel bowl over a hot water bath. You may also heat fondant in a microwave.

2   Stir constantly to ensure even heating. If using a microwave, apply short exposures, stirring between each one.

3   Heat to 165°F. If the fondant is not heated enough, it will not set firmly.

4   Add flavoring. Mint is commonly used for patties, but any nonacidic, concentrated flavor will work. Color may also be added if desired.

5   Thin to workable consistency, if necessary. Different fondants have varying consistencies. If necessary, add water or liquor to the fondant to thin it to a consistency that will flow through a piping bag or funnel, or will allow pouring (see page 16).

6   Add invertase, if desired. Invertase can be added to soften the fondant after it is coated with chocolate, as in cherry cordials.

7   Pipe, funnel, or pour the fondant onto parchment paper to make patties.

8   Dip prepared cherries for cordials. These must be preserved cherries; either maraschinos or brandied cherries are most commonly used.

9   Dip in chocolate. When using invertase, the candies must be dipped in chocolate to protect the center as it softens. If no invertase is used when making patties, dipping in chocolate is an optional step.

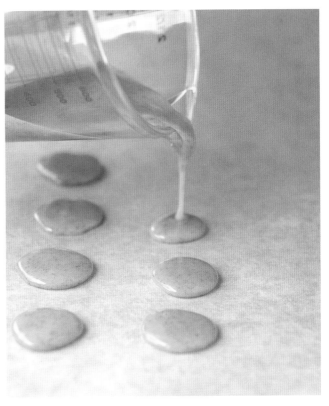

When thinned to a workable consistency, flavored fondant should easily pour onto the parchment.

1 Holding the stem, dip the preserved cherry in the fondant treated with invertase.

2 Place the dipped cherries on a tray and allow the fondant to set.

3 When using invertase, make sure that the chocolate completely covers the fondant during dipping. This will protect the center as it softens.

Pralines

AMONG THE BEST-KNOWN HOMEMADE CANDIES, pralines have become a symbol of hospitality in much of the southern United States, particularly New Orleans. Throughout most of the South, the name is pronounced PRAY-leen, but in New Orleans, the common pronunciation is PRAH-leen. Traditional pralines are made using two much beloved flavors in that part of the country: brown sugar and pecans. While this is the classic rendition, variations are not uncommon using other nuts and flavor profiles. At first glance, it would be easy to confuse pralines for cookies; both have the same general appearance. Make no mistake, however: Pralines are candies made by cooking sugar with dairy and nuts, not flour-based baked goods.

What's in it?

SUGAR Brown sugar is nearly always used, but pralines may also contain granulated white sugar.

DAIRY PRODUCT Milk, cream, and butter are used for flavor and to add fat to the candy.

NUTS The nuts used in pralines should be unsalted and must be toasted before using them, as they will not toast during the cooking process. Pecans are the most common variety of nut used.

SALT As in most nut confections, salt is added to complement the flavor.

FLAVORING The most common flavoring added to pralines is vanilla extract, but others such as coffee extract or cocoa powder may also be added.

After the praline mixture has cooled to 212°F, stir vigorously with a wooden spoon just until it begins to look creamy.

Immediately spoon or scoop the mixture onto parchment paper. The pralines can be flat or mounded, as desired.

How it's made

Like all sugar-based confections, making pralines begins by boiling the ingredients to remove water and concentrate the sugar content. The toasted nuts are included right in the boiling batch. After boiling, the mixture is cooled and stirred. The amount of stirring is critical: too little, and the candies will have a sugary texture; too much, and the batch will turn hard in the saucepan.

1. Combine the sugars and dairy product and cook, stirring constantly. Keeping the bottom of the saucepan clean will prevent scorching.

2. Add the toasted nuts at the specified temperature. The nuts must be toasted; they will not toast during the moist cooking process.

3. Cook to the desired temperature. Accuracy counts! Use a good thermometer and monitor it closely.

4. Remove from the heat and add the salt and flavoring. Flavor nuances can be lost if the flavoring is cooked with the batch.

5. Allow to cool undisturbed to 212°F. Stirring before this temperature causes a sugary texture in the finished pralines.

6. Stir vigorously with a wooden spoon. Stirring at this point causes the sugar to begin to crystallize. Stir only until the mixture begins to look creamy, 1 to 2 minutes.

How it's formed

Pralines are always scooped or spooned out onto paper or a tray. They may be flat, mounded, or somewhere in between. It is important to work quickly when scooping, as the sugar continues to crystallize while you are working. If the batch becomes too stiff to scoop, return it to the heat, stirring while heating, until it returns to a workable texture. In extreme cases, a few tablespoons of milk can be added while heating to help soften the batch.

How it's stored

Pralines are never stored for long; they are best eaten while fresh. Although they are not perishable, they tend to dry out in storage, losing quality. When storage is necessary, a tightly sealed container at room temperature is the optimum method. Like other confections, it is possible to freeze pralines, but they must be in an airtight container and allowed to return to room temperature while still sealed to prevent damage from condensation.

Rock Candy

ROCK CANDY is unique in this chapter because it is the only candy for which the goal is to produce large sugar crystals. In all of the other candies containing crystalline sugar, the desired outcome is to create many very small sugar crystals, and therefore a relatively smooth texture. With rock candy, the larger the crystals, the better! Making rock candy is a great project for kids; they can watch as the crystals grow larger each day. The finished rock candy can be used to sweeten coffee or stir into lemonade, or as ornamentation for a tray of homemade candies.

What's in it?

Pure rock candy is made of one and only one ingredient: sugar! Water is used to dissolve the sugar, sticks or strings are suspended in it, and food colors are often added for variety, but rock candy itself is 100 percent pure sucrose.

How it's made

1   Boil together sugar and water. The object is just to dissolve the sugar and to allow any impurities to rise to the surface, rather than to evaporate water as when cooking hard candy. It is critical that all utensils and receptacles be scrupulously clean to prevent unwanted crystallization of the sugar.

2   Allow the sugar syrup to partially cool without stirring. Cover the saucepan with a well-moistened towel to prevent premature crystallization of the sugar. Cooling will make the syrup easier and safer to handle.

3   Gently pour the cooled syrup into a jar or other container. Large wide-mouth glass jars are ideal for making rock candy; they allow the progress of the crystals to be monitored during the process. Any container must be perfectly clean and free from any foreign matter.

4   Suspend sticks or strings in the syrup. These can be "seeded" by brushing a little egg white on the stick and then rolling it in coarse sugar to promote crystal growth. The sticks or strings should be held in place during the process. When using a jar, this is easily accomplished by making small holes in the lid to accommodate the sticks.

5   Allow to sit at room temperature for several days or longer. Sugar crystals will begin to form on the sticks almost immediately, and after several days they should be growing large. For really large rock candy, immerse the sticks for 2 to 3 weeks. There will almost always be some sugar crystals that form on the sides and bottom of the container. These can be kept to a minimum by using a smooth-sided container such as a glass jar and cleaning the container very well prior to use.

6   Remove the rock candy and allow it to dry. One day of drying is sufficient to remove the remaining syrup from the rock candy.

How it's stored

Rock candy can be stored indefinitely at room temperature; it is not easily damaged by humidity. In extremely humid conditions, it can be sealed in an airtight container for protection. As long as it is protected from moisture, rock candy will last indefinitely without any loss of quality.

What if

What if my fudge or fondant has a grainy texture?

Allow it to cool longer before stirring, or stir longer before putting it in the pan.

What if my fudge is too soft?

Cook the next batch 2°F higher.

What if my fudge is too hard?

Cook the next batch 2°F lower.

What if my pralines are excessively sugary?

Allow the mixture to cool longer before stirring, or stir longer before scooping.

What if my fondant patties won't set?

Heat the fondant to a higher temperature before depositing.

What if my cordials won't liquefy?

Do not overheat invertase (see page 16).

Chocolate Fudge

Chocolate fudge is the classic American confection. In fact, when you say the name
fudge, it is chocolate that comes to mind. Unsweetened chocolate is used in this
recipe to supply full chocolate flavor when balanced with the sugar in the fudge.

SKILL LEVEL

2 lb (4 cups) **Sugar**

6 oz (½ cup) **Light corn syrup**

4 oz (½ cup) **Heavy cream**

8 oz (1 cup) **Milk**

6 oz (1 cup) **Unsweetened chocolate, pistoles or chopped in ½-inch pieces**

1 tsp **Vanilla extract**

8 oz (2 cups) **Chopped toasted walnuts** (optional)

---

1 Combine the sugar, corn syrup, cream, milk, and chocolate
in a 4-quart saucepan. Cook over moderate heat to 236°F,
stirring constantly.

2 Pour the mixture into a 9 × 13–inch baking pan or other pan
that will allow it to spread to create a thin layer. Leave undisturbed to cool at room temperature for 20 minutes.

3 Scrape the mixture into a large mixing bowl or into the
bowl of a mixer fitted with a paddle attachment. Add the
vanilla extract and the walnuts, if using. Mix on medium
speed, or by hand using a wooden spoon.

4 Stop mixing when the fudge begins to lose its shine and
thickens slightly. If using a mixer, it will require approximately 3 minutes of mixing. If mixing by hand, it will
require approximately 6 minutes.

5 Butter a 9-inch square baking pan, pour in the mixture, and
spread evenly with an offset palette knife.

6 Allow the fudge to crystallize for 1 hour or longer at room
temperature.

7 Cut into the desired size pieces and serve.

8 Fudge should be stored tightly covered at room temperature. It can be refrigerated, tightly sealed, for longer storage,
or frozen for maximum life.

Keys to Success

○ Be careful to cook the batch accurately; this will determine how
firm the fudge is.

○ If you like fudge slightly harder, cook the batch 2° or 3°F higher.
For softer fudge, cook a couple of degrees less.

○ Do not stir the fudge during the cooling step.

○ Stirring fudge is more of an art than a science. No clock can
tell you when it is finished. The fudge should start to lighten in
color, thicken noticeably, and lose a bit of its shine before you
pour it into the pan.

Vanilla Fudge

MAKES ONE 9-INCH SQUARE SLAB

A vanilla bean cooked with the batch gives this fudge an ethereal vanilla fragrance, with the added bonus of tiny black vanilla seeds throughout the fudge. It is like perfect vanilla ice cream transformed into candy.

SKILL LEVEL

2 lb (4 cups) **Sugar**

6 oz (½ cup) **Light corn syrup**

4 oz (½ cup) **Heavy cream**

8 oz (1 cup) **Milk**

1 tsp Salt

1 Vanilla bean

---

1 Combine the sugar, corn syrup, cream, milk, and salt in a 4-quart saucepan. Split the vanilla bean lengthwise and scrape the seeds out of the pod. Place the seeds and pod in the milk mixture. Cook over moderate heat to 236°F, stirring constantly.

2 Pour the mixture into a 9 × 13–inch baking pan, or other pan that will allow it to spread to create a thin layer. Remove the vanilla pod using a fork, and leave undisturbed to cool at room temperature for 20 minutes.

3 Scrape the mixture into a large mixing bowl or into the bowl of a mixer fitted with a paddle attachment. Mix on medium speed, or by hand using a wooden spoon.

4 Stop mixing when the fudge begins to lose its shine and thickens slightly. If using a mixer, it will require approximately 3 minutes of mixing. If mixing by hand, it will require approximately 6 minutes.

5 Butter a 9-inch square baking pan, pour in the mixture, and spread evenly with an offset palette knife.

6 Allow the fudge to crystallize for 1 hour or longer at room temperature.

7 Cut into the desired size pieces and serve.

8 Fudge should be stored tightly covered at room temperature. It can be refrigerated, tightly sealed, for longer storage, or frozen for maximum life.

ESPRESSO FUDGE *Omit the vanilla bean, dissolve 1 tbsp instant coffee in 2 tsp vanilla extract in a small bowl. Add these to the fudge when beginning to stir the batch to crystallize.*

GINGERBREAD FUDGE *Omit the vanilla bean. Add ½ tsp ground cinnamon, ½ tsp ground ginger, ¼ tsp grated nutmeg, and ⅛ tsp ground cloves to the batch before cooking. Add ¼ cup finely chopped crystallized ginger to the fudge during stirring.*

Keys to Success

○ Be careful to cook the batch accurately; this will determine how firm the fudge is.

○ If you like fudge slightly harder, cook the batch 2° or 3°F higher. For softer fudge, cook a couple of degrees less.

○ Do not stir the fudge during the cooling step.

○ Stirring fudge is more of an art than a science. No clock can tell you when it is finished. The fudge should start to lighten in color, thicken noticeably, and lose a bit of its shine before you pour it into the pan.

Root Beer Float Fudge

MAKES ONE 9-INCH SQUARE SLAB

Who can resist a perfect root beer float—scoops of vanilla ice cream lackadaisically bobbing in frosty root beer? That special indulgence is recreated here with mini marshmallows mixed into root beer–flavored fudge. You can almost hear the bubbles!

SKILL LEVEL

2 lb (4 cups) **Sugar**

6 oz (½ cup) **Light corn syrup**

4 oz (½ cup) **Heavy cream**

8 oz (1 cup) **Milk**

1 tsp **Salt**

1 **Vanilla bean**

2 tsp **Root beer flavoring** (see Keys to Success)

4 oz (2½ cups) **Mini marshmallows**

---

1 Combine the sugar, corn syrup, cream, milk, and salt in a 4-quart saucepan. Split the vanilla bean lengthwise and scrape the seeds out of the pod. Place the seeds and pod in the milk mixture. Cook over moderate heat to 236°F while stirring constantly. Add the root beer flavoring.

2 Pour the mixture into a 9 × 13–inch baking pan or other pan that will allow it to spread to create a thin layer. Remove the vanilla pod using a fork, and leave undisturbed to cool at room temperature for 15 minutes, or until the syrup has cooled to 120°F.

3 Pour the mixture into a large mixing bowl or into the bowl of a mixer fitted with a paddle attachment. Mix on medium speed, or by hand using a wooden spoon. If using a mixer, it will require approximately 3 minutes of mixing. If mixing by hand, it will require approximately 6 minutes.

4 When the fudge begins to lighten in color, lose some of its shine, and thicken slightly, stir in the mini marshmallows and stop mixing.

5 Butter a 9-inch square baking pan, pour in the mixture, and spread evenly with an offset palette knife.

6 Allow the fudge to crystallize for 1 hour or longer at room temperature.

7 Cut into the desired size pieces and serve.

8 Fudge should be stored tightly covered at room temperature. It can be refrigerated, tightly sealed, for longer storage, or frozen for maximum life.

Keys to Success

○ Root beer flavorings may vary in strength. Vary the amount to your taste.

○ Be careful to cook the batch accurately; this will determine how firm the fudge is.

○ If you like fudge slightly harder, cook the batch 2° or 3°F higher. For softer fudge, cook a couple of degrees less.

○ Do not stir the fudge during the cooling step.

○ Stirring fudge is more of an art than a science. No clock can tell you when it is finished. The fudge should start to lighten in color, thicken noticeably, and lose a bit of its shine before you pour it into the pan.

Peanut Butter Fudge

MAKES ONE 9-INCH SQUARE SLAB

Apple pie has nothing on peanut butter for sheer Americanism. If you like your peanut butter crunchy, mix chopped toasted peanuts into the batch during stirring, or sprinkle them on top of the fudge once it is in the pan.

SKILL LEVEL

2 lb (4 cups) **Sugar**

6 oz (½ cup) **Light corn syrup**

3 oz (¼ cup) **Molasses**

4 oz (½ cup) **Heavy cream**

8 oz (1 cup) **Milk**

12 oz (1½ cups) **Peanut butter**

1 tsp Vanilla extract

8 oz (2 cups) **Chopped toasted peanuts** (optional)

---

1 Combine the sugar, corn syrup, molasses, cream, milk, and peanut butter in a 4-quart saucepan. Cook over moderate heat to 236°F, stirring constantly. Remove from the heat and stir in the vanilla extract.

2 Pour the mixture into a 9 × 13–inch baking pan or other pan that will allow it to spread to create a thin layer. Leave undisturbed to cool at room temperature for 20 minutes.

3 Scrape the mixture into a large mixing bowl or into the bowl of a mixer fitted with a paddle attachment. Add the peanuts, if using. Mix on medium speed, or by hand using a wooden spoon.

4 Stop mixing when the fudge begins to lose its shine and thickens slightly. If using a mixer, it will require approximately 3 minutes of mixing. If mixing by hand, it will require approximately 6 minutes.

5 Butter a 9-inch square baking pan, pour in the mixture, and spread evenly with an offset palette knife.

6 Allow the fudge to crystallize for 1 hour or longer at room temperature.

7 Cut into the desired size pieces and serve.

8 Fudge should be stored tightly covered at room temperature. It can be refrigerated for longer storage, or frozen for maximum life.

Keys to Success

○ Be careful to cook the batch accurately; this will determine how firm the fudge is.

○ If you like fudge slightly harder, cook the batch 2° or 3°F higher. For softer fudge, cook a couple of degrees less.

○ Do not stir the fudge during the cooling step.

○ Stirring fudge is more of an art than a science. No clock can tell you when it is finished. The fudge should start to lighten in color, thicken noticeably, and lose a bit of its shine before you pour it into the pan.

Maple Fudge

Homemade fudge made with authentic maple syrup is the real
McCoy; no artificial flavors here. The walnuts are optional but add
a delightful and traditional contrast of flavor and texture.

SKILL LEVEL

1 lb (2 cups) **Sugar**

20 oz (2 cups) **Maple syrup**

2 tbsp Light corn syrup

4 oz (½ cup) **Heavy cream**

4 oz (½ cup) **Milk**

1 tsp Salt

1 tbsp Vanilla extract

8 oz (2 cups) **Chopped toasted walnuts** (optional)

---

1 Combine the sugar, maple syrup, corn syrup, cream, milk, and salt in a 4-quart saucepan. Cook over moderate heat to 236°F, stirring constantly.

2 Pour the mixture into a 9 × 13–inch baking pan or other pan that will allow it to spread to create a thin layer. Leave undisturbed to cool at room temperature for 20 minutes, or until the syrup reaches 120°F.

3 Scrape the mixture into a large mixing bowl, or into the bowl of a mixer fitted with a paddle attachment. Add the walnuts, if using. Mix on medium speed, or by hand using a wooden spoon.

4 Stop mixing when the fudge begins to lose its shine and thickens slightly. If using a mixer, it will require approximately 3 minutes of mixing. If mixing by hand, it will require approximately 6 minutes.

5 Butter a 9-inch square baking pan, pour in the mixture, and spread evenly with an offset palette knife.

6 Allow the fudge to crystallize for 1 hour or longer at room temperature.

7 Cut into the desired size pieces and serve.

8 Fudge should be stored tightly covered at room temperature. It can be refrigerated, tightly sealed, for longer storage, or frozen for maximum life.

Keys to Success

○ Be careful to cook the batch accurately; this will determine how firm the fudge is.

○ If you like fudge slightly harder, cook the batch 2° or 3°F higher. For softer fudge, cook a couple of degrees less.

○ Do not stir the fudge during the cooling step.

○ Stirring fudge is more of an art than science. No clock can tell you when it is finished. The fudge should start to lighten in color, thicken noticeably, and lose a bit of its shine before you pour it into the pan.

OPPOSITE: FUDGE, FROM LEFT TO RIGHT: Peanut Butter Fudge (page 137), Root Beer Float Fudge (page 136), Chocolate Fudge (page 134), and Vanilla Fudge (page 135)

Penuche

A traditional fudge made with brown sugar, penuche boasts the rich flavor of molasses, and can be made with toasted pecans to complete the sensation. No repertoire of fudge would be complete without it.

SKILL LEVEL

1 lb (2 cups) **Granulated sugar**

1 lb (2 cups) **Light brown sugar, packed**

2 tbsp **Light corn syrup**

4 oz (½ cup) **Heavy cream**

8 oz (1 cup) **Milk**

1 tsp **Salt**

1 tbsp **Vanilla extract**

8 oz (2 cups) **Chopped toasted pecans** (optional)

---

1 Combine the sugar, brown sugar, corn syrup, cream, milk, and salt in a 4-quart saucepan. Cook over moderate heat to 236°F, stirring constantly.

2 Pour the mixture into a 9 × 13–inch baking pan or other pan that will allow it to spread to create a thin layer. Leave undisturbed to cool at room temperature for 20 minutes, or until the syrup reaches 120°F.

3 Pour the mixture into a large mixing bowl or into the bowl of a mixer fitted with a paddle attachment. Mix on medium speed, or by hand using a wooden spoon.

4 Stop mixing when the penuche begins to lose its shine and thickens slightly. If using a mixer, it will require approximately 3 minutes of mixing. If mixing by hand, it will require approximately 6 minutes. Mix in the pecans, if using.

5 Butter a 9-inch square baking pan, pour in the mixture, and spread evenly with an offset palette knife.

6 Allow the penuche to crystallize for 1 hour or longer at room temperature.

7 Cut into the desired size pieces and serve.

8 Penuche should be stored tightly covered at room temperature. It can be refrigerated for longer storage, or frozen for maximum life.

Keys to Success

○ Be careful to cook the batch accurately; this will determine how firm the fudge is.

○ If you like penuche slightly harder, cook the batch 2° or 3°F higher. For softer penuche, cook a couple of degrees less.

○ Do not stir the batch during the cooling step.

○ Stirring penuche is more of an art than a science. No clock can tell you when it is finished. The penuche should start to lighten in color, thicken noticeably, and lose a bit of its shine before you pour it into the pan.

Firefudge

Firefudge is chocolate fudge plus a little incendiary heat, tempered by
some sweet-tart dried pineapple. A beguiling blend of intense flavors, it's
not for everyone, but it might be for you . . . if you can take the heat!

SKILL LEVEL

2 lb (4 cups) **Sugar**

6 oz (½ cup) **Light corn syrup**

4 oz (½ cup) **Heavy cream**

8 oz (1 cup) **Milk**

1 tsp Red pepper flakes (see Keys to Success)

6 oz (1 cup) **Unsweetened chocolate, pistoles or chopped in ½-inch pieces**

1 tsp Vanilla extract

6 oz (1 cup) **Chopped dried pineapple**

---

1 Combine the sugar, corn syrup, cream, milk, red pepper
flakes, and chocolate in a 4-quart saucepan. Cook over moderate heat to 236°F while stirring constantly. Remove the
pan from the heat.

2 Pour the mixture into a 9 × 13–inch baking pan or other pan
that will allow it to spread to create a thin layer. Leave undisturbed to cool at room temperature for 20 minutes.

3 Scrape the mixture into a large mixing bowl or into the
bowl of a mixer fitted with a paddle attachment. Add the
vanilla extract and the chopped dried pineapple. Mix on
medium speed, or by hand using a wooden spoon.

4 Stop mixing when the fudge begins to lose its shine and
thickens slightly. If using a mixer, it will require approximately 3 minutes of mixing. If mixing by hand, it will
require approximately 6 minutes.

5 Butter a 9-inch square baking pan, pour in the mixture, and
spread evenly with an offset palette knife.

6 Allow the fudge to crystallize for 1 hour or longer at room
temperature.

7 Cut into the desired size pieces and serve.

8 Fudge should be stored tightly covered at room temperature. It can be refrigerated for longer storage, or frozen for
maximum life.

Keys to Success

○ The heat level can be varied by increasing or decreasing the
amount of red pepper flakes.

○ Be careful to cook the batch accurately; this will determine how
firm the fudge is.

○ If you like fudge slightly harder, cook the batch 2° or 3°F higher.
For softer fudge, cook a couple of degrees less.

○ Do not stir the fudge during the cooling step.

○ Stirring fudge is more of an art than a science. No clock can
tell you when it is finished. The fudge should start to lighten in
color, thicken noticeably, and lose a bit of its shine before you
pour it into the pan.

Creamsicle Fudge

MAKES ONE 9-INCH SQUARE SLAB

Orange and vanilla intermingle to bring back the fond memories of a childhood favorite in fudge form. The only thing missing is the stick.

SKILL LEVEL

2 lb (4 cups) **Sugar**

6 oz (½ cup) **Light corn syrup**

4 oz (½ cup) **Heavy cream**

8 oz (1 cup) **Milk**

1 Vanilla bean

1 tsp Salt

2½ oz (¼ cup) **Orange juice concentrate, thawed**

1 Combine the sugar, corn syrup, cream, and milk in a 4-quart saucepan. Split the vanilla bean lengthwise and scrape the seeds out of the pod. Place the seeds and pod in the milk mixture. Cook over moderate heat to 248°F, stirring constantly.

2 Stir in the salt at the end of cooking.

3 Pour the mixture into a 9 × 13–inch baking pan or other pan that will allow it to spread to create a thin layer. Remove the vanilla pod using a fork, and leave undisturbed to cool at room temperature for 20 minutes.

4 Pour the mixture into a large mixing bowl or into the bowl of a mixer fitted with a paddle attachment. Mix on medium speed, or by hand using a wooden spoon. After approximately 1 minute of mixing, pour in the orange juice and continue mixing. If using a mixer, it will require approximately 2 minutes more of mixing. If mixing by hand, it will require approximately 5 minutes more.

5 When the fudge begins to lighten in color, loses some of its shine, and thickens slightly, stop mixing.

6 Butter a 9-inch square baking pan, pour in the mixture, and spread evenly with an offset palette knife.

7 Allow the fudge to crystallize for 1 hour or longer at room temperature.

8 Cut into the desired size pieces and serve.

9 Fudge should be stored tightly covered at room temperature. It can be refrigerated for longer storage, or frozen for maximum life.

Keys to Success

- Be careful to cook the batch accurately; this will determine how firm the fudge is.

- If you like fudge slightly harder, cook the batch 2° or 3°F higher. For softer fudge, cook a couple of degrees less.

- Do not stir the fudge during the cooling step.

- Stirring fudge is more of an art than a science. No clock can tell you when it is finished. The fudge should start to lighten in color, thicken noticeably, and lose a bit of its shine before you pour it into the pan.

Fondant

Fondant is widely used throughout the pastry and confectionery industry. You can buy tubs of premade fondant, but it is simple to make your own. Do not confuse the rolled icing commonly called fondant with real fondant; they are entirely different animals.

SKILL LEVEL

2 lb (4 cups) **Sugar**

6 oz (½ cup) **Light corn syrup**

6 oz (¾ cup) **Water**

1 Combine the sugar, corn syrup, and water in a 4-quart saucepan. Cover and bring to a boil.

2 Boil for 4 minutes covered, then remove the lid, insert a thermometer, and continue cooking without stirring until the syrup reaches 236°F.

3 Pour the syrup into a 9 × 13–inch baking pan or other pan that will allow it to spread to create a thin layer, splash lightly with cold water, and leave undisturbed to cool at room temperature for 20 minutes or until the syrup reaches 120°F.

4 Pour the syrup into the bowl of a 5-quart mixer fitted with a paddle attachment and mix on medium speed until the fondant changes from smooth, shiny, and sticky to white, opaque, and dull-looking. This will take 8 to 12 minutes and will occur suddenly during mixing.

5 Fondant may be stored tightly sealed at room temperature for up to 2 weeks. For longer storage, refrigerate.

Keys to Success

- Cook the sugar accurately; the temperature to which the syrup is cooked will determine the firmness of the finished fondant.

- Do not stir the syrup during the cooling phase.

- Slow and steady mixing will crystallize the fondant properly. Be patient.

- If you are in doubt whether the fondant has crystallized, mix a little longer. There is no concern of overmixing the fondant.

Mint Patties

Fondant patties are quick and simple to make. You can use either homemade (see page 143) or purchased fondant. While mint patties are traditional, the possibilities are nearly endless when it comes to flavorings and finishing techniques. Don't be married to tradition; use your imagination.

SKILL LEVEL

12 oz (1 cup) **Fondant**

20 **Mint leaves**

⅛ tsp **Mint extract** (optional)

12 oz (1¼ cups) **Dark chocolate, melted, tempered, or dark compound coating, melted** (optional)

---

1 Combine the fondant and mint leaves in a food processor and process until the fondant is nearly a uniform green, 3 to 4 minutes.

2 Put the fondant in a bowl and place over a hot water bath. Heat the fondant until it reaches 160°F. Stir in the extract if you want a stronger flavor than the leaves alone provide.

3 Line a sheet pan with parchment paper. Warm a 2-cup glass measuring cup. Pour the hot fondant into the warm cup.

4 Pour the hot fondant out of the cup onto parchment paper in small disks, about 1½ inches in diameter.

5 Allow the fondant disks to set, about 15 minutes.

6 Release from the parchment. If they are left uncoated, they should be stored in an airtight container.

7 If desired, coat the patties in the chocolate or compound coating using the techniques on pages 40 to 43.

COLORED FONDANTS Add liquid or paste water-based color to hot fondant as desired.

FRUIT FONDANTS Many types of fruit purees can be used to flavor fondants. When using purees to make fruit fondants, it is advisable to simmer the puree until it has been reduced to half of its volume. Two tablespoons of reduced puree will generally provide enough flavor for this recipe.

LEMON FONDANTS Add 2 tsp lemon juice, 1 tsp lemon extract, and ½ tsp grated lemon zest to the fondant just before pouring the disks. These are especially delicious when added to the mint in the recipe above.

MISCELLANEOUS FLAVORS Any number of liquid flavorings may be added to the fondant before pouring.

ORANGE FONDANTS Add 1 tbsp orange juice concentrate and ½ tsp orange extract to fondant just before pouring.

SOFT PATTIES Add ⅛ tsp of invertase (see page 16) to the fondant before pouring the disks. If you add invertase, you must coat the fondants in chocolate.

Keys to Success

- If the fondant is not heated to a high enough temperature, the patties will not harden. Use a thermometer, and be certain to heat the fondant to 160°F.

- When using an acidic flavoring such as orange, lemon, or other fruits, add the flavoring only when you are ready to pour the patties. If the acid is in contact with the fondant for too long, the patties will not harden.

- The fondant can be reheated during pouring if it gets too thick to pour.

Cherry Cordials

There is something special about cherry cordials: all of that delicious syrup waiting to be released when you bite through the chocolate. The most difficult part of making cordials is the self-control required to allow the fondant time to liquefy before you eat them all.

SKILL LEVEL

50 Maraschino cherries, stems on, drained

24 oz (2 cups) **Fondant** (see Keys to Success)

¼ tsp **Invertase** (see Keys to Success)

Water or brandy, for thinning fondant, as needed

1 lb (1½ cups) **Dark chocolate, melted, tempered, or dark compound coating, melted**

---

1 Dry the cherries thoroughly on a towel. Line a sheet pan with parchment paper and sprinkle it lightly with confectioners' sugar.

2 Heat the fondant over a water bath to 160°F.

3 Remove the fondant from the heat and add the invertase. Stir in well.

4 Holding them by the stems, dip the cherries one at a time in the fondant nearly to the top of the cherry. If the fondant becomes too thick to dip the cherries, thin it using the water or brandy.

5 Place each cherry on the prepared sheet pan. Make sure the cherries are upright when you put them down. Allow the cherries to cool until the fondant hardens, about 10 minutes.

6 Holding the cooled, fondant-coated cherries by the stem, dip them one at a time in the tempered chocolate all the way up to the stem to completely enrobe them in chocolate. Place the chocolate-dipped cherries on clean parchment. When the chocolate has set, transfer the cherries to a sealed container.

7 Leave the cherries at room temperature in the sealed container for 10 days to allow the fondant time to dissolve from the action of the enzyme.

VARIATION Cherry cordials can also be made using maraschino cherries without the stems. Dip the cherries in the heated fondant and invertase using a dipping fork (see page 42). Once the fondant sets, roll them in tempered chocolate using the technique for hand-dipping truffles shown on page 45. Roll the cherries this way three times, and after the third coat, roll them in a pan of sifted confectioners' sugar.

Keys to Success

○ Either homemade Fondant (page 143) or purchased fondant may be used.

○ Invertase (see page 16) is available at candy making supply stores and Web sites.

○ If the fondant will not stick to the cherries, dry them more thoroughly.

○ Keep the fondant hot while dipping, but do not exceed 160°F once the invertase has been added.

○ If the fondant gets too thick to dip the cherries, thin it with water or brandy.

○ Be certain to dip the cherries in chocolate the same day they are coated with the fondant.

○ If you are unable to wait for the fondant to dissolve, don't worry—they are delicious anyway!

Rock Candy

Rock candy is simple and fun to make. The longer you
leave it alone, the larger the crystals will grow.

SKILL LEVEL

9 lb (18 cups) Granulated sugar

3 lb (1½ qt) Water

6 Bamboo skewers (see Keys to Success)

1 Egg white, lightly beaten

2 tbsp Coarse sugar

---

1   Combine the sugar and water in a large clean pan and bring
to a boil.

2   Cover the pan and continue to boil for 5 minutes.

3   Remove the lid and brush any sugar crystals off the sides of
the pan using a damp pastry brush.

4   Cover the syrup and allow it to cool undisturbed for 1 hour.

5   Preheat the oven to 200°F. Line a baking sheet with parchment paper.

6   Brush the lower two thirds of each skewer with the egg
white and roll in the coarse sugar. Place the coated skewers
on the baking sheet and place in the oven for 30 minutes to
adhere the sugar to the skewers.

7   Drill or poke holes that will accommodate the bamboo
skewers in the lid of a scrupulously clean 1-gallon jar.

8   Pour the cooled syrup into the jar.

9   Place the skewers through the holes in the lid so that the
coated portion will protrude into the syrup. Place the lid
onto the jar with the skewers immersed in the syrup.

10   Place the jar in a location where it will not be moved or
shaken and let it sit for 10 days to 2 weeks.

11   Remove the skewers of rock candy from the syrup and allow
to dry overnight on a screen or on a sheet pan lined with
parchment paper.

12   The syrup may be reboiled and reused for successive
batches. To reuse the syrup, bring it to a boil and let it boil
vigorously for 10 minutes. Then proceed from step 4 above.

Keys to Success

○   The skewers need to be longer than the height of the jar so that
the lid will hold them in place.

○   Clean sugar, utensils, and containers are vital to success.

○   Make sure all the sugar crystals are removed from the sides of
the pot when boiling the syrup.

○   Avoid agitation of the syrup.

○   The less the syrup is disturbed during the process, the bigger
the crystals will be.

Chocolate-Peanut Pralines and
Pecan Pralines

Pecan Pralines

MAKES 25 PIECES

Pecan pralines are a popular and traditional candy throughout the southern United States. There are probably as many versions of these as there are people who make them, and everyone swears that theirs is the best! One thing everyone agrees on is that pralines are best enjoyed fresh.

SKILL LEVEL

8 oz (1 cup) **Granulated sugar**

8 oz (1 cup) **Light brown sugar, packed**

4 oz (½ cup) **Heavy cream**

4 oz (½ cup) **Milk**

2 oz (4 tbsp) **Butter, unsalted, soft**

6 oz (2 cups) **Chopped toasted pecans**

½ tsp **Salt**

1 tsp **Vanilla extract**

---

1 Line a sheet pan with parchment paper.

2 Combine the granulated sugar, brown sugar, cream, milk, and butter in a 4-quart saucepan. Cook over high heat, stirring constantly, until it reaches 225°F.

3 Add the pecans and continue stirring while cooking until the mixture reaches 236°F.

4 Stir in the salt and the vanilla extract and remove from the heat.

5 Allow the mixture to sit in the saucepan undisturbed until it cools to 210°F, about 20 minutes.

6 Stir vigorously using a wooden spoon until the mixture looks creamy and thickens slightly, about 45 seconds.

7 Scoop onto the prepared pan using a #50 scoop. Flatten each scoop slightly.

8 Allow the pralines to crystallize fully before trying to release them, about 20 minutes.

9 Pralines should be stored at room temperature in an airtight container.

CHOCOLATE-PEANUT PRALINES *Omit the butter. Add 1¼ oz/¼ cup cocoa powder and 2¼ oz/¼ cup peanut butter to the batch at the beginning of cooking. Substitute toasted unsalted peanuts for the pecans. Chocolate-peanut pralines require a little more stirring to set properly; stir for approximately 2 minutes before scooping.*

Keys to Success

- Sugar cooking temperature is critical; use a thermometer and cook the sugar accurately.

- Do not stir the mixture during the cooling process.

- The amount of stirring is at the heart of making pralines. When they are understirred, they will tend to have a sugary texture. If they are overstirred, they will harden in the saucepan.

- If pralines stiffen in the saucepan, reheat the batch over direct heat. If this is unsuccessful, add a few tablespoons of milk while heating.

7

Marshmallow, Nougat, and Jellies

Included in this chapter are a variety of aerated candies from divinity to nougat, marshmallow, and sponge candy, as well as candy jellies—sometimes referred to as pâte de fruit in European parlance—and a quick, practical version of candied citrus peel. To be successful with the recipes in this chapter, you will need to be familiar with the Sugar Master Techniques (see pages 28 to 32). This chapter includes some unique techniques such as whipping gelatin to make marshmallows, some unique ingredients such as gelatin, agar, pectin, and egg whites, and some unique equipment like FlexiMolds. Read about these ingredients, techniques, and tools in each new recipe before beginning the recipe.

Lighten Up with Aerated Confections

MAKING AERATED CONFECTIONS is not much different from nor more difficult than whipping a meringue and cooking sugar. If you can manage both of these elementary techniques, you can be successful in making your own nougat, marshmallow, or divinity. As in any recipe that uses cooked sugar, the temperature to which the sugar is cooked is crucial to your success: Overcook the sugar, and your nougat will be hard; undercook it and it will be too soft to cut and handle. Close attention must also be paid to the timing when making these recipes. Make sure all of your mise en place, including the pan the candy will go into, is ready before you begin cooking the sugar for the recipe; delays are ill advised once the recipe is under way.

Divinity

DIVINITY, an American classic, is the most commonly made variety of aerated candy in this book. In fact, divinity is probably made more often in homes than in professional candy shops. Like most other aerated confections, it begins with egg whites and cooked sugar combined to make a meringue. The sugar for divinity is cooked to a higher temperature than it would be for a meringue, though, resulting in a drier, firmer finished product. Divinity most often has toasted nuts added to it, usually pecans or walnuts, which contrast nicely with the sweetness of the meringue. Divinity also contains another ingredient not found in meringue: Confectioners' sugar is added after whipping to seed the meringue and cause it to recrystallize. This recrystallization is what gives divinity its short, melt-in-your-mouth texture. It is well recognized that divinity should not be attempted on very humid days, as it will remain soft and sticky instead of setting properly.

What's in it?

Divinity is a sugar syrup lightened to an ethereal foam by egg whites, with the addition of toasted nuts for texture, contrast, and substance. A few basic ingredients make up these heavenly little clouds of candy.

EGG WHITES Egg white is the aerator that makes divinity possible. Without egg whites, you could not create the foam that defines this candy. Be careful that your egg whites do not contain any yolk or fat from any other source. Room temperature whites will whip better than cold whites from the refrigerator.

SUGAR The first addition of sugar is a small amount, combined in its granulated form with the egg whites, to strengthen the egg whites as they begin whipping. This allows the cooked sugars to be added without collapsing the whites.

CREAM OF TARTAR Cream of tartar provides acidity that helps strengthen the meringue so that it does not collapse.

SUGAR . . . AGAIN This is the larger part of the sugar in the candy. This portion of the sugar is cooked with corn syrup and water and is responsible for the flavor and texture of the finished candy.

CORN SYRUP Corn syrup helps to control the recrystallization of the sugar so that it does not occur suddenly or at the wrong time.

WATER Water is the solvent that makes sugar cooking possible. Much of the water is evaporated during the cooking process so that the divinity will hold its shape and be a candy, rather than a soft meringue.

FLAVORING Vanilla extract rounds out the flavor and gives complexity to divinity.

SALT Salt is added to divinity purely for flavor, to boost the flavor of the toasted nuts and to provide contrast to the sweet candy.

TOASTED NUTS Divinity does not have to contain nuts, but they add a dimension of flavor and textural contrast most people find agreeable. Pecans are most commonly used, with walnuts a close second.

How it's made

Making divinity is just a matter of whipping a meringue while you follow the master sugar cooking technique. If you review the Sugar Master Techniques (see pages 28 to 32) and pay close attention to the order in which you work, you will be successful.

1   Combine the egg whites, the first quantity of sugar, and the cream of tartar in a clean mixer bowl with a whip attachment.

2   Combine the remainder of the sugar, the corn syrup, and water in a saucepan. Begin to cook, following the Standard Sugar Cooking Technique on page 29.

3   Begin to whip the egg whites. Timing is important here; you want the egg whites to reach soft peak consistency at the same time the sugar reaches its maximum temperature.

4   Stream the hot sugar syrup into the soft peak whites. Add the hot sugar to the whites fairly quickly. Allow the whites to continue whipping for several minutes until they cool down.

It is easiest to scoop the divinity onto the tray if you use a bowl of hot water to clean the metal spoon between scoops.

5   Add the confectioners' sugar. Mix in thoroughly, but do not overmix the sugar into the meringue.

6   Add the flavoring and the toasted pecans. These can be added either on the machine or by hand.

7   Use a spoon with a bowl of hot water to scoop the divinity into individual portions onto parchment paper. Allow to set for 30 minutes or more so that the sugar recrystallizes.

How it's stored

Divinity should be used within a couple of days of making it; this is not usually a problem. Storage during this time should always be at room temperature, protected from humidity in a sealed container. Once divinity is exposed to moisture in the air, it will become irreparably sticky and soft. Refrigeration will quickly ruin your efforts by dissolving the divinity.

Marshmallow

MARSHMALLOWS originated long ago, and while today's marshmallows bear little resemblance to their ancestors, they are nonetheless one of the world's most recognized candies. In fact, each year Americans are said to consume 90 million pounds of marshmallows! No doubt most of these marshmallows find themselves over a campfire, or maybe nestled between chocolate bars and graham crackers in a s'more. It is hard to believe that this simple yet indulgent treat began over 2,000 years ago as a medicine from the sap of a plant root.

The intriguing thing about making your own marshmallows, aside from the novelty, is the many flavor possibilities you can create. Mallows no longer need to be merely little white nondescript chewy pillows; you can make them with spice, fruit, liquor, or chocolate flavors for some unusual and decidedly grown-up combinations. Think of homemade anise marshmallows floating on and gently melting into some serious hot chocolate—no, they're not just for kids and campfires!

What's in it?

It is natural to assume that marshmallows are made by whipping a meringue with a generous amount of sugar, then adding gelatin to it. Indeed, marshmallows have been—and can be—made by this technique. More frequently, however, egg whites are forgone entirely and gelatin acts as both the aerator that creates the foam and the binder that makes handling and cutting possible.

GELATIN Gelatin acts as both aerator and binder in marshmallows. It allows them to be lightened by whipping and makes subsequent handling and cutting possible.

COLD WATER Gelatin is dehydrated when you buy it; without water it will not work in a recipe. Cold water simply returns gelatin to its natural state.

History of Marshmallow

Today's marshmallows are a simple treat with a long history. The historic roots of marshmallows are literally the roots of a plant: the marsh mallow, *Althaea officinalis*. This variety of mallow plant is a shrubby flowering plant that grows—that's right—in marshes. Today's marshmallows are descended from sweets made of the sap taken from the root of this plant. As seems to be the case with many of our modern foods, it was the ancient Egyptians who are the first documented consumers of marshmallow. Egyptians would mix together the mucilaginous sap from the root of the marsh mallow with sweeteners, probably honey; the resulting confection was deemed worthy of pharaohs and even the gods themselves. While it is not known exactly what these sweets looked like, they certainly bore little or no resemblance to the pudgy little white pillows that today are known as *marshmallows*.

The marsh mallow plant has always been valued for the healing power of its sap. Throughout history, the plant has been used to soothe respiratory ailments, as well as being generally "good for what ails you," whether sore throat, diarrhea, toothache, or indigestion. Today's herbalists still use it primarily for respiratory complaints.

In the mid-nineteenth century, French confectioners found that by mixing and cooking the mallow's root sap with egg whites and sweeteners, they could create a foam that could be molded into forms, and the first recognizable marshmallow candy was born and named *pâte de guimauve*. Of course, whipping by hand was laborious and time consuming, and mallow root sap was an expensive ingredient. It was not long after these first aerated marshmallows were created that candy makers started using a system of starch molding that greatly enhanced the efficiency of production. Around the same time, gelatin began replacing the mallow sap in the confection, increasing the availability and reducing the cost.

In 1948, Alex Doumak created an extrusion process for marshmallow production that made mass production possible. In this process, still used today, the marshmallow is extruded in a continuous long cylinder onto a bed of starch, and the individual pieces are cut off as it sets, creating the familiar shapes. Modern marshmallows contain none of the root for which they are named, but are made with sugar, corn syrup, gelatin, and flavorings. Whether you enjoy them with hot chocolate, in a s'more, or just as is, they are even more special when they are homemade.

SUGAR As in all confectionery, sugar provides sweetness, bulk, and preservation to marshmallows. Sugar also stabilizes the gelatin during whipping, just as it does when whipping egg whites to make a meringue.

CORN SYRUP Corn syrup plays its familiar role of sweetening and preventing the sugar from recrystallizing.

HONEY Honey also helps to prevent recrystallization of the sugar, as well as providing flavor. While commercial marshmallows do not contain honey, it adds complexity to the flavor and is a tribute to the candy's ancient history. If desired, honey may be omitted and replaced with an equal amount of corn syrup.

WATER Water dissolves the granulated sugar during cooking. Much of the water is then removed from the sugar through evaporation.

FLAVORING The most common flavor added to marshmallows is vanilla extract, but if you want to make true, state-of-the-art vanilla-flavored marshmallows, cook your sugar with a vanilla bean. Many other flavoring options exist, including spices, concentrated fruit purees, liquors, cocoa powder, and manufactured flavors.

COLOR Color is an optional ingredient in marshmallows and is not commonly used in the most familiar manufactured versions. Very beautiful pastel-colored marshmallows are made by artisan confectioners; adding color is entirely a personal choice.

STARCH AND CONFECTIONERS' SUGAR (COATING) You need only make marshmallows once to understand the necessity of the starch coating on the outside: Without it, they are extremely sticky and will adhere to anything they touch, including each other.

How it's made

Marshmallows begin with cooked sugar, so once again the Standard Sugar Cooking Technique (see page 29) is important to understand and follow. Unlike nougat or divinity, for which egg whites are partially whipped and the cooked sugar is streamed into the lightened whites, when making marshmallows the cooked sugar and gelatin are combined in the beginning and fully whipped together.

1   Mix the gelatin into the cold water. This allows the gelatin to rehydrate (bloom) to a usable form.

2   Combine the sugar, corn syrup, honey, and water in a saucepan and cook to the specified temperature, following the Standard Sugar Cooking Technique (see page 29). As always, be careful to cook the sugar accurately to obtain the best results.

3   Allow the syrup to cool in a mixer bowl. If you don't allow the syrup to cool, the heat will damage the gelatin.

4   Melt the gelatin over a hot water bath so that it will combine with the syrup.

5   Combine the gelatin and the syrup in the mixer bowl.

6   Whip on high speed to fully aerate the marshmallows.

7   Add flavorings at the end of whipping.

8   Spread in a pan. Marshmallows are very sticky; oil all implements used to handle them.

9   Allow to set overnight. This makes handling much easier. If necessary, refrigerate for 3 to 4 hours to cut the same day.

10 Cut. Be very generous with the starch–confectioners' sugar mixture to make cutting easier.

How it's stored

Marshmallows have a good shelf life and are actually rather forgiving of storage conditions. For storage of up to 3 or 4 weeks, simply keeping them tightly sealed in a plastic bag or a rigid container at room temperature will suffice. If for some reason you want to store them longer, sealing them in a plastic bag and freezing them is a highly effective technique; marshmallows will keep for months this way.

Whip the cooled sugar mixture and rehydrated gelatin on high speed until fully aerated.

Nougat

NOUGAT is a general term for a wide range of aerated candies. It may be chewy or short textured, very soft and tender or hard and brittle, or any texture in between. Traditional nougat is made with honey and necessarily contains nuts, but today's nougat may have inclusions such as dried or candied fruit, or may be smooth throughout. While nougat may be made in any flavor, the most common by far are the white nougats flavored with vanilla and honey, and chocolate nougat. Classic nougat is often dressed in nothing but a layer of thin wafer paper, but nougat is equally at home luxuriously draped in chocolate. The defining quality of nougat is the light texture obtained by whipping air into egg whites.

What's in it?

All nougat consists of an aerator—egg whites for the home candy maker—and a mixture of cooked sugars. To this base, flavorings, inclusions, and other ingredients are added. The additional ingredients in nougat are quite variable. Milk powder may be added for enrichment. Flavorings may be almost anything, as long as they do not contain too much water. Inclusions too must be dry; dried fruit and toasted nuts are ideal as inclusions for nougat.

EGG WHITES It is the egg whites that allow nougat to hold air, and therefore have a light texture. Egg whites are surely the heart of nougat, as they provide the defining aeration.

COOKED SUGAR MIXTURE Nougat will contain some or all of these in the sugar mixture:

> **SUGAR** Every nougat contains sugar for its clean sweet flavor and the body it adds.

> **CORN SYRUP** Although not truly traditional, most modern nougats contain corn syrup to control and prevent the recrystallization of the sugar.

> **HONEY** Honey is the original method of sweetening and flavoring nougat. It is used in traditional nougats like torrone, and may be used in more modern creations as well. Honey not only provides flavor and sweetness, but it also helps to prevent recrystallization of sugar.

> **MOLASSES** Molasses, when used in nougat, is added mainly for its unique flavor, but like honey, molasses helps to prevent the recrystallization of sugar.

ADDITIONAL INGREDIENTS Several adjunct ingredients may be used in nougat to get the desired results. The most commonly used ones are:

> **FAT** Most nougats contain fat in some quantity. Fat is added to nougat to give it a shorter texture and cleaner bite. Without fat, most nougats would be chewier than we want them to be.

> **MILK POWDER** Milk powder, if used, is added to nougat after whipping. It enriches the nougat and also promotes recrystallization, which results in a tender, short-textured nougat.

> **CONFECTIONERS' SUGAR** Like milk powder, confectioners' sugar can be added to nougat after whipping. It, too, will induce the nougat to recrystallize, resulting in a tender nougat rather than a chewy one.

> **FLAVORING** Aside from the naturally occurring flavors in the sweeteners, vanilla is the most commonly used flavor in nougats. Chocolate, peanut butter or other nut paste, spices, and manufactured flavors may all be used as well for flavoring nougat.

INCLUSIONS Any dry product may be used as an inclusion in nougat, but without question, nuts are the most common. Although some traditional nougat also contains candied fruit, dried fruit is a slightly more contemporary addition. Seeds, cereals, and dry snack foods can all be used.

WAFER PAPER Wafer paper is traditionally used to protect and present nougat. It provides an attractive edible wrapper that protects the candy from damage caused by the environment.

How it's made

While the possible flavors, textures, and inclusions in nougat are almost endless, all nougats are fundamentally made the same way: by whipping egg whites and pouring cooked sugar into them as they whip. Once this fundamental portion of the recipe is completed, the flavorings, adjunct ingredients, and inclusions determine precisely what type of nougat it will be.

1   Combine the egg whites with a small amount of sugar or corn syrup and cream of tartar. The sugar and the cream of tartar will help to strengthen the meringue as it whips.

2   Combine the remaining sugars with water in a saucepan, and begin cooking. Follow the Standard Sugar Cooking Technique (see page 29).

3   Begin whipping the egg whites. The timing here is crucial; begin whipping when the recipe specifies. The objective is to have the whites at soft peak consistency at the same moment that the sugar is cooked to its final temperature. Whites should always be whipped on the highest speed in order to aerate them well.

4   Finish cooking the sugar and stream it into the whipping whites. Add the sugar syrup to the whites in a fairly quick, steady stream down the inside edge of the bowl to avoid splashing the sugar around the inside of the bowl.

5   Allow the nougat to continue whipping. The exact time varies, but the object is to incorporate more air into the nougat and to allow the mixture to begin to cool. Usually 3 to 4 minutes is ample time.

6   Add the dry ingredients, such as confectioners' sugar or cocoa powder, if they are in the recipe. Mix just until combined.

7   Add the melted fat or chocolate to the nougat. If it is used in the recipe, fat or chocolate should be added once the nougat is fully aerated.

8   Stop whipping once the fat or chocolate is incorporated. If you continue mixing once the fat or chocolate is incorporated, the nougat will lose aeration and become dense.

9   Mix in the inclusions by hand. Better results are generally obtained by mixing inclusions in by hand, not on the machine.

10 Form as desired. Nougat may be sandwiched between wafer paper for a simple and traditional finish, or it may be spread in a pan, allowed to cool, and cut and dipped in chocolate later.

1 With the whites whipping at high speed, add the cooked sugar in a quick, steady stream against the inside of the bowl to avoid splashing.

2 The best results are achieved when inclusions, such as nuts, are mixed into the nougat by hand.

3 Spread the nougat in a pan lined with wafer paper.

4 Wafer paper can be applied while the nougat is warm for a traditional finish.

How it's stored

Regardless of the type or flavor of nougat, it must always be protected from the atmosphere. When exposed to air, the quality will always suffer. Some varieties will pick up moisture and become sticky; some will dry out. Either situation is to be avoided. When nougats are dipped in chocolate, the chocolate becomes a protective layer. Wafer paper, too, offers some protection from the elements. When properly protected, nougat has a quality shelf life of many weeks—much longer than home candy makers usually need.

Sponge Candy

SPONGE CANDY is a very old-fashioned sweet that goes by many different names. Whether you know it as sponge candy, cinder block, fairy food, or seafoam, sponge candy is always a slightly caramelized sugar mixture lightened into a foam by the addition of baking soda; it has a unique, delicate, crispy texture and a distinctive flavor of caramel with a hint of honey.

Sponge candy enjoys regional popularity in America. Buffalo, New York, and the surrounding area is home to sponge candy; many candy shops in that region boast excellent versions. Abroad, sponge candy is a center for at least two candy bars, one made by Cadbury (Crunchie) and one made by Nestlé (Violet Crumble); these are sold primarily in Britain and Australia, respectively. Whether you have a mass-produced version, a local candy maker's, or make it in your own kitchen, those who know and love it always appreciate sponge candy.

What's in it?

Sponge candy contains few ingredients. It is unique among the aerated candies because it is lightened by the addition of a chemical leavener, baking soda, rather than by whipping an aerator such as egg whites or gelatin.

GELATIN A very small amount of gelatin used in sponge candy helps to make the hot syrup more elastic and therefore able to hold more of the gas from the baking soda, resulting in a lighter candy.

SUGAR Providing sweetness, caramelization, and bulk, sugar is the major ingredient in sponge candy, as in most candies.

CORN SYRUP The addition of corn syrup helps to prevent sponge candy from crystallizing, in addition to providing sweetness and caramelization.

HONEY An optional ingredient in sponge candy, honey may be present in small quantities, purely for flavor.

BAKING SODA Well known as a leavener in baked goods, the baking soda releases CO_2 gas when added to the hot sugar mixture, which immediately foams up and forms the unique spongy texture that is the hallmark of the candy. Baking soda should always be sifted before being added to sponge candy.

How it's made

Making sponge candy is not much more difficult than cooking sugar, but preparation is essential to ensure good results. Always prepare the pan before you begin cooking the sugar, use a saucepan that allows for expansion once the baking soda is added, and be careful not to disturb the sponge candy while it is in the crucial cooling stage, or it may collapse.

1   Hydrate the gelatin in cold water. There is no need to melt the gelatin; the hot sugar will do that for you.

2   Combine the sugars and water in a saucepan and cook. The sugar mixture is cooked to hard crack stage (see page 31) to ensure that the candy will be crisp when it is finished. When using honey, it is usually added late in the cooking to prevent burning.

As soon as the baking soda is fully incorporated, pour the foamy sugar into a pan. Allow it to continue to rise and cool undisturbed.

When thoroughly cooled, sponge candy can be broken by hand or sliced into pieces with a sharp chef's knife.

3   Remove from the heat and allow to cool slightly. A slightly cooler sugar mixture will hold aeration better than one that is scorching hot.

4   Stir in the hydrated gelatin. You will immediately notice that the sugar becomes elastic. Be sure the gelatin is thoroughly mixed into the sugar.

5   Whisk in the sifted baking soda. Whisk vigorously to ensure that the soda is thoroughly mixed into the sugar and that no lumps form. Return briefly to heat.

6   Immediately pour into the prepared pan. The foamy sugar should still be rising when it goes into the pan.

7   Allow to cool undisturbed until thoroughly cooled. This will take at least a couple of hours, and it is fine to leave it overnight, as long as it is protected from humidity.

8   Break or cut into pieces and dip in chocolate, if desired. Home candy makers usually do not attempt to cut regular-shaped pieces from sponge candy; they break it into irregular chunks. Dipping in chocolate is optional, but the chocolate not only provides flavor, it protects the sponge candy from humidity.

How it's stored

Like most sugar candies, sponge candy is very easily ruined by exposure to humidity. Once the pieces are coated in chocolate, they are safe from moisture in the air, but before coating, every effort must be taken to prevent moisture or humidity from damaging the sponge candy. Tightly sealed plastic bags or containers are the best method to avoid this environmental damage.

Jellies

MAKING JELLIES is not too much different from cooking any other sugar mixture, except that jellies contain a binding agent that will cause them to thicken and hold their shape once they have cooled. It is again crucial to cook to the proper temperature to achieve the desired texture. There are three basic types of jellies presented in this book: those using pectin as a binding agent, those using starch, and those using agar. Each has its own advantages and disadvantages. Pectin has a great mouthfeel but can be finicky about setting. Starch is predictable and available, but can only be used to make a limited range of jellies. Agar is easy to work with, works with any type of flavoring, and agar jellies can have a very fresh flavor; however, agar jellies have a texture that not everyone loves. Using any of these basic recipes with different fruits, you can make multilayered jellies of different flavors and colors, or you can make any molded shape you want.

Starch Jellies

Jellies thickened with starch are commonplace in the world of manufactured candies. Spearmint leaves, gumdrops, orange slices, as well as Swedish Fish are all commercial examples of starch jellies. All of these candies are made using special starches that have been modified to behave exactly as the manufacturer wants them to. The home candy maker, however, does not have access to these modified starches, so there is really only one type of starch jelly likely to be made in home kitchens: Turkish Delight.

Turkish Delight (also known as *lokom*) is, without doubt, one of the first types of gelled candies ever created. It is frequently made with rose flavoring and pistachios, honoring its historical and geographical roots, but many different flavors are common today, and inclusions are optional. Give this one a try! At its best, Turkish Delight is soft, tender, and subtle—a true delight.

What's in it?

SUGAR Cane sugar is the only sweetener used in traditional Turkish Delight. It is the base of the syrup that will be thickened by the starch.

WATER Like any candy for which sugar must be cooked, the water dissolves the sugar. More water is left in Turkish Delight after cooking than in many other candies, resulting in a softer candy.

CREAM OF TARTAR Cream of tartar plays two vital functions in Turkish Delight: It helps to prevent the sugar from recrystallizing, and it breaks down the starch slightly, so that the jellies maintain a good texture after cooling.

STARCH Jellies are really flavored syrups thickened with a binding agent, and Turkish Delight uses cornstarch as that binder.

FLAVORING Flavor in Turkish Delight might be from a liquid flavoring such as rose water, or from a spice cooked with the batch such as vanilla bean or cardamom. Manufactured flavors may also be used in Turkish Delight and are added after cooking when used.

COLOR Color is a strictly optional ingredient in Turkish Delight. When used, it should be in moderation; Turkish Delight is not generally a vibrantly colored candy.

INCLUSIONS The only inclusions commonly used in Turkish Delight are unsalted nuts. Dried fruit may also be used.

SUGAR-STARCH BLEND A mixture of 2 parts confectioners' sugar and 1 part cornstarch protect the candies from sticking together.

How it's made

Cooking Turkish Delight involves three discrete operations: Cooking the sugar, cooking the starch, and combining the two mixtures and cooking them together. The greatest care must be taken with the starch portion; because it is so thick, it will burn very easily.

Cut Turkish Delight with a chef's knife, then roll the pieces in the confectioners' sugar–cornstarch mixture to keep them from sticking together.

1 Cook the sugar portion. Follow the Standard Sugar Cooking Technique (see page 29). Be sure to avoid the introduction of sugar crystals into the cooked syrup. Cream of tartar helps to prevent recrystallization.

2 Cook the starch portion. The starch mixture must be whisked vigilantly during cooking to prevent scorching; it is a very thick mixture. Cream of tartar begins to break down the starch to improve the texture of the jelly.

3 Cook the two portions together. Gentle heat and vigorous stirring are required for this operation; there is no substitute for a long, slow cook. The mixture will appear lumpy in the early stages of cooking, but it will become smooth and clear as the cooking progresses.

4 Mix in the liquid flavoring, color, and inclusions. Liquid flavor is added after cooking so that it does not evaporate during cooking.

5 Pour into a prepared pan. The pan should be lined with plastic wrap to prevent sticking.

6 Allow to cool overnight. The jellies should sit overnight to fully form a gel.

7 Cut and roll in confectioners' sugar–starch blend. The sugar blend prevents the pieces from sticking together.

How it's stored

Turkish Delight is always stored well protected from the atmosphere; it tends to dry out if exposed to air. It should be stored with plenty of the sugar-starch blend around it to prevent the pieces from sticking together.

Pectin Jellies

Pectin jellies are considered by many to possess the finest quality of any of the jellies. Pectin has a mouthfeel that is to most people's liking. These jellies should always use fruit juices or purees rather than manufactured flavors for superior flavor; pectin jellies can be made using a wide variety of fruits.

What's in it?

The very best pectin jellies contain nothing but fruit juices or purees, sugar, and pectin. Additional acid in the form of lemon juice is frequently added to these jellies to aid in setting.

FRUIT JUICE OR PUREE The juice or puree not only provides the flavor and color of the jelly, it also contains the water needed for cooking. When using a juice such as pomegranate or grape, applesauce is added to the jelly to provide a better texture.

SUGAR Sugar in pectin jellies not only adds sweetness, but is a necessary ingredient for the pectin to bind properly. Cutting down on the sugar in a pectin jelly recipe will cause it not to set properly.

PECTIN Pectin is the binding agent in these jellies. Standard liquid pectin of the variety found in grocery stores should be used for the recipes in this book, not a low-sugar version.

LEMON JUICE In addition to a high sugar content, pectin requires a relatively high level of acidity in order to form a gel. Lemon juice is added at the end of cooking to induce the pectin to set.

How it's made

Like all jellies, pectin jellies are a flavored syrup with a binding agent. The unique qualities of pectin jellies are that they contain no water other than that from the fruit puree or juice and that they use pectin for a binder.

1   Cook the fruit puree with the sugar. This removes water through evaporation and concentrates the sugar content and the fruit flavor. It is crucial to stir during cooking to prevent scorching.

2   Add the liquid pectin and cook briefly. Make sure the pectin comes to a boil and continues to boil for about 1 minute. Stirring will prevent scorching.

Pour the mixture into a pan prepared with cooking spray and granulated sugar.

3   Pour into a prepared pan and top with granulated sugar. Sugar should be sprinkled over the top before the jellies begin to cool so that it adheres to the jellies.

4   Allow to cool completely. It is perfectly acceptable to allow the jellies to cool overnight in the pan.

5   Remove from the pan, cut, and roll in granulated sugar. The granulated sugar will prevent the individual pieces from sticking together.

How it's stored

Once coated with granulated sugar, pectin jellies are not very susceptible to damage from air or humidity. It is nonetheless advisable to store them in an airtight container. Like any true confection, pectin jellies need not be refrigerated, and doing so usually damages the sugar coating.

Agar Jellies

Although widely used in Asian cuisines, agar or agar-agar (see page 12) is a binding agent frequently overlooked in American candy making. Derived from sea vegetables, agar is an easy-to-use binder that creates brilliantly clear, firm jellies with a short texture. There is no system of standardization for agar, so there may be differences between agars from different sources. If your jellies are a bit too firm or too soft, simply alter the amount of agar in the next batch to control the texture.

What's in it?

Like most candies, agar jellies have pretty fundamental ingredients. The only one the least bit out of the ordinary is the agar itself.

SUGAR Sugar sweetens, preserves, and provides bulk to the agar jellies.

CORN SYRUP Corn syrup not only provides sweetness and prevents recrystallization, it also helps improve the short texture of the jellies.

AGAR This is the binding agent that causes the jellies to set.

FLAVORING While agar jellies can be made using manufactured flavors, the most commonly used flavorings are fruit purees. Because the flavoring is not cooked with the batch, agar jellies can have a particularly fresh, fruit flavor.

How it's made

Like other jellies, agar jellies are a flavored syrup with a binding agent, in this case agar. The most important consideration unique to agar jellies is that the flavoring must not be added to the batch until after it is cooked and has cooled slightly. Cooking the flavoring with the agar will prevent the jellies from setting properly.

1   Soak the agar in water. This step is greatly reduced when using powdered agar. Nevertheless, it is a good idea to put the agar in cold water while measuring out the remainder of the ingredients. Soaking helps the agar to dissolve thoroughly and then to thicken the mixture.

2   Add the sweeteners and stir while cooking. As always, cooking concentrates the sugar content to the proper level. In addition, cooking is necessary to activate the agar and to thicken the jelly.

3   Remove from the heat and allow to cool slightly. The jelly should cool to approximately 180°F before adding the flavoring.

4   Add the flavoring. Fruit juices or purees are the flavorings most commonly used for agar jellies. They are added after cooking because they are acidic and would damage the agar if cooked with it.

5   Pour into a lined pan or into flexible molds, sprinkle sugar on top, and allow to set. Agar jellies set quickly, usually within 30 minutes or so. Allow them to cool to room temperature before cutting.

6   Cut and roll in granulated sugar. The individual pieces should be rolled in sugar to form a skin that will prevent them from sticking together.

7   Allow to dry overnight on a screen. Drying overnight at room temperature creates a light crust on the outside of the candies. Omitting this step will usually result in wet jellies.

How it's stored

Properly made and dried agar jellies will not require special storage conditions; simply protecting them from moisture and extremes of temperature will be sufficient protection. Under these conditions they should have a shelf life of several weeks, if desired. Do not fall into the trap of refrigerating them—you will most certainly have wet jellies when they come out.

Citrus Confit

FULLY CANDYING FRUIT is an arduous process involving at least ten days—and usually much more—of careful attention to the project. Making citrus confit is a simple and quick way to make orange or lemon peels that, while not truly candied, are perfectly acceptable to use in baked goods or as centers of chocolates, or enjoyed on their own. It is a great way to utilize a product that normally goes to waste, and once the confection has been made, it can be stored for weeks without any loss of quality.

What's in it?

The citrus peels are themselves the stars of the show here. The only other ingredients are the sugar, corn syrup, and water that make up the syrup that sweetens and preserves them.

CITRUS PEELS Orange and lemon peels give the best results for confit, although other types of citrus can be used. Oranges used for juicing, such as valencias, will make a better-tasting confit than navel oranges.

SUGAR Sugar in citrus confit sweetens and preserves the peels.

CORN SYRUP Because of the high sugar content, corn syrup is needed to help prevent recrystallization of the sugar.

How it's made

Citrus confit is simple to make and can be stored as is or dried for use inside of a chocolate.

1   Quarter and peel the citrus. Cutting the fruit into quarters makes it easy to peel off uniform portions for candying. Be sure that the skins are peeled cleanly, leaving no residue of fruit on the inside.

2   Blanch the peels in fresh water three times. Blanching will remove bitter oils contained in the pith, which would ruin the flavor of the finished product.

3   Simmer the peels gently in the syrup. The peels should not be boiled in the syrup, but very gently simmered. Boiling will cause the skins to turn leathery and firm. Approximately 90 minutes of simmering is usually required for the skins to begin to turn translucent.

4   Cool the confit in the syrup in which it was simmered, then refrigerate.

How else can I use it?

Citrus confit has uses beyond its starring role as a center for chocolate: It can be cut into the desired size and shapes, dried slightly in a low oven, and used as an inclusion in other candies, including nougat, fudge, marzipan, and others. Outside of confectionery, confit is used in baked goods. Holiday breads like pannetone and stollen both welcome diced confit, and the classical Florentine cookies benefit from the bright fresh flavors of confit.

For use as a center, citrus confit can be cut into julienne, dried in a very low oven, and dipped in chocolate.

1   After simmering, cool the peels to room temperature in the syrup.

2   The peels can be julienned, rolled in sugar, and enjoyed on their own.

3   Citrus confit can be julienned, dried in a very low oven, and dipped in chocolate as desired.

How it's stored

Citrus confit is best stored refrigerated in the syrup in which it was simmered. When kept under these conditions, it will have a shelf life of many weeks.

What if

What if my egg whites for nougat or divinity won't whip?

There is probably some fat or yolk contaminating them. Clean all bowls and equipment well, wipe out the bowl using vinegar to remove any traces of fat, and start again with fresh whites.

What if my marshmallow firmed up during whipping and won't spread evenly in the pan?

The mixture got too cool during whipping and the gelatin set. You may be able to save it by warming the bowl and mixture over a water bath while stirring, until it once again is smooth. It can then be spread in the pan.

What if my aerated candy is too firm?

The sugar was most likely overcooked. Next batch, cook the sugar a couple of degrees lower.

What if my pectin jellies did not set?

The batch was probably undercooked. Boil the mixture for 4 to 5 minutes more while stirring, add lemon juice again at the end of boiling, and pour them into the pan to set again.

What if my Turkish Delight looks lumpy?

You must be vigorous about whisking it as the two portions cook together. Whisk more, and continue cooking.

What if my agar jellies turned wet after a day?

Either they were undercooked, or they were not allowed to dry overnight on a screen. Roll in granulated sugar again and allow to dry overnight on a screen.

What if my citrus confit has firm spots that have not absorbed the syrup?

The skins were boiled rather than simmered, or they were not simmered long enough. Try adding a little bit of water to the syrup and very gently simmer for another 20 minutes or until the spots absorb the syrup.

Chocolate Marshmallows

Marshmallows

Making your own marshmallows is surprisingly simple. In addition to the standard vanilla, many flavor variations are possible, including spices, chocolate, and fruit.

SKILL LEVEL

¾ oz (3 tbsp; 3 envelopes) **Gelatin**

4 oz (½ cup) **Cold water**

12 oz (1½ cups) **Granulated sugar**

9 oz (¾ cup) **Light corn syrup**

3 oz (¼ cup) **Honey**

4 oz (½ cup) **Water**

1 tbsp **Vanilla extract**

2 oz (½ cup) **Confectioners' sugar, unsifted**

2 oz (½ cup) **Cornstarch**

---

1 Stir the gelatin into the cold water in a stainless-steel bowl. Set aside. Oil a 9-inch square baking pan, a rubber spatula, and an offset palette knife.

2 Combine the granulated sugar, corn syrup, honey, and water in a 2-quart saucepan. Cook to 250°F, following the Standard Sugar Cooking Technique (see page 29). Remove from the heat.

3 Pour the hot syrup into a 5-quart mixer bowl. Allow to cool undisturbed until a thermometer in the syrup reads 210°F, about 15 minutes.

4 While the syrup is cooling, melt the gelatin over a hot water bath.

5 When the syrup reaches 210°F, add the melted gelatin.

6 Whip on highest speed until very light, about 6 minutes. Whip in the vanilla extract.

7 Remove the marshmallow from the bowl using an oiled rubber spatula and place in the prepared baking pan. Spread in an even layer with the oiled offset palette knife.

8 Allow to set at room temperature for at least 2 hours. The marshmallows are easier to cut if they set overnight.

9 Sift together the confectioners' sugar and cornstarch.

10 Remove the slab of marshmallow from the pan and dredge in the sugar-starch mixture.

11 Cut into 1-inch squares using scissors.

12 Dredge the marshmallows in the sugar-starch mixture to prevent them from sticking together. Remove any excess by shaking the marshmallows in a sifter.

13 Store in an airtight container.

CHOCOLATE Add 1½ oz/¼ cup sifted cocoa powder to the marshmallows at the end of whipping.

RASPBERRY, PASSION FRUIT, OR OTHER FRUIT Reduce fruit puree by half over low heat on the stove. Add 2 oz/¼ cup reduced puree to marshmallows at the end of cooking.

SPICE Add 1½ tsp ground spice (anise, cinnamon, etc.) to the sugars at the beginning of cooking.

FLAVORED Manufactured flavors or extracts may be added to marshmallows near the end of whipping to create an array of flavors.

COLORED Food colors may be added to marshmallows near the end of whipping.

A VARIETY To create different colored and flavored marshmallows from a single batch, divide the batch and mix in the desired food colors and flavors into each portion.

MARBLED Marbled marshmallows may be created by swirling two different batches together after whipping in Step 6.

Keys to Success

- Sugar cooking temperature is critical. Use an accurate thermometer to cook the sugar.

- If you want slightly firmer marshmallows, cook the sugar mixture to a temperature 3° to 4°F higher. For softer marshmallows, cook the sugar mixture to a temperature 3° to 4°F lower.

- Be sure to allow the sugar to cool to the proper temperature before adding the gelatin.

- Always whip marshmallows on the the mixer's highest speed to achieve the best aeration.

- The marshmallows are very sticky. Any implement used to handle them must be well oiled.

- Work with the marshmallows promptly, before the gelatin sets.

- If desired, the marshmallows may be left overnight before cutting. This will make them easier to cut.

Divinity

A bit like a cross between marshmallow, nougat, and fudge, divinity is a light aerated candy that has a short, fudge-like texture. It is not much more difficult to make than a meringue and is best enjoyed fresh, when it lives up to its name.

SKILL LEVEL

MERINGUE

2 Large egg whites

2 oz (¼ cup) Granulated sugar

½ tsp Cream of tartar

SYRUP

1 lb (2 cups) Granulated sugar

6 oz (½ cup) Light corn syrup

4 oz (½ cup) Water

ADDITIONS AND INCLUSIONS

2 tsp Vanilla extract

1 tsp Salt

1 oz (⅛ cup) Confectioners' sugar

8 oz (2 cups) Roughly chopped toasted pecans

---

1 Line a sheet pan with parchment paper. Lightly sift confectioners' sugar over the parchment.

2 Combine the egg whites, granulated sugar, and cream of tartar for the meringue in a 5-quart mixer bowl fitted with a whip attachment. Do not begin to mix yet.

3 Combine the granulated sugar, corn syrup, and water for the syrup in a 2-quart saucepan. Stir over heat until it comes to a boil. Cover and boil for 3 minutes.

4 Remove the cover, insert a thermometer, and cook to 230°F without stirring.

5 When the syrup reaches 230°F, begin whipping the egg whites on high speed.

6 Continue cooking the syrup to 260°F.

7 Pour the hot syrup into the whipping whites in a constant stream. Continue whipping on high speed for 6 minutes.

8 Add the vanilla extract, salt, and confectioners' sugar to the whipping whites.

9 Remove from the machine and mix in the pecans by hand using a wooden spoon.

10 Using a spoon dipped in warm water each time, scoop the mixture into roughly egg-shaped portions and place on the prepared sheet pan.

11 Allow the divinity to set at room temperature for an hour or more before serving.

12 Store in an airtight container to protect from humidity.

COCOA NIBS DIVINITY *Replace the pecans with 4 oz/1 cup cocoa nibs.*

Keys to Success

○ Divinity is based on meringue making: Make sure all ingredients, tools, and equipment are free from oil or egg yolk before beginning.

○ Cook the sugar accurately to the proper temperature using a reliable thermometer.

○ Always use clean egg whites without a trace of yolk.

○ Be certain that the mixer bowl and whip attachment are free of fat.

○ Stream the hot syrup down the inside edge of the mixing bowl so that it goes into the whites and not on the whip or bowl.

○ Add the hot syrup to the egg whites in a moderate stream, neither very slowly nor in one gush.

○ Begin to scoop the divinity as soon as it is mixed for the best results. Have the pan, spoon, and warm water ready.

Chocolate Nougat

MAKES ONE 9 × 13-INCH SLAB

This is a soft chocolate nougat, similar to what is found in some well-known candy bars, except this one has more chocolate flavor. It is the fourth musketeer, the one with attitude, the one the others were jealous of, and you make it in your own kitchen! The nougat becomes more tender a day or two after it is made.

SKILL LEVEL

MERINGUE

2 Large egg whites

3 oz (¼ cup) Light corn syrup

1 tbsp Vanilla extract

ADDITIONS

1½ oz (¾ cup) Milk powder

2 oz (½ cup) Cocoa powder

1 oz (¼ cup) Confectioners' sugar

4 oz (6 tbsp) Melted unsweetened chocolate

SYRUP

1 lb (2 cups) Granulated sugar

6 oz (¾ cup) Water

18 oz (1½ cups) Light corn syrup

COATING

24 oz (2½ cups) Dark chocolate, melted, tempered, or dark compound coating, melted

---

1 Lightly oil a 9 × 13–inch baking pan.

2 Combine the egg whites, corn syrup, and vanilla extract for the meringue in a 5-quart mixer bowl fitted with a whip attachment. Do not begin whipping yet.

3 Sift together the milk powder, cocoa powder, and confectioners' sugar. Set aside.

4 Combine the sugar, water, and corn syrup for the syrup in a 2-quart saucepan. Cover the pan and bring to a boil. Boil covered for 3 minutes, remove the lid, insert a thermometer, and continue to cook over high heat without stirring.

5 When the syrup reaches 233°F, begin whipping the egg whites on high speed.

6 When the syrup reaches 257°F, remove immediately from the heat and pour the hot syrup into the whipping whites in a constant stream. Continue whipping on high speed for 8 minutes.

7 Turn off the mixer, add the sifted dry ingredients, and mix together on low speed just to combine.

8 Add the unsweetened chocolate and mix on low speed just to combine. If there are still white streaks of meringue, mix in the chocolate by hand with a rubber spatula.

9 Press into the prepared baking pan in an even layer.

10 Allow the nougat to cool completely to room temperature, about 2 hours, or allow to rest overnight.

11 Cut into 1-inch squares for individual candies or 1 × 4½–inch strips for bars.

12 Dip in chocolate or coating as desired, using the technique shown on page 44.

13 Mark the tops with the dipping fork (see page 46).

Keys to Success

○ Sugar cooking temperature is always critical. Use an accurate thermometer to cook your sugar.

○ If you want slightly firmer nougat, cook the sugar mixture to a temperature 3° to 4°F higher. For softer nougat, cook the sugar mixture to a temperature 3° to 4°F lower.

○ Make certain that the bowl is free of fat and that the egg whites do not have any yolk in them.

○ Whip the egg whites on the mixer's highest speed to achieve the best aeration.

○ Stream the hot syrup down the inside edge of the mixing bowl so that it goes into the whites and not on the whip or bowl.

○ Add the hot syrup to the egg whites in a moderate stream, neither very slowly nor in one gush.

○ Do not mix the nougat for a long time after the chocolate has been added. Mix only until incorporated.

Peanut Butter Nougat

MAKES ONE 9 × 13-INCH SLAB

All of the goodness of peanut butter in a light nougat—nothing could be better,
except maybe adding some chocolate. This nougat pairs well with both dark and milk
chocolate. The texture of the nougat will improve a day or two after it is made.

SKILL LEVEL

MERINGUE

1 Large egg white

3 oz (¼ cup) Light corn syrup

1 tbsp Vanilla extract

SYRUP

1 lb (2 cups) Granulated sugar

6 oz (¾ cup) Water

12 oz (1 cup) Light corn syrup

6 oz (½ cup) Molasses

ADDITIONS AND COATING

2 oz (¾ cup) Milk powder

2 oz (½ cup) Confectioners' sugar

9 oz (1 cup) Peanut butter

1 lb (1½ cups) Dark or milk chocolate, melted, tempered, or dark or milk compound coating, melted

Chopped toasted unsalted peanuts (optional), for garnish, as needed

---

1 Lightly oil a 9 × 13–inch baking pan and an offset palette knife.

2 Combine the egg white, corn syrup, and vanilla extract for the meringue in a 5-quart mixer bowl fitted with a whip attachment. Do not begin whipping yet.

3 Combine the granulated sugar, water, corn syrup, and molasses for the syrup in a 2-quart saucepan, cover, bring to a boil without stirring, and insert a thermometer.

4 When the syrup reaches 233°F, begin whipping the egg white on high speed.

5 Continue cooking the sugar until it reaches 255°F. Remove immediately from the heat and pour the hot syrup into the whipping egg white in a constant stream.

6 Continue whipping for 4 minutes after all the syrup has been added.

7 While the whites whip, sift together the milk powder and confectioners' sugar.

8 Remove the bowl from the mixer and fold in the milk powder mixture by hand using a rubber spatula.

9 Mix in the peanut butter by hand using a rubber spatula.

10 Spread in the prepared baking pan using the offset palette knife.

11 Allow the nougat to cool completely to room temperature, about 2 hours, or allow to rest overnight.

12 Cut into 1-inch squares for individual candies or 1 × 4½–inch strips for bars.

13 Dip in chocolate or coating as desired, using the technique shown on page 44.

14 Mark the tops with the dipping fork (see page 46), and, if desired sprinkle a little of the peanuts on top of each piece before the chocolate sets.

DOUBLE PEANUT NOUGAT *To provide a crisp texture, add 6 oz/1 cup chopped toasted (salted or unsalted) peanuts in Step 9.*

Keys to Success

- Sugar cooking temperature is critical to achieve the right firmness from the nougat.

- If you want slightly firmer nougat, cook the sugar mixture to a temperature 3° to 4°F higher. For softer nougat, cook the sugar mixture to a temperature 3° to 4°F lower.

- Mix egg whites on the mixer's highest speed to achieve the best aeration.

- Stream the hot syrup down the inside edge of the mixing bowl so that it goes into the whites and not on the whip or bowl.

- Add the hot syrup to the egg whites in a moderate stream, neither very slowly nor in one gush.

Nougat Torrone

Torrone is a nougat with a long history. Dating back to the Roman Empire, it is still a popular confectionery treat today. Containing honey, sugar, and egg whites, and wrapped in wafer paper, this version honors the ingredients and flavors of the original.

SKILL LEVEL
■ ■ ■ □

24 oz (5 cups) **Toasted whole unblanched almonds**

4 sheets **Wafer paper, 8 × 11 inches**

MERINGUE

2 **Large egg whites**

2 oz (¼ cup) **Sugar**

½ tsp **Cream of tartar**

SYRUP

18 oz (1½ cups) **Honey**

24 oz (3 cups) **Sugar**

6 oz (½ cup) **Light corn syrup**

4 oz (½ cup) **Water**

1 **Vanilla bean, split and scraped**

1 oz (2 tbsp) **Cocoa butter, melted**

---

1 Place the toasted almonds in a large ovenproof bowl and put in an oven set at 250°F until ready for use. Line the bottom of a 9 × 13–inch baking pan with a single layer of wafer paper, cutting it as needed. Set aside.

2 Combine the egg whites, sugar, and cream of tartar for the meringue in a 5-quart mixer bowl fitted with a whip attachment. Do not begin whipping yet.

3 Warm the honey to nearly a boil either in a microwave oven or on the stove in a saucepan.

4 Combine the sugar, corn syrup, water, and vanilla bean pod and seeds for the syrup in a 2-quart saucepan. Cover and bring to a boil. Turn down the heat and boil for 3 minutes, covered. Remove the lid, insert a thermometer, and continue to cook uncovered on high heat without stirring.

5 When the syrup reaches 300°F, begin whipping the egg whites on high speed.

6 Add the hot honey to the syrup. Continue cooking until the mixture once again reaches 300°F. Remove from the heat.

7 Using tongs, pick the vanilla pod out of the syrup. Pour the hot syrup into the whipping whites in a constant stream.

8 Continue whipping on high speed for 3 minutes.

9 Add the cocoa butter and mix until the nougat is once again smooth. Remove the bowl from the mixer.

10 Remove the almonds from the oven. Scrape the nougat into the warm bowl of almonds using a rubber spatula. Mix with the rubber spatula until the almonds are evenly distributed throughout the nougat.

11 Pour the hot nougat into the prepared baking pan, on top of the wafer paper. Cover the top of the nougat with a single layer of wafer paper, cutting the sheets as needed.

12 Allow the nougat to cool at room temperature until it is just slightly warm to the touch and very stiff, about 45 minutes.

13 Remove the nougat from the pan by prying it out with a spatula or bench scraper.

14 Trim the edges of the nougat to make it uniform and cut into the desired size pieces, either individual bites or bars. Or allow to cool completely and break into irregular pieces.

15 Wrap the nougats individually, or store them at room temperature in an airtight container. The texture of the nougat improves a day or two after it is first made.

Keys to Success

- Be careful to have all mise en place ready as per the instructions. Once you begin the process, it should not be interrupted until the nougat is cooling.

- Make sure that the egg whites for whipping are clean and do not contain any yolk.

- Be certain that all utensils and bowls, and the whipping attachment are scrupulously clean and free from any fat residue.

- Whip egg whites on the mixer's highest speed to achieve the best aeration.

- Sugar cooking temperature is critical. Use an accurate thermometer and cook the sugars carefully. The sugar may foam when the honey is added, so add the honey slowly at first.

- If you like torrone a little softer, cook the syrup only to 290°F rather than 300°F, which yields a very firm nougat.

- Stream the hot syrup down the inside edge of the mixing bowl so that it goes into the whites and not on the whip or bowl.

- Exercise great caution with both the syrup and the nougat while they are hot. Either one can cause severe burns.

- Do not mix the nougat for a long time after the cocoa butter has been added. Mix only until incorporated.

- Keeping inclusions warm before adding them to the nougat will help making mixing easier.

Turkish Delight

MAKES ONE 9 × 13-INCH SLAB

In the classic children's books *The Chronicles of Narnia*, a little boy loves Turkish Delight so much that he trades his family for it. No need to swap your family or friends—they will surely thank you for sharing this delight with them.

SKILL LEVEL

SUGAR SYRUP

2 lb (4 cups) Granulated sugar

8 oz (1 cup) Water

1 tsp Cream of tartar

STARCH PASTE

4½ oz (1 cup) Cornstarch

1 tsp Cream of tartar

24 oz (3 cups) Water

FLAVORING, COLORING, AND INCLUSION

2 tsp Rose water

2–3 drops Pink or red coloring

12 oz (1½ cups) Shelled unsalted undyed pistachios

COATING

2 oz (½ cup) Confectioners' sugar

1 oz (¼ cup) Cornstarch

---

1 Lightly oil a 9 × 13–inch baking pan, line with plastic wrap (see page 51), and oil the wrap. Set aside.

2 Combine the sugar, water, and cream of tartar for the sugar syrup in a 2-quart saucepan. Bring to a boil, cover, and allow to boil for 4 minutes undisturbed.

3 Remove the lid from the pan, insert a thermometer, and continue cooking until the sugar reaches 260°F. Remove from the heat, cover, and leave undisturbed.

4 Mix together the cornstarch, cream of tartar, and water for the starch paste in a 4-quart saucepan.

5 Stir constantly with a whisk over medium heat until the mixture thickens and boils. (It will be a very pasty, thick mixture.) Continue to stir and cook for 2 to 3 minutes.

6 Stream the cooked sugar syrup into the starch paste while whisking on the heat.

7 Bring the mixture to a gentle boil and continue whisking and cooking on low heat until the mixture is smooth and clear. This will take 20 to 25 minutes.

8 Remove from the heat, stir in the rose water, coloring, and pistachios.

9   Pour into the prepared pan, lay a piece of plastic wrap directly on top of the candy, and leave it to cool for at least 4 or 5 hours, or overnight.

10 Sift together the confectioners' sugar and cornstarch for the coating. Cut the candy into the desired size pieces, and roll in the coating mixture.

11 Store airtight at room temperature.

CARDAMOM AND CASHEW *Omit the rose water and the pink color. Add 2 tsp ground cardamom to the sugar when it is first cooked. Replace the pistachios with toasted whole cashews.*

ORANGE-ALMOND *Replace the rose water with orange blossom water, and replace the pistachios with lightly toasted blanched almonds, either whole or chopped.*

SAFFRON *Omit the rose water and the pink color. Add ¼ tsp of saffron threads to the sugar syrup when it is first cooked.*

VARIOUS FLAVORS *Any manufactured flavor can be used to make Turkish Delight. Simply replace the rose water with the desired flavor, and, if desired, use a color compatible with the chosen flavor. Nuts may be included or omitted.*

Keys to Success

○ Sugar cooking temperature is critical to success. Use a good thermometer to ensure accuracy.

○ The starch gets very thick when cooked. Adjust the heat to prevent scorching.

○ When the sugar and starch are first combined, the mixture looks lumpy and separated. Whisk vigorously while cooking, until the candy becomes smooth and transparent. Be patient and use a low heat.

Molded Agar Jellies (page 192) and Turkish Delight

Sponge Candy

Sponge candy enjoys regional popularity in the United States, and there are at least two candy bars made of sponge candy sold mainly in the United Kingdom. With a little practice, you can make sponge candy every bit as light and airy as these.

SKILL LEVEL

¼ tsp **Gelatin**

1 tsp **Cold water**

24 oz (3 cups) **Sugar**

12 oz (1 cup) **Light corn syrup**

8 oz (1 cup) **Water**

1½ oz (2 tbsp) **Honey**

½ oz (2 tbsp) **Baking soda, sifted**

24 oz (2¼ cups) **Milk chocolate, melted, tempered, or milk compound coating, melted, for dipping**

---

1 Brush a 9 × 13–inch baking pan with soft butter and dust with flour. Shake out the excess flour.

2 Mix the gelatin into the cold water in a small bowl or cup. Set aside.

3 Combine the sugar, corn syrup, and water in a 4-quart saucepan. Cover and bring to a boil.

4 Boil covered for 4 minutes, uncover, insert a thermometer, and continue cooking without stirring until it reaches 280°F.

5 Add the honey and continue cooking until the syrup reaches 310°F. Remove from the heat and allow to sit undisturbed until the bubbling stops, about 2 minutes.

6 Whisk the gelatin into the hot sugar. Be certain that it has been mixed in well.

7 Whisk the baking soda into the mixture. Whisk vigorously to thoroughly incorporate the baking soda.

8 Return the batch to the heat and whisk over the heat for 30 seconds. The mixture will rise up in the pan.

9 Pour immediately into the prepared baking pan and leave undisturbed to cool at room temperature for at least 2 hours, or overnight.

10 Invert the pan on a piece of parchment paper and tap out the sponge candy.

11 Break into the desired size pieces using a knife.

12 Dip in milk chocolate or coating as desired, using the technique shown on page 44.

Keys to Success

- Be sure that the gelatin has been thoroughly mixed into the hot syrup.

- Whisk vigorously when adding the baking soda to distribute it evenly.

- Do not disturb the sponge candy as it cools; too much motion will cause it to collapse.

- If the air is humid, protect the sponge candy from exposure during the cooling stage by enclosing the pan in an airtight container.

Pectin Jellies

Known in Europe as *pâte de fruit,* pectin makes jellies with an excellent texture.
Whether you make your own puree or buy it, this recipe will work with almost any fruit,
allowing you to take advantage of the best that the season—or freezer—has to offer.

SKILL LEVEL

1 lb (2 cups) **Fruit puree** (berries, stone fruit, etc.)

24 oz (3 cups) **Sugar, for the jellies**

6 oz (2 envelopes; 3 oz each) **Liquid pectin** (see Keys to Success)

1 tbsp Lemon juice

2 oz (¼ cup) **Sugar, for coating**

1 Lightly oil a 9-inch square baking pan, line with plastic wrap (see page 51), and oil the wrap. Set aside.

2 Combine the puree and 24 oz/3 cups sugar in a 2-quart saucepan. Stir constantly while cooking to 238°F.

3 Add the pectin, return to a boil while stirring, and boil for 1 minute.

4 Stir in the lemon juice and remove from the heat.

5 Pour into the prepared pan and sprinkle a thin layer of the coating sugar on the top of the jelly.

6 Allow to set at room temperature until completely cool, 2 hours or longer. Leaving overnight is acceptable.

7 Turn the pan upside down to release the jelly. Peel off the plastic wrap.

8 Coat the jelly with more of the sugar. Cut into the desired size pieces and roll each piece in the sugar.

9 Store in an airtight container at room temperature.

PECTIN JELLIES MADE USING JUICE *When using a juice such as pomegranate or grape, use 10 oz/1¼ cups juice, and 8 oz/¾ cup of unsweetened applesauce in place of the puree.*

Keys to Success

○ Sold under brand names such as Certo and Ball, liquid pectin is commonly available in grocery stores.

○ The instructions on the pectin envelopes are not for confectionery jellies, so disregard them when making these jellies.

○ Open the envelopes of pectin and have them ready so that they can be added quickly and easily when needed.

○ Jellies scorch easily. Moderate the heat during boiling, and keep the bottom of the saucepan clean using a heat-resistant rubber spatula.

○ Be sure to have your pan prepared before beginning to cook; the jellies begin to set immediately once they are cooked.

Agar Jellies

MAKES 25 PIECES

Using agar is an easy way to make fresh-tasting, brightly colored jellies. The flavor stays fresh because the fruit is added without cooking. Layering two or more flavors and colors together creates a dramatic effect.

SKILL LEVEL

1½ tbsp **Agar powder**

12 oz (1½ cups) **Sugar**

16 oz (2 cups) **Water**

18 oz (1½ cups) **Light corn syrup**

12 oz (1½ cups) **Fruit puree or juice** (see Keys to Success)

1 tbsp **Lemon juice**

8 oz (1 cup) **Sugar, for sanding**

---

1. Lightly oil a 9 × 13–inch baking pan, line with plastic wrap (see page 51), and oil the wrap. Set aside.

2. Mix the agar and 12 oz/1½ cups sugar. Stream them into the water in a 2-quart saucepan off the heat while whisking.

3. Add the corn syrup and put over high heat. Stirring constantly with a heat-resistant rubber spatula, bring to a boil. Insert a thermometer.

4. Lower the heat to medium, continue stirring, and cook until the temperature reaches 223°F.

5. Remove from the heat, and whisk in the fruit puree and lemon juice. Pour into the prepared pan.

6. Immediately sprinkle a little of the sanding sugar on top of the jelly before it cools.

7. Leave undisturbed to cool at room temperature for at least 1 hour, or until fully cooled.

8. Remove from the pan by pulling out the plastic liner. Remove the plastic liner from the jellies and cut them into 1-inch square pieces, or as desired.

9. Toss the pieces in the remaining sugar and place on a screen to dry uncovered overnight.

10. Store at room temperature in a tightly sealed container.

MOLDED AGAR JELLIES *Prepare the desired molds by spraying them with nonstick cooking spray, then dusting them with granulated sugar. Pour the jelly into the molds while hot and allow to set. Unmold, roll in sugar, and dry on a screen overnight.*

Keys to Success

- Either a freshly made puree or a purchased frozen one will perform well in this recipe. Strongly flavored fruits like raspberry, blackberry, mango, and apricot provide the best flavor.

- Agar scorches easily as it cooks. Be careful to moderate the heat and to stir well to keep the bottom of the saucepan clean.

- Sugar cooking temperature is critical. Use an accurate thermometer and cook to the required temperature.

- Allowing the finished jellies to dry on a screen overnight will prevent them from weeping.

Citus Confit

Citrus confit is an easy way to make a candy or baking ingredient out of what is normally a waste product. Whether you dry it and dip it in chocolate, dice it and use it in baked goods, or simply roll it in sugar to nibble, confit is sure to please citrus lovers.

SKILL LEVEL

5 Oranges, lemons, or grapefruits

24 oz (3 cups) Sugar

24 oz (2 cups) Light corn syrup

16 oz (2 cups) Water

1 Quarter the fruits and peel the skins off the interior. Reserve the interiors for another use.

2 Put the skins in a 4-quart saucepan and cover them with cold water. Bring to a boil, remove from the heat, and drain. Repeat this step two more times, using fresh water each time.

3 Combine the sugar, corn syrup and water in another 4-quart saucepan and bring to a simmer. Add the blanched citrus peels, cover, and return to a simmer.

4 Simmer the skins gently for 90 minutes, stirring occasionally.

5 Remove from the heat and allow to cool to room temperature in the syrup.

6 Store refrigerated in the syrup in a sealed container. Confit will keep refrigerated for at least 4 weeks.

Keys to Success

○ Use good-quality citrus fruit with unblemished skins. Thinner skinned citrus makes better confit than thick skinned citrus.

○ Gently simmer during cooking. Do not boil, as this toughens the skins.

○ Stir occasionally to be sure that all of the skins are cooked evenly.

Chocolate-Coated Confit

MAKES 48 PIECES

Who would have imagined that a humble citrus peel could be elevated to such a rarified stature? All it takes is some well-made citrus confit and a little tempered chocolate and you have a classic flavor combination for a first-rate candy.

SKILL LEVEL

8 quarters Citrus Confit (page 193)

1 lb (1½ cups) Milk, dark, or white chocolate, melted, tempered, or compound coating, melted, for dipping

---

1 Cut the citrus confit on a slight bias into strips ¼-inch wide.

2 Place on a screen and dry in a 200°F oven for 30 minutes.

3 Allow the confit to cool to room temperature.

4 Dip in the tempered chocolate or compound coating using one of the variations below.

5 Store at room temperature.

BLACK-AND-TAN DIPPED CONFIT Hold the strips by one end and dip into the tempered dark chocolate three quarters of the way to the end. Place on a parchment paper–lined sheet pan and allow the chocolate to set. Once set, hold the strips by the previously dipped end and dip into the tempered milk chocolate just to overlap the dark chocolate. Place on a parchment paper–lined sheet pan and allow to set. These will keep for at least a week at room temperature.

FULLY DIPPED CONFIT Dip the strips in the chocolate using the technique on page 44 to fully cover them with one type of chocolate. These will keep for at least a week at room temperature.

THREE QUARTERS DIPPED CONFIT Hold the strips by one end and dip into the tempered chocolate three quarters of the way to the end. Place with zest side facing up on a parchment paper–lined sheet pan. Store at room temperature and consume within 3 days.

Keys to Success

- Make sure the confit is neither dry and brittle nor soaking wet when dipping.

- Allow the confit to cool fully before dipping in chocolate.

- The chocolate must be properly tempered to ensure proper appearance.

- Both of the fully dipped confits will keep at room temperature for at least a week, but the one with the exposed peel must be consumed within several days.

8

Nuts!

The traditional combination of chocolate and nuts never goes out of style. Toasted nuts provide a perfect flavor complement to chocolate, and when the nuts are left whole or in larger pieces, they give a satisfying crunch to any confection. Nut confections can be broadly separated into two categories: nuts that are ground to a paste, and nuts that are whole or in pieces. Confections that use ground nuts include two great classics of confectionery: marzipan and gianduja, as well as buckeyes, an American regional favorite. Whole nut candies include rochers or clusters, dragées or caramel-coated nuts, and the American classic, turtles. Because this chapter focuses on nut confections, you should be familiar with the information on buying and storing nuts in Chapter 1, and also with the master technique of toasting nuts in Chapter 3. The most important thing you can do to ensure the best-quality products from the recipes in this chapter is to buy fresh nuts, store them properly, and toast them to perfection.

Marzipan

MARZIPAN is a traditional candy made from almonds ground into a paste with sugar. It is often molded into fruits, vegetables, or flowers to be used as both a decoration and a confection. While professional confectioners combine cooked sugar and grind it with almonds to make their own marzipan, it is much more practical for the home confectioner to use store-bought almond paste as the base for marzipan candies. The marzipan recipes in this book use almond paste and combine it with various other ingredients to create a range of marzipan-filled chocolates.

What's in it?

Marzipan contains little more than almonds and sugar. For convenience, almond paste is used in the recipes in this book. In order to provide flavor and textural variety, assorted toasted nuts and fruits can be kneaded into marzipan.

ALMOND PASTE This is the form of almonds that can be turned easily into marzipan by simply kneading in a little more confectioners' sugar.

CONFECTIONERS' SUGAR When kneaded into almond paste, confectioners' sugar makes marzipan malleable and easy to handle.

KIRSCH This is a traditional German unsweetened cherry brandy. It is not mandatory in marzipan, but the flavor complements almonds nicely. When not using kirsch, you may substitute another spirit; if alcohol is not desired, corn syrup may also be used to moisten the marzipan.

COLORS Colors are an optional ingredient in marzipan and are commonly used when the marzipan is for modeling. Any food-grade color will work with marzipan, but paste colors are generally the most effective, due to their low moisture content.

INCLUSIONS In order to make marzipan confections with a variety of flavors and textures, inclusions may be added. Most commonly these will be chopped toasted unsalted nuts, but dried or candied fruit or citrus confit also make good inclusions for marzipan.

How it's made

Making marzipan from almond paste is a simple matter of kneading together all of the ingredients. The only thing to be careful of is how much liquid to add to make marzipan smooth yet firm. If your marzipan becomes oily, add liquid (in the form of kirsch or corn syrup) to it a little at a time until the marzipan becomes smooth again. Adding liquid to separated marzipan seems a bit counterintuitive, but it is the correct remedy for oily marzipan.

1   Cut the almond paste in small pieces. Cutting the almond paste will make it easier to incorporate it with the sugar.

2   Combine the almond paste with the sugar by hand. Knead the almond paste into the sugar. It will require persistent kneading with some force to make it come together.

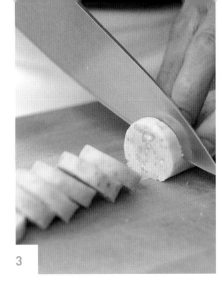

1   Use a rolling pin to roll the marzipan into an even sheet that can be cut into any desired shapes.

2   Rolled marzipan can be sliced with a chef's knife, then sliced evenly to form squares.

3   Use your hands to roll the marzipan into a log, then slice the log using a chef's knife.

3   If necessary to make a smooth mixture, add a little liquid. Sprinkle kirsch or another liquid on the marzipan to make a smooth dough. Always add as little of the liquid as possible to make marzipan that will hold its shape; too much liquid makes the marzipan too soft to handle.

How it's formed

In the recipes in this book, marzipan is either rolled into a sheet or formed into a log, cut in pieces, and dipped in chocolate with or without an additional garnish. These recipes are made to produce the maximum yield with the minimum waste or reworked product. After rolling, it is also possible to cut shapes using cutters, and then to rework the leftover material and cut more pieces.

How else can I use it?

Marzipan can be used in many ways. Traditionally, it is often modeled into fruit shapes and painted; it can be made into roses for cake decorations; and it can be rolled and used to coat cakes or pastries. It is a versatile preparation that has many uses in the worlds of baking, pastry, and confectionery.

How it's stored

Marzipan is not a product that spoils easily, but it will dry out if it is not handled and stored properly. From the instant it is made, marzipan should always be kept tightly covered with plastic wrap to prevent drying. For storage, it should be wrapped tightly in plastic wrap and sealed in either a plastic bag or an airtight container. It can be stored at room temperature indefinitely without concern for spoilage under these conditions.

Some people opt to store marzipan in the refrigerator, which is acceptable but not necessary. The only danger of storing marzipan refrigerated is that it can pick up moisture from condensation, making it too soft.

Gianduja

GIANDUJA (jhan-DOO-ya) is a delicious mixture of chocolate and finely ground nuts. It is most likely Italian in origin and is traditionally made with dark chocolate and hazelnuts. While it is possible to toast and grind nuts and add the resulting paste to chocolate, it is simpler to make and smoother when a preground nut butter is added to chocolate. Not only is this simpler, but it opens the door for many flavor combinations. Praline paste is the most frequently used nut paste in gianduja. Health food stores and some grocery stores carry nut butters made from a variety of nuts. and any of them may also be used to create gianduja.

Because gianduja is high in cocoa butter from the chocolate, it requires tempering just as chocolate does, and for all of the same reasons. Untempered gianduja will not set quickly, will be soft, will have a grainy texture, and will bloom, just like untempered chocolate. There are different ways to temper gianduja, but for the recipes in this book the method is to begin with tempered chocolate, add the nut paste, and stir well to ensure that the gianduja will set properly. You may want to review the chocolate tempering procedure on page 36 before beginning the gianduja recipes.

What's in it?

Gianduja contains chocolate (milk, dark, or white) and ground nuts, which may be any variety. It may also contain additional sugar. When sugar is added to gianduja in these recipes, confectioners', not granulated, sugar is used for a smooth texture.

CHOCOLATE Gianduja may be thought of as nut-flavored chocolate. When milk or white chocolate is used to make gianduja, slightly more chocolate is required to obtain the same firmness from the product.

NUT PASTE Almond butter or praline paste are the most traditional nut pastes to use when making gianduja at home, but there is nothing that says you cannot and should not use cashew butter, peanut butter, or any other form of nut paste that you like.

CONFECTIONERS' SUGAR An optional ingredient, confectioners' sugar will make the gianduja sweeter, but too much will also make it slightly less smooth in the mouth due to the particle size of confectioner's sugar.

INCLUSIONS Any type of dry inclusion may be used in gianduja; toasted nuts and dried fruit are the most commonly used ones.

How it's made

Fundamentally, gianduja is made by simply mixing the ingredients together. To ensure that the gianduja sets properly, the recipes in this book begin with tempered chocolate.

1   Temper the chocolate to be used. Follow the master technique on page 36, and be sure to test the chocolate to verify that it is fully tempered.

2   Mix in the room temperature nut paste and optional ingredients. It is important that the nut paste be at room temperature. If it is too cold, the chocolate will set immediately and you will not be able to make a smooth mixture. If the nut paste is above 85°F, you run the risk of taking the chocolate out of temper.

Using more nut paste and less chocolate yields a gianduja that can be spread to create layered confections.

Pipe the gianduja into nickel-size domes and place three toasted nuts on top of each.

3 Stir the mixture for an additional 3 minutes. The additional agitation helps to make sure the gianduja is tempered.

How it's formed

Gianduja can be spread in a prepared pan and allowed to set before unmolding and cutting. It may be dipped in chocolate if desired, but unlike many other centers, it is not necessary to dip it. Gianduja left exposed to the atmosphere will not be damaged by humidity nor by drying, so dipping in chocolate is optional.

How else can I use it?

Gianduja may be mixed with butter and piped into shapes, as when making Amigos (page 221), or it can be made using more nut paste and less chocolate to make a softer mixture, which can be used as a filling for shell-molded chocolates or chocolate cups.

How it's stored

Because gianduja contains no water, it is not prone to spoilage and has a very long shelf life. It should be protected from heat, moisture, and light and stored at room temperature. Like chocolate itself, gianduja should not be refrigerated—it will be damaged by moisture from condensation.

Buckeyes

BUCKEYES are a regional favorite candy indigenous to Ohio. They are named for their resemblance to the nut of the buckeye or horse-chestnut tree, which is in turn named for its resemblance to the eye of a male deer. Buckeye candies are balls of a peanut butter center dipped nearly to the tops in chocolate so that they look like buckeye nuts. The legends surrounding the nuts say that they are good-luck charms and will cure rheumatism when carried in your pocket. This may be a little far-fetched, but there is no question that balls of peanut butter dipped in chocolate will raise your spirits.

What's in it?

The ever-popular combination of peanut butter and chocolate is honored in buckeyes. The peanut butter center itself is made with confectioners' sugar and melted butter, so they have a short texture rather than a sticky peanut butter mouthfeel.

PEANUT BUTTER Regular supermarket-variety creamy salted peanut butter is used in these candies.

BUTTER The butter helps the centers set so that they are firm and easier to handle.

VANILLA EXTRACT Vanilla extract adds an element of complexity to the flavor of buckeyes.

CONFECTIONERS' SUGAR Sugar provides a short texture to the centers. The amount of sugar may vary slightly with each batch, and it should be added until the proper texture is achieved.

How it's made

Buckeyes are simple to make; adding the correct amount of confectioners' sugar is the crucial step in making the centers. If too little sugar is used, the centers will not hold their shape properly; too much, and they will crumble during shaping. Test the consistency frequently as you near the full amount of sugar.

1   Cream the peanut butter, soft butter, and vanilla extract together. These should be mixed just until homogeneous, not to incorporate air.

2 Add the sifted confectioners' sugar in stages. The sugar can be added in large increments at first, but as the mixture approaches the proper consistency, it should be added slowly. Evaluate the consistency by making balls, as for the candy, to see if it is a workable texture. Overall, it is preferable to have the mixture too dry rather than too moist.

How it's formed and finished

The finished filling is rolled into balls about 1¼ inches in diameter. These are dipped in tempered chocolate, either dark or milk, leaving an "eye" exposed on the top. To dip the buckeyes, lightly chill them and impale with a toothpick to use as a handle, or dip using a dipping fork. Either way, they aren't buckeyes if they don't have the eye at the top.

How it's stored

Like most chocolates, buckeyes should be stored at room temperature. If this is not possible, they can be refrigerated, but their appearance will be damaged slightly by moisture from condensation.

Using a toothpick as a handle, dip the chilled centers in tempered chocolate, leaving an eye exposed at the top.

Rochers

ROCHER (row-SHAY) means "rock" in French, so these little clusters of toasted nuts and other ingredients are meant to resemble edible stones. They are simple to make and may be made from any type of chocolate and many different types of centers. Rochers are an excellent way to utilize tempered chocolate left over after dipping the centers from another recipe. In common English usage, rochers are often called clusters or, when they are made using coconut, haystacks. Regardless of the name, they are a great addition to an assortment of homemade chocolates.

What's in it?

Any ingredient used to make rochers must be dry and shelf stable. Other than this requirement, there are few limitations to the centers that may be used to make rochers. Any type of chocolate can be used in making rochers: milk, dark, white, or even gianduja; it is purely a matter of preference. The most commonly used inclusions are toasted nuts or seeds, dried or candied fruit, and cereal or snack foods. Because of the flexibility, rochers present great opportunity for creativity and for utilizing leftover products.

INCLUSIONS The possibilities are nearly endless—you should mix and match to create chocolates to your liking.

> **TOASTED UNSALTED NUTS** are the most common inclusions for rochers. A great technique for getting extra flavor is to moisten the nuts with a liquor and sprinkle them with sugar before toasting.

> **DRIED FRUIT** provides both textural and flavor contrast to rochers, bringing both sweet and tart flavors to the party.

> **CEREAL** adds a crisp element of lightness to rochers. Puffed rice or corn flakes are the most commonly used cereals, but many other types may be used.

> **SNACK FOODS** such as pretzels, crackers, or even tortilla chips can bring a salty surprise to your products.

CHOCOLATE Any variety of chocolate can be used for rochers. Make sure it is properly tempered so that it sets with the desired snap and shine.

How it's made

Rochers are made by mixing a small amount of tempered chocolate to cover the inclusions, then spooning them out in individual portions. The most crucial factors when making rochers are to temper the chocolate and to work with a small amount at a time to obtain the best appearance.

1   Prepare and mix all of the inclusions. Nuts must be toasted and allowed to cool, and generally fruit should be cut in pieces nearly the same size as the other inclusions used. All inclusions should be at room temperature and mixed together in a bowl.

2   Temper the chocolate (see page 36). Compound coating may also be used to make rochers.

3   Warm a small bowl or cup. The bowl should be warmed to about 85°F so that the chocolate will not set as soon as it touches a cold bowl.

4   Place about ½ cup of inclusions in the warmed bowl. Working with a small amount of ingredients at a time will result in a smoother finish on the products.

5   Add enough tempered chocolate to coat the inclusions. The inclusions should be completely coated with, but not swimming in, the chocolate.

How it's formed

Once the inclusions are mixed with the chocolate, use a spoon to drop individual pieces onto a pan lined with parchment paper. Work quickly with each batch so the chocolate doesn't begin to set in the bowl; rewarm the bowl as needed.

How it's stored

Rochers are stored the same way other chocolate-coated centers are: at room temperature, protected from moisture and extremes of temperature. Refrigeration should always be a last resort because the moisture from condensation will diminish the appearance of the pieces.

Once the inclusions are covered in chocolate, use a spoon to drop individual mounds.

Turtles

LIKE TRUFFLES AND BUCKEYES, turtles are a confection named for its resemblance to another object—this one a torpid reptile. Also like truffles and buckeyes, chocolate turtles are one of the most widely recognized and appreciated homemade chocolates. Turtles are usually made with pecans or cashews because they give the desired shape, but other nuts can be used as well. To make turtles, you will need to be familiar with making soft caramels (see page 120).

What's in it?

Turtles are made using five toasted nuts strategically placed to resemble the legs and head of a turtle, onto which warm soft caramel is poured to hold them together and create the body. Once cooled, the turtles get their shell of tempered chocolate spooned or piped onto the caramel. Occasionally, turtles are dipped fully in chocolate so that they are entirely coated.

PECANS Pecans are the nuts most commonly used in turtles, cashews make a nice variation, and other nuts may be used if desired. Whatever the variety, the nuts must be properly toasted to develop full flavor. Salting is optional.

SOFT CARAMEL The soft caramel for turtles should be cooked to a relatively firm consistency so that it holds the finished turtle together.

TEMPERED CHOCOLATE Turtles are nearly always finished using dark chocolate, but other varieties could be used. Compound coating would be a distant second choice.

Arrange the nuts on a sheet pan and carefully pour the warm caramel over the nuts.

Pipe or spoon tempered chocolate onto the caramel, leaving the turtle's "head" and "feet" exposed.

How it's made

To make turtles, the nuts are placed in a cluster, the caramel is cooked and then cooled to the optimum temperature, and the chocolate is tempered and applied. Each step requires attention to detail, but the resulting turtles are well worth the effort.

1 Cook the soft caramel. Use a spoon test (see page 30) to make sure the caramel is cooked firm enough to hold the turtle together when it is finished. Set it aside to cool slightly. The caramel performs best when it is applied at around 145°F.

2 Lay the toasted nuts out in groups of five on a sheet pan lined with parchment paper or plastic wrap to resemble the legs and head of a turtle. The nuts within each group should be touching, but leave a little space between the groups.

3 Pour the warm caramel onto the center of each group of the nuts. Do not cover the nuts entirely, but use the caramel to bind the group together with the end of each nut protruding. Allow the caramel to cool fully to room temperature.

4 Pipe or spoon the tempered chocolate onto the caramel, leaving the feet and head exposed. Alternatively, dip each piece in the tempered chocolate to fully enrobe.

How it's stored

Store turtles in single layers in airtight containers with waxed or parchment paper between to prevent them from sticking together. Turtles have a long shelf life and may be kept for several weeks if desired.

Dragées

THE WORD *dragée* means "dredged." Dragéed nuts have been dredged in caramel, chocolate, or both. Dragéed almonds or hazelnuts are some of the most practical and delicious chocolates that a home candy maker can produce. Practical because the nuts are chocolate-coated without individual dipping, and delicious because freshly toasted nuts, crisp caramel, and chocolate all together is pretty close to heaven. Other varieties of nuts may also be caramel-coated; the technique differs slightly depending on the nuts used. Also included in this category are a few savory/sweet treats that do not use chocolate, such as caramel-coated popcorn.

What's in it?

In general terms, dragées require a center, usually a nut; they require caramelized sugar; and they may or may not include chocolate for further coating. The variety of nut can be altered to suit personal tastes, as can any optional seasonings that might be added.

CENTERS Nuts are the classic, but many other possibilities exist, such as coriander or anise seeds, coffee beans, and, of course, popcorn. A mixture of several different centers may also be dragéed.

SUGAR The sugar for dragées is caramelized, either before or after the centers are added. Either way, it makes a thin caramel coating on the center. This may complete the dragées, or they may be further coated in chocolate.

BUTTER Dragéed centers almost always contain butter. Flavor is actually the secondary reason for the butter; it is mainly used to prevent the centers from sticking together.

FLAVORING Vanilla extract is the most commonly used flavoring in dragées, but many other possibilities exist, including spices, either savory or sweet. When using spices, care must be taken about when to add them so that the high heat of the caramel does not burn them.

CHOCOLATE Not every dragéed item is coated in chocolate. The most common example is caramel-coated popcorn, which seldom wears chocolate. When used, though, a chocolate coating not only provides flavor, it also protects the caramelized sugar from humidity, making the dragées less particular about storage conditions.

COCOA POWDER OR CONFECTIONERS' SUGAR These are used to dust the finished pieces when they have been chocolate-coated.

How it's made and formed

There are two different techniques that can be used to make dragées; the type of center determines which technique you should use. When using hard centers with a smooth surface such as almonds or hazelnuts, the preferred method is to use untoasted nuts and to caramelize the sugar directly on the nuts (Technique #1). This technique is slightly more difficult than Technique #2, but gives better results for these centers. When using a softer center such as popcorn, or a center with a wrinkled surface such as pecans or walnuts, the preferred technique is to make the caramel first, then add the center to cover it with the caramel (Technique #2). In either case, the final step of finishing with several coats of chocolate is optional.

dragée technique #1

1 Combine sugar and water in a large saucepan. Cook over high heat to the thread stage (see page 31). The amount of sugar will be so small that you will not be able to use a thermometer easily. Look for the boiling syrup to thicken but not to brown, or use a spoon test (page 30).

2 Add the untoasted nuts to the sugar and stir vigorously. The sugar will crystallize on the nuts, creating a frosty white coating on each individual nut.

3 Stir constantly over medium heat. The object is to caramelize the sugar and to simultaneously toast the nuts in the pan. Continue stirring until the sugar has created an even, light brown, smooth varnish coating each nut. Turn the heat lower as the nuts cook to prevent scorching.

4 Add the butter. The butter is added only after the sugar has caramelized so that it coats the outside of the centers, making them easier to separate.

5 Pour the coated centers onto an oiled sheet pan. They must be separated into individual kernels before the sugar on the outside hardens. Wearing vinyl or latex food-handling gloves and working quickly is the best way to accomplish this.

6 Allow the individual nuts to cool. Whether using them with just the caramel coating or coating with chocolate, you must let the nuts cool completely before storing, serving, or coating them.

7 If coating with chocolate, refrigerate the nuts briefly. Five minutes in the refrigerator will make chocolate coating much easier.

8 Pour one-third of the chocolate over the nuts in a large bowl.

9 Stir vigorously until the chocolate sets and the nuts break apart into individual kernels.

10 Refrigerate briefly again, and repeat the chocolate-coating step. Repeat this three times until all of the chocolate for the recipe has been used on the nuts.

11 Coat with a dusting of cocoa powder, confectioners' sugar, or a combination of the two. This coating provides a finish and an additional flavor note to the completed pieces.

dragée technique #2

1 Prepare the centers. Nuts should be toasted; any center should be warmed so that it combines easily with the caramel.

2 Caramelize the sugar using either the dry technique (page 32) or the wet technique (page 29). If using the dry technique, the sugar should be fully melted so that it is completely smooth, and it should be a medium-brown color. When using the wet technique, cook to the temperature specified in the recipe.

3 Mix the centers into the caramel. Stir over low heat until the centers are fully coated with the caramel.

1 Mix the nuts into the caramel, stirring over low heat until the nuts are completely coated (Technique #2).

2 Pour the coated nuts onto an oiled sheet pan.

3 Wearing food-handling gloves, work quickly to separate the individual nuts before the caramel hardens.

4 Stir until the chocolate sets and the nuts break apart into individual kernels.

4   Add the flavorings, if used. Spices must be added at the end of the process to prevent burning and bitter flavors.

5   Add the butter. Do not overmix; keep the butter on the outside of the caramel, rather than mixing it into the sugar.

6   Pour the coated centers onto an oiled sheet pan. They must be separated into individual kernels before the sugar on the outside hardens. Wearing vinyl or latex food-handling gloves and working quickly is the best way to accomplish this.

7   Allow the individual nuts to cool. Whether using them with just the caramel coating or coating with chocolate, you must let the nuts cool completely before storing, serving, or coating them.

8   Coat with chocolate, if desired. See the technique on page 206.

How else can I use it?

An alternative use for dragéed centers is to group them together into clusters, either to use alone or to dip in tempered chocolate; caramel corn may be formed into balls.

How it's stored

Dragéed centers that are not chocolate-coated should be stored at room temperature, carefully protected from humidity or moisture, like any sugar-based candy. Centers that have been chocolate-coated are far more tolerant of moisture but will be adversely affected by warm temperatures.

Caramel-Coated Popcorn

CARAMEL-COATED POPCORN, or a popcorn-nut mixture, is a simple-to-make, delicious treat involving little more than caramelizing sugar, adding flavorings, and stirring together with the popcorn mixture. Although caramel corn is often enjoyed almost immediately, it can be stored for longer periods when it is wrapped to protect it from humidity (and eager hands!).

What's in it?

WATER As always when cooking sugar, water is used to dissolve the sugar. In the case of caramel corn, virtually all of the water is removed during cooking to create a crisp texture.

SUGAR Sugar provides the sweetness and the coating for the popcorn. In this process, the sugar is caramelized.

BROWN SUGAR In addition to sweetness, brown sugar contributes molasses flavor and additional browning to caramel for popcorn.

CORN SYRUP Corn syrup helps to prevent the recrystallization of sugar.

BUTTER Butter not only adds flavor and contributes to a more tender bite, but also helps to prevent the pieces in the mixture from sticking together.

SALT Popcorn (and nuts) without salt are just incomplete to most people, even when coated with caramel.

BAKING SODA Baking soda aerates caramel, giving it a more delicate bite. It also promotes browning and flavor development.

POPCORN This is the center to be coated with the caramel mixture. Any other type of center can be added, provided it is dry (so as not to dissolve the caramel) and is firm enough to stand up to the stirring required to coat it with the caramel. Some other suggested centers include nuts, cereals, seeds, crackers, and pretzels.

How it's made

Making this popular treat is a simple matter of caramelizing sugar and mixing in the popped corn, followed by butter. Once the popcorn is coated with caramel, the individual kernels are separated by hand and allowed to cool until they are no longer sticky. Because you are working with hot sugar, extreme caution must be exercised when handling the sugar; gloves, whether rubber or leather, must be worn for this part of the process. Should the caramel corn become too cool to separate, it can be rewarmed in a 250°F oven to soften it so that the process can be completed.

Stir the caramel into the warm popcorn until the corn is completely coated.

1   Combine the popcorn and nuts and place in a 250°F oven to keep warm.

2   Combine the sugars and water and cook to 300°F to begin caramelization.

3   Mix in the salt.

4   Add the baking soda to the sugars off the heat.

5   Add the caramel to the warm popcorn. Stir until the corn is coated with the caramel, reheating as necessary.

6   Add the butter to the batch and mix lightly.

7   Pour the mixture onto an oiled countertop or sheet pan, and while it is still warm, separate into individual kernels.

How it's stored

Caramel-coated popcorn has a good shelf life, provided it is protected from humidity. The finished treats should be sealed tightly in airtight containers as soon as they have cooled to prevent damage from moisture in the air.

What if

What if my marzipan is oily and cracks?

The marzipan has separated and requires the addition of a little bit of liquid, such as simple syrup, a spirit, or corn syrup.

What if my gianduja doesn't set?

The chocolate used to make the gianduja was not tempered properly. The gianduja can be reheated to 105°F, cooled to 80°F while stirring over a cool water bath, stirred vigorously, and respread. This procedure should temper the gianduja so that it sets properly.

What if my buckeyes are too soft to dip?

They must be refrigerated briefly to firm them for dipping.

What if my rochers do not set properly?

The chocolate was not tempered. Always use tempered chocolate to make rochers.

What if the chocolate on my dragées will not set?

Either the chocolate was not tempered, or the nuts are too warm. In either case, put the bowl of nuts over ice and stir vigorously until the chocolate sets.

What if I cannot separate my caramel corn into individual pieces?

Rewarm in a 250°F oven to soften the caramel, and continue separating.

Marzipan

Marzipan is a fragrant mixture of almond paste and sugar. It can be used many different ways, from modeling into edible roses or fruits to rolling sheets for coating cakes, or as a center for dipping in chocolate. This master recipe is used as a basis for the confections that follow.

SKILL LEVEL

3 oz (⅓ cup) **Almond paste**

3 oz (¾ cup) **Confectioners' sugar**

About ½ oz (1 tbsp) **Kirsch or other spirit** (see Keys to Success), **or as needed**

---

1 Cut the almond paste into pieces of approximately ½ inch. Place in a mixing bowl.

2 Sift the confectioners' sugar over the almond paste.

3 Working by hand, knead the almond paste and the confectioners' sugar together to form a ball.

4 If the marzipan seems very dry, or will not form a ball, sprinkle with kirsch and continue working until a ball is formed.

5 Once mixed, the marzipan should be kept tightly wrapped, as it will dry out when left exposed to the air.

Keys to Success

○ Kirsch is unsweetened cherry brandy and is traditional in marzipan. If unavailable or undesired, you may substitute another spirit, simple syrup, or even corn syrup.

○ Be persistent with the kneading! It takes some effort to blend the sugar and almond paste together.

○ If kirsch or other liquid is added, add the minimum amount necessary so that the marzipan is not too soft.

○ If the marzipan develops an oily appearance, do not add more sugar; add kirsch or other liquid and knead until the oil reincorporates into the marzipan.

Cherry-Almond Marzipan

MAKES 36 PIECES

The tart flavor of dried cherries harmonizes beautifully with toasted almonds in this marzipan. If you think that you do not like marzipan, this one might just change your mind.

SKILL LEVEL

2 oz (½ cup) **Toasted almonds, chopped ⅛ inch**

2 oz (¼ cup) **Dried cherries, chopped ⅛ inch**

1 Full recipe **Marzipan** (page 211)

Confectioners' sugar, for dusting table, as needed

10 oz (1 cup) **Dark chocolate, melted, tempered, or dark compound coating, melted, for dipping**

36 **Dried cherry halves**

1 Line a sheet pan with parchment paper.

2 Knead the chopped almonds and cherries into the marzipan by hand.

3 Sift confectioners' sugar over the work table to prevent the marzipan from sticking to the surface. Roll the marzipan by hand into a log 1 inch in diameter and 9 inches long.

4 Slice the marzipan log into ¼-inch-thick disks using an oiled chef's knife.

5 Dip the disks in the tempered chocolate or compound coating using the technique shown on page 44. Place on the prepared sheet pan.

6 Before the chocolate fully sets, place 1 dried cherry half on top of each piece. Allow to set completely.

Keys to Success

○ If the marzipan is too dry to work with without cracking, knead in a little kirsch, amaretto, or corn syrup to moisten it.

○ Use a sharp knife to cut the log so that the pieces aren't misshapen.

Tropical Marzipan Squares

A truly unexpected and refreshing combination: marzipan and tropical flavors. Sure to inspire you to plan your next island getaway.

SKILL LEVEL

2 oz (½ cup) **Macadamia nuts, chopped ⅛ inch**

1 **Full recipe Marzipan** (page 211)

Confectioners' sugar, for dusting table, as needed

10 oz (1 cup) **Milk chocolate, melted, tempered, or milk compound coating, melted, for dipping**

5 **Candied pineapple rings, whole**

1 Line a sheet pan with parchment paper.

2 Knead the chopped macadamia nuts into the marzipan by hand.

3 Sift confectioners' sugar over the work table to prevent the marzipan from sticking to the surface. Roll the marzipan into a 6-inch square.

4 Brush or spread a thin coat of tempered chocolate or compound coating on the top of the marzipan square. Let the coating set.

5 Turn the marzipan over onto a piece of parchment paper so that the chocolate is on the bottom. Cut into 1-inch strips using an oiled chef's knife. Cut each strip into 6 equal triangles.

6 Cut each pineapple ring into 8 equal wedges.

7 Dip the marzipan triangles in the tempered chocolate or compound coating using the technique shown on page 44. Place on the prepared sheet pan.

8 Before the chocolate fully sets, place a candied pineapple wedge on top of each triangle. Allow to set completely.

Keys to Success

○ If the marzipan is too dry to work with without cracking, knead in a little rum or corn syrup to moisten it.

○ Be sure the nuts have cooled before adding them to the marzipan.

○ Square up the edges of the marzipan as you are rolling it to get a uniform square shape.

Walnut Marzipan

MAKES 32 PIECES

Here is a sophisticated variation on traditional marzipan. The walnuts provide a welcome complement to the sweet, fragrant marzipan.

SKILL LEVEL

2 oz (½ cup) untoasted Walnuts, chopped ⅛ inch

1 Full recipe Marzipan (page 211)

Confectioners' sugar, for dusting table, as needed

10 oz (1 cup) Dark chocolate, melted, tempered, or dark compound coating, melted, for dipping

32 untoasted Walnut halves

1 Line a sheet pan with parchment paper.

2 Knead the chopped walnuts into the marzipan by hand.

3 Sift confectioners' sugar over the work table to prevent the marzipan from sticking to the surface. Roll the marzipan by hand into a log 1 inch in diameter and 8 inches long.

4 Slice the marzipan log into ¼-inch-thick disks using an oiled chef's knife.

5 Dip the disks into the tempered chocolate or compound coating using the technique shown on page 44. Place on the prepared sheet pan.

6 Before the chocolate fully sets, place 1 walnut half on top of each piece. Allow to set completely.

Keys to Success

○ If the marzipan is too dry to work with without cracking, knead in a little light rum or corn syrup to moisten it.

○ Use a sharp knife to cut the log so that the pieces aren't misshapen.

Toasted Hazelnut Squares

MAKES 36 PIECES

Hazelnuts' bold flavor stands up to even the highest percentage
chocolate. Try dipping these in a 70 percent chocolate and you will
be rewarded with a very adult, sophisticated confection.

SKILL LEVEL

2 oz (½ cup) **Toasted hazelnuts, chopped ⅛ inch**

1 Full recipe Marzipan (page 211)

Confectioners' sugar, for dusting table, as needed

10 oz (1 cup) **Dark chocolate, melted, tempered, or dark compound coating, melted, for dipping**

36 Toasted whole blanched hazelnuts

1 Line a sheet pan with parchment paper.

2 Knead the chopped hazelnuts into the marzipan by hand.

3 Sift confectioners' sugar over the table to prevent the marzipan from sticking to the surface. Roll the marzipan into a 6-inch square.

4 Brush or spread a thin coat of tempered chocolate or compound coating on the top of the marzipan square. Let the coating set.

5 Turn the marzipan over onto a piece of parchment paper so that the chocolate is on the bottom. Cut into 1-inch squares using an oiled chef's knife.

6 Dip the squares in the tempered chocolate or compound coating using the technique shown on page 44. Place on the prepared sheet pan.

7 Before the chocolate fully sets, place 1 whole hazelnut on top of each square. Allow to set completely.

Keys to Success

- If the marzipan is too dry to work with without cracking, knead in a little hazelnut liqueur or corn syrup to moisten it.

- Be sure the nuts have cooled before adding them to the marzipan.

- Square up the edges of the marzipan as you are rolling it to get a uniform square shape.

Pistachio Squares

Pistachios bring their texture, flavor, and vibrant color to this marzipan.
Save the brightest, greenest nuts for the garnish on top of each piece.

SKILL LEVEL

2 oz (½ cup) unsalted Pistachios, chopped ⅛ inch

1 Full recipe Marzipan (page 211)

Confectioners' sugar, for dusting table, as needed

10 oz (1 cup) Dark chocolate, melted, tempered, or dark compound coating, melted, for dipping

36 Whole peeled undyed unsalted pistachios (see Keys to Success)

1 Line a sheet pan with parchment paper.

2 Knead the chopped pistachios into the marzipan by hand.

3 Sift confectioners' sugar over the work table to prevent the marzipan from sticking to its surface. Roll the marzipan into a 6-inch square.

4 Brush or spread a thin coat of tempered chocolate or compound coating on the top of the marzipan square. Let the coating set.

5 Turn the marzipan over onto a piece of parchment paper so that the chocolate is on the bottom. Cut into 1-inch strips using an oiled chef's knife.

6 Dip the squares in the tempered chocolate or compound coating using the technique on page 44. Place on the prepared sheet pan.

7 Before the chocolate fully sets, place 1 whole peeled pistachio on top of each square. Allow to set completely.

Keys to Success

○ To peel pistachios, drop them into boiling water and allow to boil for 1 minute. Strain them out of the water, and when slightly cooled, squeeze the skins off of each nut individually.

○ If the marzipan is too dry to work with without cracking, knead in a little light rum or corn syrup to moisten it.

○ Square up the edges of the marzipan as you are rolling it to get a uniform square shape.

Cherry-Almond Marzipan (page 212), Pistachio Squares,
Toasted Hazelnut Squares (page 215), Tropical Marzipan
Squares (page 213), and Walnut Marzipan (page 214)

Basic Gianduja

Nuts paired with chocolate is always a winning combination. When you buy gianduja, it is always made using either hazelnuts or almonds, but chocolate can be mixed with any nut paste to make delicious gianduja. Let your own taste be your guide. These basic giandujas can be used in many different ways.

SKILL LEVEL

10 oz (1 cup) **Praline paste**

8 oz (¾ cup) **Dark chocolate, melted, tempered**

1 Line a 9-inch square baking pan with plastic wrap (see page 51).

2 Stir the praline paste into the tempered chocolate.

3 Spread the gianduja in the pan. Allow to set fully at room temperature.

4 Cut into the desired size pieces.

ALMOND GIANDUJA Combine 1 lb/1½ cups melted, tempered white chocolate with 8 oz/¾ cup almond butter (available in health food stores).

CASHEW GIANDUJA Combine 1 lb/1½ cups melted, tempered milk chocolate with 8 oz/¾ cup cashew butter (available in health food stores).

PEANUT BUTTER GIANDUJA Mix 1 lb/1½ cups melted, tempered milk chocolate with 8 oz/¾ cup peanut butter that has been warmed to 85°F.

INCLUSIONS Any of the giandujas can be used with inclusions such as toasted chopped nuts or chopped dried fruit. Mix these in after combining the nut butter and the chocolate.

Keys to Success

○ Temper the chocolate to use for gianduja or it will not set up properly.

○ Stir the nut butter well to homogenize it before mixing with the chocolate.

○ Cut the gianduja the same day you make it or it will be too firm to cut cleanly.

Layered Gianduja

The basic giandujas are even better when they are layered together to make one extraordinary confection. This rendition uses three different types of gianduja, but it can be made using two instead if you want to make a slightly quicker version. Either way, it is an irresistible piece that also looks great.

SKILL LEVEL

8 oz (¾ cup) **Dark chocolate, melted, tempered**

10 oz (1 cup) **Praline paste**

1 lb (1½ cups) **Milk chocolate, melted, tempered**

8 oz (¾ cup) **Peanut butter**

1 lb (1½ cups) **White chocolate, melted, tempered**

8 oz (¾ cup) **Almond butter**

1 Line a 9-inch square baking pan with plastic wrap (see page 51).

2 Mix together the dark chocolate and praline paste and pour into the prepared pan. Allow to set for 30 minutes at room temperature.

3 Mix together the milk chocolate with the peanut butter and pour on top of the first layer of gianduja. Allow to set for 30 minutes at room temperature.

4 Mix together the white chocolate with the almond butter and pour on top of the second layer of gianduja. Allow to set for 1 hour at room temperature.

5 Remove from the pan by lifting out the plastic wrap. Remove the plastic wrap and cut into 1-inch square pieces.

Keys to Success

○ Be certain that each chocolate is tempered before you mix the nut butter into it. If not, the gianduja will not set properly.

○ Allow each layer to set before pouring on the next to ensure that the layers are even.

○ Cut the gianduja the same day you make it or it will be too firm to cut cleanly.

Layered Gianduja (page 219) and Amigos

Amigos

MAKES 25 PIECES

Gianduja can be made a bit softer than usual by the addition of butter. Once it is made up, it is an ideal consistency for piping, whether from a star tip or a round one. Top the piped gianduja with toasted nuts, dip in chocolate, and enjoy!

SKILL LEVEL

8 oz (¾ cup) **Praline paste or other nut butter**

6 oz (⅔ cup) **Dark chocolate, melted**

2 oz (4 tbsp) **Butter, unsalted, soft**

4 oz (75 each; 1 cup) **Whole toasted blanched hazelnuts**

1 lb (1½ cups) **Dark chocolate, melted, tempered, for dipping**

---

1 Line 2 sheet pans with parchment paper. Fit a piping bag with a #4 round tip.

2 Combine the praline paste and melted chocolate in the bowl of a 5-quart mixer fitted with a paddle attachment. Mix on low speed for 5 minutes.

3 As the mixer turns, add the butter in 3 or 4 additions. Continue mixing until the gianduja stiffens slightly.

4 Transfer the gianduja to the piping bag and pipe into nickel-size domes onto a prepared sheet pan.

5 Before the gianduja sets, place 3 toasted hazelnuts on top of each dome. Allow to set completely, about 20 minutes at room temperature.

6 Dip in tempered dark chocolate using the technique shown on page 44. Place on another prepared sheet pan. Allow to set completely, about 10 minutes.

ALMOND AMIGOS Use 8 oz/¾ cup of white chocolate, 8 oz/¾ cup of almond butter, and 2 oz/4 tbsp butter. Place a single whole toasted blanched almond on the top of each gianduja. Dip in tempered dark chocolate.

CASHEW AMIGOS Use 8 oz/¾ cup of milk chocolate, 8 oz/¾ cup of cashew butter, and 2 oz/4 tbsp butter. Place a single whole cashew on the top of each gianduja. Dip in tempered milk chocolate.

PEANUT BUTTER AMIGOS Use 8 oz/¾ cup of milk chocolate, 8 oz/¾ cup of peanut butter, and 2 oz/4 tbsp butter. Place three whole toasted peanuts on the top of each gianduja. Dip in tempered milk chocolate.

Keys to Success

○ Mixing the gianduja in the machine tempers it. Make sure it mixes slowly and for at least 10 minutes total.

○ If the gianduja hardens in the pastry bag, massage it by hand until it is malleable.

○ Place the nuts on top before the gianduja sets.

Buckeyes

A popular iconic treat from Ohio, buckeyes combine peanut butter and chocolate in a unique shape resembling horse chestnuts. You don't have to be from the Buckeye State to love these little jewels.

SKILL LEVEL

9 oz (1 cup) **Peanut butter**

4 oz (8 tbsp) **Butter, unsalted, soft**

1 tsp **Vanilla extract**

12 oz (3 cups) **Confectioners' sugar, sifted** (see Keys to Success)

1 lb (1½ cups) **Dark chocolate, melted, tempered**

---

1 Line 2 sheet pans with parchment paper.

2 Cream together the peanut butter, butter, and vanilla extract in a mixer fitted with a paddle attachment on medium speed.

3 Add the confectioners' sugar slowly until the mixture forms a workable dough. Add up to ½ cup more sugar if necessary.

4 Remove the mixture from the machine. Using a #100 scoop or teaspoon, scoop out balls of the buckeye mixture. Place the portions on a prepared sheet pan.

5 Using your hands, roll the portions into round balls 1¼ inches in diameter. Return to a sheet pan.

6 Chill the formed buckeyes for approximately 20 minutes.

7 Impale each buckeye lightly with a toothpick to use as a handle for dipping in chocolate. Holding a buckeye by the protruding toothpick, dip it in the tempered chocolate, leaving a ½-inch circle of the center uncoated on top. Place on a prepared sheet pan. Remove the toothpick and smooth the small hole that it left in the top of the candy. Allow the chocolate to set completely.

8 Store at room temperature, tightly sealed.

Key to Success

○ The consistency of the peanut butter center is the key to making buckeyes. Add confectioners' sugar until the mixture will roll up between your hands to a uniform ball that holds its shape and does not crumble. The amount of confectioners' sugar may vary.

Rochers

Rocher is French for "rock," and these chocolates just might be named
that because they do! There is no limit to the possible combinations of
nuts, dried fruit, seeds, and cereals that can be made into rochers. These
are just a few—use your vision to create your own unique rochers.

SKILL LEVEL

4 oz (1 cup) **Chopped unsalted nuts**

1 tsp **Liquor**

1 tbsp **Sugar**

3 oz (½ cup) **Chopped dried fruit**

4 oz (⅜ cup) **Chocolate, melted, tempered, or compound coating, melted**

---

1 Preheat the oven to 350°F. Line 2 sheet pans with parchment
paper.

2 Moisten the chopped nuts with the liquor and toss with the
sugar. Spread on a sheet pan.

3 Bake until lightly toasted. Stir occasionally during toasting
to ensure even browning. Remove from the oven and allow
to cool to room temperature.

4 Stir together the nuts and fruit.

5 Warm a small bowl or a cup to 85°F. In the warmed bowl,
combine one quarter of the nut-fruit mixture with one
quarter of the chocolate. Mix together to entirely cover the
nuts and fruit.

6 Working quickly before the chocolate sets, use a spoon to
deposit tablespoon-size mounds of the chocolate-coated
mixture on a sheet pan.

7 Repeat in one-quarter increments with the remaining nut-
fruit mixture and chocolate. Allow the rochers to cool and
set completely.

SUGGESTED COMBINATIONS

Chopped cashews, rum, chopped pineapple, and milk chocolate

Chopped hazelnuts, brandy, apricots, and dark chocolate

Sliced almonds, kirsch, dried cherries, and dark chocolate

Toasted shredded sweetened coconut and 6 oz/⅔ cup milk
chocolate

Keys to Success

○ Be sure that the nuts have completely cooled before mixing with
the chocolate.

○ Warm the bowl for mixing slightly, only to 85°F, to prevent the
chocolate from setting too quickly.

○ Spoon the rochers out quickly so that the chocolate doesn't
begin to set.

○ Try to make attractive shapes with a little height to them for
better-looking rochers.

Almond Dragées

MAKES 250 PIECES

This is a slightly simplified version of dragées for home use. You can substitute
hazelnuts for the almonds in this recipe for an equally delicious rendition.
This is an efficient way to make chocolates for a group of people.

SKILL LEVEL

1 lb (2 cups) Lightly toasted whole blanched almonds

4 oz (½ cup) Granulated sugar

2 oz (¼ cup) Water

½ tsp Lemon juice

½ oz (1 tbsp) Butter, unsalted, soft

12 oz (1¼ cups) Dark chocolate, melted, tempered

1 tbsp Cocoa powder, sifted, or confectioners' sugar, sifted, for dusting

1   Place the almonds into a 300°F oven in a baking pan or ovenproof bowl to warm them. Lightly oil a sheet pan.

2   Combine the sugar, water, and lemon juice in a 4-quart saucepan. Bring to a boil and continue cooking until the sugar has caramelized to a light golden color (see page 32).

3   Add the almonds to the caramel and stir constantly over low heat to coat the nuts with the caramel.

4   When the nuts are evenly coated, add the butter and stir gently to melt the butter and coat the nuts.

5   Pour the nuts onto the prepared pan. Before they cool completely, separate them into individual nuts.

6   Allow the nuts to cool completely to room temperature, about 30 minutes. Put the nuts in the refrigerator for 5 minutes.

7   Place the chilled nuts in a large bowl. Add one third of the tempered chocolate. Stir vigorously until the nuts gather together in one mass, then break back apart into individual pieces.

8   Place the nuts in the refrigerator for 5 minutes. Repeat step 7 with another third of the chocolate.

9   Place the nuts back in the refrigerator for 5 minutes. Add the remaining chocolate and once again stir vigorously until the nuts gather together in one mass, and then break back apart into individual pieces.

10 Sprinkle the cocoa powder or confectioners' sugar on the nuts and stir lightly.

11 Shake the excess powder off the nuts. Store at room temperature.

Keys to Success

○ Begin with properly toasted almonds.

○ Be sure the almonds are hot when you add them to the caramel.

○ Keep the heat on low when coating the nuts with the caramel.

○ Do not stir excessively when adding the butter to the nuts. It is intended to coat them and make them easier to separate, not to mix into the caramel.

○ To avoid burns, wear food-handling gloves when separating the caramel-coated nuts.

- Chilling the almonds before adding chocolate and between coats of chocolate speeds the process and reduces the amount of stirring required.

- When adding the chocolate, be sure to stir until the nuts break apart into individual pieces.

Chili Pecans

A little Southwest flavor is evident in these savory-sweet nuts. Are they
a snack? Are they a candy? They could be either—you decide. If you like
them a little spicier, add a little cayenne or chipotle powder.

SKILL LEVEL

12 oz (3 cups) **Toasted pecan halves**

2½ oz (⅓ cup) **Sugar**

1 oz (2 tbsp) **Water**

2 tsp **Lemon juice**

2 tbsp **Light corn syrup**

2½ oz (5 tbsp) **Butter, unsalted, soft**

1 tbsp **Chili powder**

¼ tsp **Garlic powder**

1 tsp **Salt**

---

1 Put the toasted pecans in a 300°F oven to warm them.
Lightly oil a sheet pan.

2 Combine the sugar, water, and lemon juice in a 4-quart
saucepan. Bring to a boil and continue cooking until it
turns to a light caramel color (see page 32).

3 Lower the heat and add the corn syrup and 2 oz/4 tbsp of
the butter. Stir to incorporate.

4 Add the pecans and stir over low heat to cover the nuts
entirely with the caramel.

5 Combine the chili powder, garlic powder, and salt and
sprinkle on the pecans. Stir to distribute the spice mixture.

6 Add the remaining butter. Stir gently to coat the nuts with
the melted butter.

7 Pour the hot nuts onto the prepared pan. Separate into individual pieces before they cool.

8 Store at room temperature in an airtight container.

TAMARI-SESAME ALMONDS Substitute toasted whole
almonds for the pecans. Omit the chili and garlic powders
and the salt. After coating the nuts, add ¼ cup sesame seeds
and allow them to toast lightly. Stir in 2 tbsp tamari and 1 tsp
toasted sesame oil.

Keys to Success

○ Begin with properly toasted pecans.

○ Heating the pecans makes it easier to coat them with the caramel.

○ To prevent burning, be sure to lower the heat once the pecans
are added.

○ Do not stir excessively when adding the butter to the nuts. It is
intended to coat them, not to mix into the caramel.

○ To avoid burns, wear food-handling gloves when separating the
nuts.

Caramel Corn

It is a familiar childhood treat, but it never gets old. Caramel corn is always certain to delight. It becomes more sophisticated with the addition of a variety of nuts, and for true indulgence, try the chocolate variation below.

SKILL LEVEL

8 oz (5 qt) **Popped popcorn**

8 oz (1 cup) **Granulated sugar**

4 oz (½ cup) **Light brown sugar, packed**

6 oz (½ cup) **Light corn syrup**

2 oz (¼ cup) **Water**

1½ oz (3 tbsp) **Butter, unsalted, soft**

1 tsp **Baking soda**

1 tsp **Salt**

---

1 Place the popcorn in a large ovenproof bowl. Place in a 350°F oven.

2 Combine the sugar, brown sugar, corn syrup, water, and 1 oz/2 tbsp of the butter in a 2-quart saucepan.

3 Stir while cooking to 300°F.

4 Remove the caramel from the heat and stir in the baking soda and salt. Mix well.

5 Remove the popcorn from the oven. Pour the caramel over the popcorn while stirring with a wooden spoon.

6 Continue to mix until the caramel begins to stiffen too much to stir.

7 Return the bowl to the oven for 10 minutes, remove, and stir the mixture again. Repeat until the popcorn is well coated with caramel.

8 Add the remaining butter, stir gently to allow it to melt and to distribute it.

9 Pour the caramel corn onto a clean countertop and separate the individual kernels before they harden.

10 Store in airtight containers at room temperature.

CARAMEL CORN WITH NUTS Substitute up to 6 cups toasted nuts such as peanuts, cashews, or brazil nuts for an equal volume of popped corn.

CHOCOLATE CARAMEL CORN For the ultimate in caramel corn, drizzle the cooled caramel corn with 1 lb/1½ cups of melted, tempered dark chocolate using a pastry bag or pouring it in a fine stream. Allow to set fully before packaging.

POPCORN BALLS Rather than separating the kernels, gather them into balls. Insert sticks, if desired.

Keys to Success

○ Keeping the popcorn hot while working with it will make it easier to distribute the caramel evenly.

○ Hold the hot bowl with a pad and stir the hot corn with a wooden spoon.

○ Do not stir excessively when adding the butter to the popcorn. It is intended to coat it and make the corn kernels easier to separate, not to mix into the caramel.

○ To avoid burns, wear food-handling gloves when separating the kernels of popcorn.

Coconut Joys

This coconut filling is similar to some well-known candy bars. It can be dipped in either milk or dark chocolate, depending on your taste. Placing a whole almond on each piece before dipping adds a nice crunch.

SKILL LEVEL

2 oz (¼ cup) **Water**

6 oz (¾ cup) **Sugar**

12 oz (1 cup) **Light corn syrup**

12 oz (4 cups) **Sweetened shredded coconut**

2 oz (½ cup) **Marshmallow creme**

1 tsp Vanilla extract

1 lb (1½ cups) **Dark or milk chocolate, melted, tempered, for dipping**

---

1 Lightly oil a 9-inch square baking pan and line it with plastic wrap using the technique on page 51.

2 Combine the water, sugar, and corn syrup in a 2-quart saucepan and bring to a boil, stirring constantly. Cover the pan and continue boiling for 3 minutes. Remove the lid, insert a thermometer, and continue cooking until the mixture reaches 245°F.

3 Remove from the heat and stir in the coconut. Mix in the marshmallow creme and vanilla extract.

4 Pour the mixture into the prepared baking pan. Allow it to cool completely to room temperature, about 1 hour. It is acceptable to leave it overnight, covered.

5 Remove from the baking pan by pulling the plastic wrap out of the pan. Invert onto a sheet of parchment paper. Peel the plastic wrap off the coconut.

6 Cut the coconut into 1-inch squares using an oiled chef's knife.

7 Dip each square into the tempered chocolate using the technique shown on page 44.

8 Garnish each square with a fork mark (see page 46) and a few shreds of coconut before the chocolate sets.

Keys to Success

○ Cook the sugar accurately to ensure proper texture.

○ Allow the sheet to fully cool before unmolding.

○ If the mixture is too soft to cut cleanly, chill it in the refrigerator for 15 minutes before cutting.

1 When the sugar mixture reaches the proper temperature, add to the coconut followed by the marshmallow creme and vanilla extract.

2 Use the plastic wrap to remove the coconut sheet from the pan.

3 Before the chocolate sets, garnish with a wave and a few shreds of coconut.

Turtles

These classics can be made using cashews or pecans. Soft caramel is the
glue that cements the turtle into shape, and chocolate makes the shell.
Coat just the tops in chocolate if you know you are using them right away,
or dip them entirely in chocolate if you prefer more chocolate.

SKILL LEVEL
■ ■ □

2 oz (¼ cup) **Water**

8 oz (1 cup) **Sugar**

½ **Vanilla bean, split and scraped**

7 oz (½ can; ⅔ cup) **Sweetened condensed milk**

6 oz (½ cup) **Light corn syrup**

3 oz (6 tbsp) **Butter, unsalted, soft**

½ tsp **Salt**

1¼ lb (5 cups) **Toasted pecan halves**

1 lb (1½ cups) **Dark chocolate, melted, tempered** (see Keys to Success)

---

1 Combine the water, sugar, vanilla bean seeds and pod, condensed milk, corn syrup, and butter in a heavy-bottomed 2-quart saucepan and bring to a boil, stirring constantly.

2 Continue stirring while cooking until the batch reaches 245°F. This is a good estimation of the required temperature. When the thermometer reads 240°F, begin testing the caramels using the spoon technique outlined on page 30. The cooled piece on the spoon should be firm but not hard when the caramel is properly cooked.

3 Stir in the salt.

4 Remove from the heat. Shock the saucepan in cold water, remove the vanilla pod using tongs, and set aside to allow the caramel to cool slightly.

5 Line a sheet pan with parchment paper. Place the toasted pecans on the pan in groups of 5 to resemble a turtle—its legs and head. You should be able to make 60 turtles.

6 When the caramel has cooled to a thick but fluid consistency (140° to 150°F), spoon a tablespoon of the caramel onto each group of pecans to form the body of the turtle. Allow the turtles to cool completely.

7 Spoon or pipe the tempered chocolate on top of the cooled caramel, leaving the pecans exposed. If preferred, dip them entirely in tempered chocolate using the technique on page 44.

8 Store in a single layer in an airtight container.

Keys to Success

- If you don't want to make this many, make the number of turtles you want and pour the remaining caramel into an oiled baking pan to cool. Once it has cooled, cut and wrap or dip in chocolate as desired.

- Caramel scorches easily. Stir constantly during cooking with a heat-resistant rubber spatula, and moderate the heat to prevent scorching.

- A few degrees can make a big difference in the finished product: Undercooked caramel will be too soft and will not hold its shape.

- If the caramel gets too thick to pour, rewarm by stirring over heat.

- If the turtles are not to be used within a few days, dipping them entirely in chocolate will help to keep them fresh. If dipping entirely, you will need 2 lb/3 cups melted, tempered chocolate.

- If you prefer cashews, use 1 lb/4 cups cashews instead of the pecans.

9

Chocolate Molds and Cups

Using chocolate molds or foil cups is a great way to add variety and color to an assortment of chocolates. Chocolate molds are available in countless shapes and sizes to fit any preference or occasion. When properly used, chocolate molds provide a shine, finish, and uniformity unequaled by any other technique. In addition, applying colored cocoa butter or different varieties of chocolate to the mold can result in the most dramatic and colorful chocolates you can make. Shell molding is a technique that can help you to make chocolates with the highest degree of polish and professionalism—it is well worth the effort. Both shell molding and using foil cups permit the use of pleasantly soft centers for great textural contrast and mouthfeel.

Chocolate Molds

UNTIL FAIRLY RECENTLY, chocolate molds were always made of steel and lined with tin to provide a smooth surface. These metal molds are no longer made but are still widely available, and if in good condition, they are perfectly capable of turning out first-rate chocolates. Today's molds are made from plastics and range from flimsy inexpensive molds to rigid polycarbonate molds that should last for generations. The inexpensive molds work well but do not last as long as the polycarbonate molds do. Any style of chocolate mold can work well provided the interior of the mold is in good condition. The crucial thing to remember is that *chocolate makes a mirror image of whatever it sets on;* if the interior of the mold is shiny and smooth, the chocolates that come out of the mold will also be shiny and smooth. If the mold is scratched, dented, or pitted, then every chocolate that comes out of that mold will exhibit those same defects.

Care of chocolate molds

Regardless of what type of chocolate molds you own, the most important factor in cleaning and care is that the inside of the mold must never be scuffed, scratched, or damaged in any way. If a chocolate should stick in a mold, never use any type of probe to remove it from the mold; if it is hopelessly stuck, washing the mold will be the only answer.

It is common practice for professional chocolatiers not ever to wash their chocolate molds; when properly used, they need not be washed. Chocolate will release cleanly from the inside of the mold, leaving no visible residue behind. In fact, some professionals maintain that the shine of the products actually improves the more the mold is used without washing. If the molds are not going to be washed, any excess chocolate can be scraped from the outside of the mold with a scraper or palette knife.

Proper washing of molds does not harm them, however, and because in a home kitchen the molds are not used as frequently, most home candy makers prefer to clean their chocolate molds after each session. When washing, always use warm water, gentle soap, and a soft cloth. Never use anything abrasive on the interior of the molds, and never put them in a dishwasher. A rule of thumb is: If you would not use it on your skin, do not use it on your chocolate molds. Follow this guideline and your molds will turn out perfect chocolates for many years to come.

Lining a chocolate mold

1   Temper the chocolate (see page 36). It is vital that the chocolate be well tempered for it to shrink and release from the mold.

2   Polish the mold. If they have been washed before use, polish the mold with a soft lint-free cloth such as cheesecloth.

3   Warm the mold slightly. This step is optional, but for the best results the mold should be near 80°F when the chocolate is poured into it. A hair dryer is a good way to warm the mold, but be careful not to overheat it. Remember that 80°F is below your body temperature, so the mold should still feel slightly cool to the touch.

4   Fill the mold cavities. Use a spoon or a ladle and allow the chocolate to fill all the cavities of the mold.

5   Scrape off the excess chocolate. Remove the chocolate from the top of the mold. There is nothing wrong with using a scraper on the top of the mold, just not inside of the mold cavities.

6   Vibrate the mold on the table. This step will remove any trapped air pockets that could mar the finish of the finished products.

7   Allow the mold to sit. This allows the shell of chocolate to begin to form. The precise amount of time varies with the chocolate used, the room temperature, and the mold. Usually for small molds, 1 to 2 minutes is sufficient. (If making solid chocolate molds, at this point go to step 3 of Sealing a Chocolate Mold on page 240.)

8   Pour the excess chocolate out of the mold. Tapping the mold lightly will remove more of the chocolate.

9   Scrape off the excess chocolate. Clean the top of the mold using a scraper again.

10   Invert the mold. Place the mold upside down, elevated, so that the excess chocolate can drain. Leave it inverted for about 5 minutes or until the chocolate is no longer flowing.

11   Clean the top of the mold . . . again. Scrape the top of the mold so that the top edge of each cavity is clean and uniform.

Congratulations! You have lined the molds and are ready to move on to filling them.

Filling a chocolate mold

Many different fillings may be used in molded chocolates—including no filling at all, resulting in a solid chocolate piece. The most commonly used fillings are ganache, soft caramel, and ground nut pastes. A filling that will remain soft results in a crisp shell surrounding a creamy center, which is one of the biggest pleasures of molded chocolates. Remember that no matter what filling you use, it should be slightly fluid at the time it goes into the mold so that it will self-level and can be capped easily.

1   Prepare the filling. The filling must be somewhat soft when it is piped into the shells. In the case of a ganache or soft caramel, the filling will have to be slightly warm to obtain the right viscosity. The target temperature is 80°F; if you use a filling warmer than this, it will damage the chocolate shell.

2   Pipe the filling into the lined cavities. It is crucial that there is ⅛ inch between the top of the filling and the top of the mold so that the mold can be sealed.

3   Allow the filling to firm. If the filling was warmed for use, it will firm as it cools. Having the filling firm before moving on to sealing will make that step much easier. If you need to accelerate this process, refrigeration for a short time (about 15 minutes) is an acceptable option.

The molds are now filled and ready to be sealed.

Using Chocolate Molds

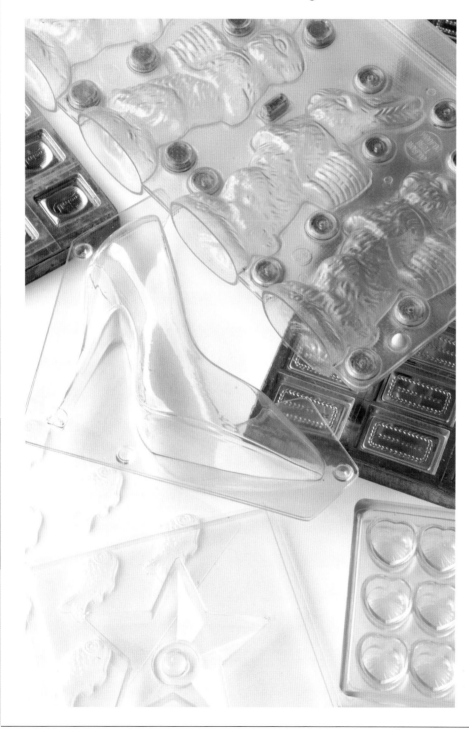

It is the contraction of tempered chocolate when it sets that makes using chocolate molds possible. Whenever using molds, you want to create a situation where the chocolate will contract well and pull away from the inside of the mold so that it releases. The keys to contraction are:

PROPERLY TEMPERED CHOCOLATE
When chocolate is optimally tempered, it contracts the most when it sets. If the chocolate is either untempered, or is tempered but cold and thick, it will not shrink sufficiently when it sets and won't release from the molds.

CLEAN, POLISHED MOLDS Molds that have residues of fillings or water spots will not easily release the chocolate. Always polish the molds if they have been washed before use or if they have any visible spots in them.

TYPES OF MOLDS, CLOCKWISE FROM TOP LEFT:
Magnetic molds, antique metal molds, polycarbonate molds, and vacuumed molds.

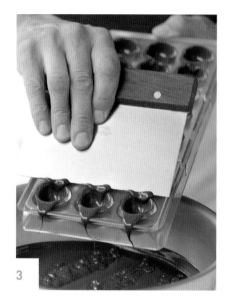

1 Use a spoon or piping bag to fill all of the cavities of the mold with tempered chocolate.

2 When a shell has begun to form, pour the excess chocolate out of the mold, lightly tapping the back of the mold if necessary.

3 Use a scraper to clean the top of the mold.

4 Pipe a filling into the lined molds, being careful to stop ⅛ inch below the top of each cavity.

5 Pipe tempered chocolate to cover each filled cavity.

6 Place a flat pan on top of the mold, invert the pan and mold together, then lift the mold off the pan to free the chocolates.

Sealing a chocolate mold

Sealing the molds is the final step before unmolding. It is important that the filling be entirely contained by the chocolate so that it does not leak out after the chocolates are unmolded.

1   Pipe tempered chocolate over the top of each cavity in the mold. Allow the chocolate to cover each filled cavity. If the filling is a soft variety, such as caramel cream, do not tilt the mold or the filling will run and will mix with the chocolate.

2   Allow the chocolate to set at room temperature for 15 minutes. The chocolate you just applied should set at room temperature.

3   Refrigerate the mold for approximately 20 minutes. Refrigeration will contract the chocolate and make the finished products easy to release.

Unmolding

How you remove the chocolates from the mold is just as important as any other step in making molded chocolates. All of the work you have done to create the filled pieces will be wasted if they are not unmolded properly.

1   Flex the chilled molds slightly. You should not have to flex them much—just a little twist to loosen the chocolates from the mold.

2   Place a flat pan on top of the mold. The pan will be the surface onto which the chocolates are unmolded, and will help to protect them during unmolding.

3   Invert the mold and pan together. Tap the pan and mold lightly on the table. The pan will prevent the chocolates from falling out of the mold prematurely.

4   Lift the mold off the pan. All or most of the chocolates should have come free from the mold, and are now sitting free on the pan.

5   If some of the chocolates did not come out of the mold, refrigerate the mold for another 15 minutes. This will further shrink the chocolate. Repeat steps 1 through 4.

1

2

3

Decorating Techniques for Shell-Molded Chocolates

1 Wearing food-handling gloves, smear colored cocoa butter in the cavities of the mold before lining with chocolate.

2 Use a clean brush to speckle powdered food-safe color in the cavities of the mold before lining.

3 Adding color to a mold is an easy technique for a striking effect on the finished chocolates.

Making Large Hollow Chocolate Molds

Making large chocolate molds is not much different from making filled shell-molded chocolates. All of the same principles and steps apply, with only a few minor differences.

1 Temper the chocolate.

2 Polish the mold.

3 Warm the mold slightly.

4 Brush the inside of each half of the mold with tempered chocolate. Brushing the molds will prevent the formation of air bubbles.

If the mold has an open base when it is clipped together, follow these steps:

1 Clip the two halves of the mold together.

2 Invert the mold so that the opening is facing up.

3 Fill the mold completely with tempered chocolate.

4 Allow the chocolate to sit for 3 to 5 minutes at room temperature.

5 Invert the mold so that excess chocolate runs out.

6 Clean the base and refrigerate for 20 minutes.

7 Unclip the mold and unsnap the mold from the finished piece.

If the mold is totally enclosed when it is snapped together, follow these steps:

1 Fill one half of the mold nearly to the top with tempered chocolate.

2 Clip the other half of the mold on the top of the first. Make sure it is well sealed.

3 Gently turn the mold so that the chocolate inside evenly coats the mold.

4 Continue turning until the chocolate has thickened and is set in place. This will take 10 to 15 minutes, depending on the size of the mold.

5 Refrigerate the mold for 20 minutes.

6 Unclip the molds and unsnap the mold from the finished piece.

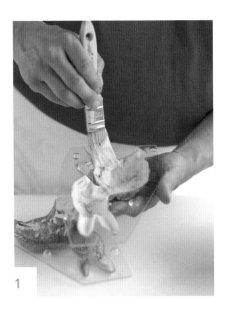

1

2

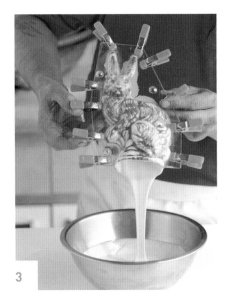

3

4

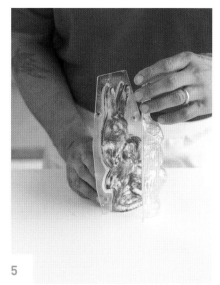

5

1 Use a clean pastry brush to brush a layer of tempered chocolate on all areas of the mold's cavity.

2 Clamp the edges of the mold securely closed and fill the cavity with tempered chocolate.

3 When the chocolate has begun to set to for a shell, invert the mold to remove all excess chocolate.

4 To cap the bunny, pour a small pool of tempered chocolate on a piece of parchment paper and set the cavity's opening in the chocolate.

5 To unmold, remove the clamps and gently pull off each side of the mold.

Lining foil cups

Lining foil cups with chocolate and then filling them is a technique very similar to shell molding, but rather than unmolding the finished chocolate, the container is part of the presentation. The centers in foil cups are usually sealed entirely in chocolate, but if they are going to be used within a day or two, the center may be piped in and left exposed for simplicity or for a unique finish.

Always work with the cups in the same order for each step of the procedure.

1   Temper the chocolate to be used. Untempered chocolate will not be strong enough to pull the foil cup away without breaking. Chocolate that is too cool and thick will make shells thicker than they should be, leaving insufficient room for the filling.

2   Use a piping bag to fill 8 to 10 foil cups at a time. Fill the cups to within 1/16 inch of the tops.

3   Invert each cup to remove the excess chocolate from the cup. Shake them lightly to remove the chocolate.

4   Place the cups upside down on a screen. Allow the excess chocolate to drain.

5   Remove each cup from the screen. You must pick up the cups before the chocolate sets, so you only have 4 to 5 minutes. Place the lined cups upright and allow the chocolate to set.

The lined cups are now ready to be filled.

Fill each cup with tempered chocolate, allow it to begin to form a shell, then invert the foil cup to remove the excess.

Filling foil cups

1 The filling must be a soft consistency. The filling must be soft enough to go through a piping bag. If the cups are to be capped, it should be soft enough to level itself. In this case, the filling may need to be warmed slightly. It should never exceed 80°F, however, or it will soften the chocolate shells. If the cups are not to be capped, the filling should be a consistency that will hold its shape.

2 Fill the lined cups to within ⅛ inch of the top. This will allow room for sealing them. If you are not sealing the tops with chocolate, pipe on a rosette of tempered chocolate using a small star tip or other design.

3 Allow the filling to firm. If the filling was warmed for use, it will firm as it cools. Having the filling firm before moving on to sealing will make that step much easier. If you need to accelerate this process, refrigeration for a short time (about 15 minutes) is an acceptable option.

4 Pipe tempered chocolate on top of the filling to seal. This is best done using a paper cone (see page 47). Garnish as desired; piped dots of chocolate or toasted nuts are popular choices.

The filled cups are finished and ready either for enjoying or storing.

Pipe the filling into the foil cups to within ⅛ inch of the top.

When the filling is firm, pipe tempered chocolate on top to seal.

How it's stored

Both shell-molded chocolates and foil cups must be stored in the same manner as any other filled chocolate: at room temperature, protected from humidity and extremes of temperature. The shelf life varies depending on the filling. If ganache is the filling, they have a shelf life of 2 weeks; a soft caramel or peanut butter filling has a much longer shelf life.

Caramel Cream Filling

UNLIKE SOFT CARAMELS, which contain no actual caramel, caramel cream is made by adding other liquid ingredients to caramelized sugar. Excellent-quality versions such as this use cream and butter for those liquid ingredients; lesser-quality manufactured versions often add corn syrup instead of dairy products.

What's in it?

Caramel cream is caramelized sugar enriched and softened by the addition of cream and butter. When it is made properly, it has a thick but flowing texture when it has cooled to room temperature.

SUGAR It is the sugar that gives caramel flavor and bulk to this filling.

LEMON JUICE A small amount of lemon juice added to the sugar before cooking will make it easier to caramelize without forming lumps.

CREAM Cream adds both moisture and butterfat to the caramel cream, both of which prevent the caramel from hardening into organic glass when it cools. In addition, cream contributes dairy flavor to the blend.

BUTTER The additional fat in butter is what makes this filling especially indulgent.

LIQUEUR (OPTIONAL) This filling needs no additional flavor, but it is possible to add liqueur, if desired, to create different flavor profiles.

How it's made

The master technique that will be most important in making caramel cream is the Dry Sugar Cooking Technique (see page 32). Spending time reviewing this technique will ensure your success when making this filling.

1   Preheat the cream. Heating the cream will make it easier to incorporate into the hot caramel. Do not boil it or you will evaporate too much water. Just heat it nearly to a boil and remove it from the heat.

2   Preheat the saucepan. Preheating for several minutes will greatly speed the process of caramelizing the sugar.

3   Work the lemon juice together with the sugar. Rub the lemon juice into the sugar by hand. Working the lemon juice in will evenly distribute it so that it will prevent lumps.

4   Pour the sugar into the hot saucepan. Be prepared to stir immediately with a wooden spoon; the sugar will begin to caramelize immediately when it hits the hot pan.

5   Stir vigorously until the sugar has melted. It is important to keep the sugar moving so that it melts and caramelizes evenly. If necessary, turn the heat down during cooking to ensure an even result.

6   Make sure all of the sugar crystals have melted. The crystals must have completely melted, and the sugar should have a medium amber, transparent color.

7   Stir in the hot cream over low heat. Add the cream in a steady stream and stir with a wooden spoon to make sure the cream and caramel combine.

8   Add the butter. Turn off the heat and stir the butter into the caramel.

9   Cool the caramel cream at room temperature. Pouring the caramel cream into a flat container such as a baking pan will accelerate the cooling process.

10   Add liqueur, if desired.

How else can I use it?

Caramel cream may be used in any molded shell or foil cup where it will be contained by the preformed chocolate shell. It may also be used as a filling in pastries, and if thinned with a little milk and/or liqueur, it makes an excellent base for sauce to use with desserts.

How it's stored

Caramel cream may be stored in a tightly sealed container at room temperature for a week or more. For longer-term storage, refrigeration is an acceptable option.

Dulce de Leche

DULCE DE LECHE, literally "milk candy," is a traditional Latin American preparation that can be used as a dessert sauce, part of a frozen dessert, or as a center for shell-molded or foil cup chocolates. In the traditional version, sugar and milk are stirred constantly while simmering for 3 to 4 hours. The longer it cooks, the more of a caramel flavor it develops and the firmer it will be when it cools. Few of us have the time or inclination to make dulce de leche by the traditional technique anymore, but an excellent rendition can be made by heating sweetened condensed milk in simmering water and holding it there for about 4 hours. In order to avoid the dangerous possibility of an exploding can, always open the can first so that it is not entirely sealed, and heat it in a water bath, never on direct heat. Making dulce de leche by this technique may not be the most traditional method, but it results in a first-rate product without having to stand at the stove for hours at a time. Once made, the dulce should be refrigerated until it is needed.

What if

What if my chocolates won't release from the molds?

There can be several causes. Untempered chocolate, dirty molds, or just impatience can all cause this condition. In any case, the solution is to refrigerate the filled molds for another 20 minutes and try again to release them.

What if the filling is leaking through the bottom of my molded chocolates?

The bottom coat is too thin or it is uneven. If they are still in the molds, spread more tempered chocolate on the flat, exposed portion of the molds. If they have already been released from the molds, spread or pipe chocolate on the base of each leaking piece.

What if my large molded chocolates bloom?

The chocolate may have been untempered.
The mold was not refrigerated in time when they were setting.

What if there is a thick shell on my molded chocolates or foil cups?

The chocolate was too cool and thick when the molds or cups were filled.
The chocolate sat in the molds too long before you emptied out the excess.

What if there is an excessively thin shell on my molded chocolates or foil cups?

The chocolate was not in the molds or cups long enough before emptying.
The molds were too warm when filled.

What if there are bubbles on the surface of my molded chocolates?

The chocolate was too thick and cool when you filled the molds.
The molds were too cold when you lined them.

Buttercreams

Made with fresh butter, just enough fondant, and the flavoring of your choice, these are the way buttercreams are supposed to be: flavorful, smooth, and melt-in-your-mouth soft. Flavoring options make the possibilities endless.

SKILL LEVEL

1 lb (1½ cups) **Milk, dark, or white chocolate, melted, tempered, for lining and sealing molds**

12 oz (24 tbsp; 3 sticks) **Butter, unsalted, soft**

6 oz (½ cup) **Fondant** (see Keys to Success)

Flavoring (see Variations), **as needed**

1 Line 2 chocolate molds with the tempered chocolate.

2 Mix the butter and fondant in a mixer or by hand until smooth. Mix in the flavoring. Transfer to a piping bag with a small opening cut at the tip of the bag.

3 Pipe the filling into the prepared molds to within ⅛ inch of the top. If necessary, tap the mold on the table to flatten the filling.

4 Refrigerate the molds for 20 minutes to allow the filling to firm.

5 Seal the molds using the tempered chocolate.

6 Allow the molds to set at room temperature for 20 minutes. Refrigerate for 20 minutes more.

7 Remove the finished chocolates from the mold.

VARIATIONS *Many different flavors of buttercream can easily be created from this one recipe. Any type of jam may be used; stir in ¼ to ½ cup, to taste. Orange juice concentrate (¼ cup), praline paste (¼ cup), or peanut butter (½ cup) also make excellent flavorings.*

Keys to Success

- Either homemade Fondant (page 143) or purchased fondant may be used for this recipe.

- Be certain that the chocolate for lining and sealing the molds is properly tempered (see page 36).

- Be sure that the buttercream does not protrude above the top of the molds. If it does, tap the molds until it levels out.

- If the molds do not release easily, give them 5 minutes more in the refrigerator.

Molded Cherry Cordials

MAKES 48 PIECES

Cherry cordials can be made either by dipping (see page 40) or by molding. Molded cordials usually contain more of the liquid center that makes these chocolates unique.

SKILL LEVEL

48 Maraschino cherries, stems removed, drained

1 lb (1½ cups) **Dark chocolate, melted, tempered, for lining and sealing molds**

12 oz (1 cup) **Fondant** (see Keys to Success)

¼ tsp Invertase

---

1 Dry the cherries thoroughly on a towel.

2 Line 2 cherry cordial molds with the tempered chocolate.

3 Warm the fondant over a hot water bath to 80°F. Add the invertase and mix in thoroughly. Transfer to a piping bag with a small opening cut at the tip of the bag.

4 Pipe fondant into the bottom of each lined mold cavity one quarter of the way to the top of the mold.

5 Place 1 maraschino cherry in each filled cavity.

6 Pipe the warm fondant into each mold to within ⅛ inch of the top of the molds. If necessary, tap the mold on the table to flatten the filling.

7 Refrigerate the molds for 20 minutes to allow the fondant to firm.

8 Seal the molds with the chocolate.

9 Allow the molds to set at room temperature for 20 minutes. Refrigerate for 20 minutes more.

10 Remove the finished chocolates from the molds.

Keys to Success

○ Either homemade Fondant (page 143) or purchased fondant may be used for this recipe.

○ Be certain that the chocolate for lining and sealing molds is properly tempered (see page 36).

○ Make sure the fondant is very close to 80°F when it is piped into the molds. If necessary, reheat it when topping off the molds after the cherries are added.

○ You may need to remelt and retemper the chocolate for sealing the molds due to the time that has elapsed while filling them.

Dark Chocolate Peanut Butter Cups

Peanut Butter Bombs

Peanut butter is always a popular filling, and peanut butter cups are one of the most beloved uses of it. This recipe uses chocolate molds to create a slightly more polished version of the perennial favorite.

SKILL LEVEL

1 lb (1½ cups) **Milk chocolate, melted, tempered, for lining and sealing molds**

9 oz (1 cup) **Peanut butter**

2 oz (½ cup) **Confectioners' sugar, sifted**

4 oz (8 tbsp) **Butter, unsalted, soft**

2 oz (1½ tbsp) **Milk chocolate, melted**

---

1 Line 2 chocolate molds with the tempered chocolate.

2 Warm the peanut butter to 85°F over a hot water bath.

3 Stir in the sifted confectioners' sugar, butter, and melted milk chocolate. Mix by hand or in a mixer fitted with a paddle attachment on medium speed for 4 minutes. Transfer to a piping bag with a small opening cut at the tip of the bag.

4 Pipe the filling into the prepared molds to within ⅛ inch of the top. If necessary, tap the mold on the table to flatten the filling.

5 Refrigerate the molds for 20 minutes to allow the filling to firm.

6 Seal the molds with the tempered chocolate.

7 Allow the molds to set at room temperature for 20 minutes. Refrigerate for 20 minutes more.

8 Remove the finished chocolates from the mold.

VARIATIONS *If desired, chopped toasted peanuts may be added to the filling for textural contrast. Dark chocolate may be substituted for milk chocolate for lining and sealing.*

PEANUT BUTTER CUPS *may be made using the same filling piped into a foil cup lined with milk or dark chocolate (see opposite). Garnish with a half of a roasted peanut, if desired.*

Keys to Success

- Be certain that the chocolate for lining and sealing molds is properly tempered (see page 36).

- Be sure that the filling does not protrude above the top of the molds. If it does, tap the molds until it levels out.

- If the molds do not release easily, give them 5 minutes more in the refrigerator.

Belle Helene

Poire Belle Helene is a classical symphony of pears and chocolate. The dessert may be somewhat time-worn, but these chocolates will always delight.

SKILL LEVEL

1 lb (1½ cups) **Dark chocolate, melted, tempered, for lining and sealing molds**

4 oz (½ cup) **Heavy cream**

1½ oz (2 tbsp) **Light corn syrup**

12 oz (2 cups) **Dark chocolate, chopped in ½-inch pieces**

½ oz (1 tbsp) **Butter, unsalted, soft**

1 oz (2 tbsp) **Poire William or other pear liqueur**

50 **Dried pear pieces, cut to fit the cavities**

---

1 Line 2 chocolate molds with the tempered chocolate.

2 Combine the cream and corn syrup in a small saucepan. Bring to a boil.

3 Remove from the heat. Add the chopped chocolate to the cream mixture off the heat. Stir until all of the chocolate melts and the mixture is smooth. If some of the chocolate does not melt, heat the mixture over a hot water bath, not direct heat.

4 Stir in the butter. Add the Poire William and stir until incorporated.

5 Allow the ganache to cool to 75°F. Transfer to a piping bag with a small opening cut at the tip of the bag.

6 Fill the molds one quarter of the way with the ganache. Place 1 piece of dried pear in each cavity on top of the ganache.

7 Fill the molds with ganache to within ⅛ inch of the top. If necessary, tap the mold on the table to flatten the filling.

8 Refrigerate the molds for 20 minutes to allow the ganache to firm.

9 Seal the molds with the tempered chocolate.

10 Allow the molds to set at room temperature for 20 minutes. Refrigerate for 20 minutes more.

11 Remove the finished chocolates from the mold.

Keys to Success

○ Be certain that the chocolate for lining and sealing the molds is properly tempered (see page 36).

○ Make sure the ganache is very close to 75°F when it is piped into the molds. If necessary, reheat it when topping off the molds after the pears are added.

○ You may need to remelt and retemper the chocolate for sealing the molds due to the time that has elapsed while filling them.

○ If the molds do not release easily, give them 5 minutes more in the refrigerator.

Assorted molded chocolates

Black Pearls

As rich and indulgent as pearls! Caramel, cognac, milk chocolate, and dark chocolate commingle to create a true luxury. You don't need to open any oysters to get these, just use a few of the master techniques to capture your prize.

SKILL LEVEL

1 lb (1½ cups) **Dark chocolate, melted, tempered, for lining and sealing molds**

4 oz (½ cup) **Heavy cream**

1½ oz (2 tbsp) **Light corn syrup**

2 oz (¼ cup) **Sugar**

½ tsp **Lemon juice**

8 oz (1⅓ cups) **Milk chocolate, chopped in ½-inch pieces**

1 oz (2 tbsp) **Cognac**

---

1 Line 2 chocolate molds with the tempered dark chocolate.

2 Combine the cream and corn syrup in a small saucepan. Heat to just below a boil. Remove from the heat and set aside to keep hot.

3 Preheat a 2-quart saucepan until hot. Put the sugar and lemon juice into the hot saucepan. Stir constantly over medium heat until the sugar completely melts and a medium-dark caramel color is obtained.

4 Pour the hot cream into the caramel over low heat while stirring constantly. When the caramel is thoroughly blended into the cream, remove from the heat.

5 Add the chopped milk chocolate to the cream mixture off the heat. Stir until all of the chocolate melts and the mixture is smooth. If some of the chocolate does not melt, heat the mixture over a hot water bath, not direct heat.

6 Add the cognac and stir until incorporated.

7 Allow the ganache to cool to 75°F. Transfer to a piping bag with a small opening cut at the tip of the bag.

8 Fill the molds to within ⅛ inch of the top. If necessary, tap the mold on the table to flatten the filling.

9 Refrigerate the molds for 20 minutes to allow the ganache to firm.

10 Seal the molds with the tempered dark chocolate.

11 Allow the molds to set at room temperature for 20 minutes. Refrigerate for 20 minutes more.

12 Remove the finished chocolates from the mold.

Keys to Success

- Be certain that the chocolate for lining and sealing the molds is properly tempered (see page 36).

- Add the hot cream to the caramel in a steady stream while stirring. If the caramel hardens, maintain a low heat and stir until it dissolves in the cream.

- Make sure the ganache is very close to 75°F when it is piped into the molds.

- You may need to remelt and retemper the chocolate for sealing the molds due to the time that has elapsed while filling them.

- If the molds do not release easily, give them 5 minutes more in the refrigerator.

Gianduja Molds

Any type of gianduja may be used in a molded chocolate. Gianduja for molding may be made with extra nut butter to give it an even better flavor and softer texture than when it is spread in a pan.

SKILL LEVEL

1 lb (1½ cups) **Milk, dark, or white chocolate, melted, tempered, for lining and sealing molds**

8 oz (¾ cup) **Milk, dark, or white chocolate, melted**

2 oz (½ cup) **Confectioners' sugar**

8 oz (1 cup) **Nut butter** (see Keys to Success)

2 oz (4 tbsp) **Butter, unsalted, soft**

1 Line 2 chocolate molds with the tempered chocolate.

2 In the bowl of a mixer fitted with a paddle attachment, combine the melted chocolate, confectioners' sugar, and nut butter. As it is mixing on medium speed, add the softened butter in 3 portions, allowing the butter to be fully incorporated before making the next addition. Continue mixing on medium speed for 4 minutes more.

3 Transfer the gianduja to a piping bag with a small opening cut at the tip of the bag. Pipe the gianduja into the prepared molds to within ⅛ inch of the top. If necessary, tap the mold on the table to flatten the gianduja.

4 Refrigerate the molds for 20 minutes to allow the gianduja to firm.

5 Seal the molds with tempered chocolate.

6 Allow the molds to set at room temperature for 20 minutes. Refrigerate for 20 minutes more.

7 Remove the finished chocolates from the molds.

VARIATIONS Many different inclusions may be added to the gianduja for flavor and textural contrast. Chopped dried fruits, toasted nuts, or even crushed cereal can all add interest to these chocolates. Using a variety of inclusions, you can create several types of chocolates from one batch of gianduja.

Keys to Success

○ Many different types of nut butter are available, often from health food stores. Cashew and almond are frequently found, and praline paste may also be used. Try different nuts with different chocolates to create your own unique confections.

○ Be certain that the chocolate for lining and sealing molds is properly tempered (see page 36).

○ Be sure that the gianduja does not protrude above the top of the molds. If it does, tap the molds until it levels out.

○ If the molds do not release easily, give them 5 minutes more in the refrigerator.

Assorted molded chocolates

Dish of Dulce

Dulce de leche is a caramelized milk mixture that traditionally requires hours
of simmering and stirring. Heating sweetened condensed milk in a pan of
water will create a more convenient and equally indulgent filling.

SKILL LEVEL

1 can (14 oz) **Sweetened condensed milk**

1 lb (1½ cups) **Dark chocolate, melted, tempered, for lining and sealing molds**

---

1 Preheat the oven to 350°F. Use a can opener to create 2 vents in the top of the can of milk. Cover the can with aluminum foil.

2 Place the can in an ovenproof saucepan and pour in water to within ½ inch of the top of the can. Bring the water to a simmer on the stove.

3 Tightly cover the pan with foil and put in the oven. Leave undisturbed in the oven for 4 hours.

4 Remove from the oven, remove the can from the water, and allow it to cool to room temperature. (The filling may be prepared up to 2 days ahead; store in the refrigerator until needed. Bring back to room temperature before using.)

5 Line 2 chocolate molds with the tempered chocolate.

6 Place the dulce de leche in a piping bag with a small opening cut at the tip of the bag. Fill the molds to within ⅛ inch of the top. Refrigerate the molds for 15 minutes.

7 Seal the molds with the tempered chocolate.

8 Allow to set at room temperature, then refrigerate for 30 minutes.

9 Release the finished chocolates from the molds.

Keys to Success

- Be sure to create the vents in the can to prevent bursting.
- The dulce de leche should be at room temperature for filling the molds.
- Be certain that the chocolate for lining and sealing molds is properly tempered (see page 36).
- If the molds do not release easily, give them 5 minutes more in the refrigerator.

Lattes

A crisp toasted hazelnut brings a surprising textural element to this molded chocolate.
If your molds won't accommodate a whole nut, use the largest pieces that will fit.

SKILL LEVEL

1 lb (1½ cups) **Dark chocolate, melted, tempered, for lining and sealing molds**

4 oz (½ cup) **Heavy cream**

1½ oz (2 tbsp) **Light corn syrup**

2 tsp **Instant coffee granules**

1 tsp **Hot water**

8 oz (1⅓ cups) **Milk chocolate, chopped in ½-inch pieces**

50 **Toasted whole blanched hazelnuts**

---

1 Line 2 chocolate molds with the tempered dark chocolate.

2 Combine the cream and corn syrup in a small saucepan. Bring to a boil.

3 Dissolve the coffee in the water. Add to the cream mixture.

4 Remove from the heat. Add the chopped milk chocolate to the cream mixture off the heat. Stir until all of the chocolate melts and the mixture is smooth. If some of the chocolate does not melt, heat the mixture over a hot water bath, not direct heat.

5 Allow the ganache to cool to 75°F. Transfer to a piping bag with a small opening cut at the tip of the bag.

6 Fill the molds one quarter of the way with the ganache. Place 1 hazelnut in each cavity on top of the ganache.

7 Fill the molds with ganache to within ⅛ inch of the top. If necessary, tap the mold on the table to flatten the filling.

8 Refrigerate the molds for 20 minutes to allow the ganache to firm.

9 Seal the molds with the tempered chocolate.

10 Allow the molds to set at room temperature for 20 minutes. Refrigerate for 20 minutes more.

11 Release the finished chocolates from the molds.

Keys to Success

○ Be certain that the chocolate for lining and sealing the molds is properly tempered (see page 36).

○ Make sure the ganache is very close to 75°F when it is piped into the molds. If necessary, reheat it when topping off the molds after the hazelnuts are added.

○ You may need to remelt and retemper the chocolate for sealing the molds due to the time that has elapsed while filling them.

○ If the molds do not release easily, give them 5 minutes more in the refrigerator.

Solid molded chocolates

Passions

The tart, crisp flavor of passion fruit is the perfect foil for rich white chocolate.
If you prefer, you can substitute dark chocolate for the shells in this recipe.

SKILL LEVEL

1 lb (1½ cups) **White chocolate, melted, tempered, for lining and sealing molds**

2 oz (¼ cup) **Heavy cream**

1 oz (2 tbsp) **Light corn syrup**

2 oz (¼ cup) **Passion fruit puree**

12 oz (2 cups) **White chocolate, chopped in ½-inch pieces**

1 oz (2 tbsp) **Butter, unsalted, soft**

1 Line 2 chocolate molds with the tempered white chocolate.

2 Combine the cream and corn syrup in a small saucepan. Bring to a boil.

3 Add the passion fruit puree and remove from the heat.

4 Add the chopped white chocolate and butter to the cream mixture off the heat. Stir until all of the chocolate melts and the mixture is smooth. If some of the chocolate does not melt, heat the mixture over a hot water bath, not direct heat.

5 Allow the ganache to cool to 75°F. Transfer to a piping bag with a small opening cut at the tip of the bag.

6 Fill the molds with the ganache to within ⅛ inch of the top.

7 Refrigerate the molds for 20 minutes to allow the ganache to firm.

8 Seal the molds using tempered white chocolate.

9 Allow the molds to set at room temperature for 20 minutes. Refrigerate for 20 minutes more.

10 Remove the finished chocolates from the mold.

Keys to Success

○ Be certain that the chocolate for lining and sealing the molds is properly tempered (see page 36).

○ Make sure the ganache is very close to 75°F when it is piped into the molds.

○ You may need to remelt and retemper the chocolate for sealing the molds due to the time that has elapsed while filling them.

○ If the molds do not release easily, give them 5 minutes more in the refrigerator.

10

Layers of Flavors

The layered candy bar, consisting of several types of center all enrobed in chocolate, is a uniquely American creation. The first layered candy bar may well have been the Goo Goo Cluster, created in Nashville, Tennessee, in 1912. Regardless of when or where the layered confection began, it has become a beloved part of the food culture, and candy bars are now manufactured in an ever-increasing range of flavors and textures; almost everyone has a favorite candy bar. The popularity is well founded: A candy bar provides more than a bite or two of sustenance; layering different types of centers permits nearly endless possibilities for flavors and textures; and the use of inclusions such as nuts or dried fruit only increases the potential for variety and enjoyment.

Homemade candy bars may represent the crowning achievement for the home candy maker. While they are not substantially more difficult to make than any other chocolate-coated candy, they can be the most impressive chocolates in a home candy maker's repertoire. The recipes in this chapter may either be cut into bars as directed in the recipe, or cut into individual pieces, as desired. Success with layered pieces requires only the same skills and understanding as each of the individual components alone does. If you can cook caramels and make coconut filling, you can combine them to make Cocomels (page 283). Read the information in previous chapters about each center that you are using, and step by step you can build any layered bar you can envision.

What should go into it?

Layered candy bars may have any number of different centers in them. Among the most popular are caramel and various forms of nuts. There is little to prevent you from putting together any of the centers used in this book to create your own unique candy bar. These are some key points to consider if you want to make your own candy bar recipes.

CONSIDER MOISTURE One minor obstacle that must be considered when planning a layered candy is the moisture content in each of the fillings. When a relatively moist filling such as ganache is layered with a center that attracts moisture such as a caramel, the caramel will soak up the moisture from the ganache to the detriment of both centers. In this scenario, the ganache would become dry and crumbly and the caramel would at first get sticky, and would later recrystallize. This does not mean that you cannot combine centers with disparate moisture qualities; it just means that you must protect them from each other. The easiest way to prevent a loss of quality from moisture migration is simply to brush a thin layer of fat between layers where there might be a problem. Any type of hard fat can be used; cocoa butter is ideal and coconut fat is perfectly acceptable. If you are in doubt about how the layers of fillings might interact, brush with fat. This will eliminate any potential damage that could occur after the piece is coated with chocolate.

DESIGN FLAVOR PROFILES The flavor profile of a layered bar may range from the classical, like nougat and caramel, to the funky, like Firefudge (page 141) with mango jelly. Whether you want to create the homemade equivalent of a well-known candy bar or something totally different, think about which centers will best achieve your desired result. If you want a strong fruit flavor, a jelly is your best bet. For a melt-in-your-mouth chocolate flavor, either ganache or a meltaway is best.

CONTRAST TEXTURES While a uniformly smooth texture can make a good candy bar, combining two or more textures can result in a great one. A short-textured nougat with chewy caramel is a good example of pleasing textural contrast; add peanuts for crunch and you have added a whole new dimension to the experience.

USE INCLUSIONS When using inclusions in a candy bar for texture and flavor, remember that the inclusions must be low in moisture or they can cause your bars to spoil. Nuts are the most commonly used inclusions, but any shelf-stable product could be used; consider cereals, seeds, crackers, and dried fruit. Another caution about inclusions is that some products, such as cereal or crackers, will get soggy if they are used in a filling that contains moisture, such as ganache. This type of inclusion should be reserved for low-moisture centers like nut pastes, meltaways, or gianduja.

How it's formed

Because layered candy bars may include many different centers, there is no one standard method for assembling them. All of the layered bars in this book are assembled in a 9 × 13–inch baking pan. They may be built upside down in the pan or right side up—it makes little difference in the finished pieces. Even with all of this flexibility, there are still guidelines to making layered pieces.

BE AWARE OF TEMPERATURE When you are using one center that must be poured into the pan while hot, like a caramel or a jelly, and another that cannot tolerate heat, like peanut butter filling or ganache, it is important to deposit the hot layer first and allow it to thoroughly cool before depositing the next layer. Do not be concerned about which side will ultimately be the top; it can easily be turned over when finished.

THINK ABOUT TEXTURE When one layer is firm, such as gianduja, and another is soft, like marshmallow, the firmer layer should usually be the bottom of the finished bar. Having the firmer layer on top makes the bar more difficult to eat.

Spread each layer evenly to a thickness of no more than ⅜ inch.

CONSIDER THE HEIGHT When making a bar that has two or more layers, it is easy to wind up with a bar far too thick once all of the layers are combined and the chocolate is applied. In general, each layer should be not much more than ¼ inch to ⅜ inch thick to avoid winding up with a very heavy finished piece.

How it's finished

Once again, there is no single set-in-stone way to finish layered candy bars. Different centers and inclusions require slightly different handling techniques. In general, however, follow these steps to finish your own candy bars:

1   Remove the slab from the pan. This step is made much simpler by first lining the pan with plastic wrap (see page 51).

2   Precoat the bottom of the entire slab. Whichever side is to be the bottom of the finished bars must be coated with a thin layer of tempered chocolate or melted compound coating. Use the same chocolate in which you will enrobe the bars; for example, if enrobing in milk chocolate, precoat in milk chocolate.

After precoating the slab, place it right side up and cut into pieces with a sharp knife.

One popular finishing technique is to make waves, then garnish with toasted nuts.

3 Cut to the desired sizes. Most bars are best cut with a sharp chef's knife on a cutting board while they are right side up. When cutting a piece that contains caramel, oiling the knife lightly will help to prevent sticking.

4 Enrobe on a screen. Place the cut bars on an icing screen over a piece of parchment paper or a sheet pan. Use a ladle to pour chocolate over the bars one at a time. Allow the chocolate to run over the entire piece and let the excess run onto the paper or pan below. Any excess chocolate can be reclaimed and this ensures that the entire bar is coated with chocolate.

5 Remove from the screen. Remove each bar from the screen shortly after enrobing. If the chocolate is allowed to set on the screen the bar will be hopelessly glued to the screen and will not release in one piece. Place the freshly enrobed pieces on parchment paper to set.

6 Garnish. Bars may be garnished by any of the techniques used for any other chocolate-dipped candy (see Garnishing Master Techniques, page 42). Using a fork to make waves on the tops, sprinkling chopped nuts on the chocolate before it sets, or piping stripes of contrasting chocolate after the enrobing has set are all popular ways to finish candy bars.

7   Package. Your homemade candy bars are special, and they deserve packaging that is both attractive and protective. Package them within a day of enrobing to preserve the best freshness and appearance. Many colors and sizes of foil sheets designed for packaging candy are available and are ideal for wrapping candy bars. Cellophane sheets allow you to see the bar, and boxes that fit several bars not only protect their cargo but make an impressive presentation as a gift.

How it's stored

The storage requirements for candy bars are no different from any other chocolate-dipped candy. They must be stored at a cool room temperature and protected from humidity, temperature extremes, and light. The shelf life of candy bars depends on the centers used and can range from two weeks for a bar containing ganache to months for a bar that uses gianduja and marzipan.

Kitchen Sink Bars

Yes, everything is in here . . . peanuts, pretzels, caramel, peanut butter, and, of course, chocolate. It may seem like overkill until you try one—then you are likely to become a believer. Truly indulgent.

SKILL LEVEL

INCLUSIONS

4 oz (2½ cups) **Thin salted pretzel sticks**

6 oz (1 cup) **Dry roasted, salted peanuts**

CARAMEL

2 oz (¼ cup) **Water**

8 oz (1 cup) **Sugar**

½ **Vanilla bean, split and scraped**

7 oz (½ can; ⅔ cup) **Sweetened condensed milk**

6 oz (½ cup) **Light corn syrup**

3 oz (6 tbsp) **Butter, unsalted, soft**

½ tsp **Salt**

GIANDUJA

8 oz (¾ cup) **Peanut butter**

1 lb (1½ cups) **Milk chocolate, melted, tempered**

ENROBING AND GARNISHING

2 lb (3 cups) **Milk chocolate, melted, tempered**

---

1   Lightly brush a 9 × 13–inch baking pan with oil and line with plastic wrap (see page 51).

2   Sprinkle the pretzels and peanuts over the pan in an even layer.

3   Combine the water, sugar, vanilla bean, condensed milk, corn syrup, and butter for the caramel in a heavy-bottomed 4-quart saucepan and bring to a boil, stirring constantly.

4   Continue stirring while cooking until the batch reaches 245°F. This is a good estimation of the required tempera-ture. When the thermometer reads 240°F, begin testing the caramel using the spoon technique outlined on page 30. The cooled piece on the spoon should be firm but not hard when the caramel is properly cooked.

5   Remove from the heat and carefully remove the vanilla bean using tongs. Stir in the salt. Pour into the baking pan directly over the pretzels and peanuts so that they become embedded in the caramel.

6 Allow the caramel to cool completely to room temperature, 1 hour or longer.

7 To make the gianduja, warm the peanut butter over a hot water bath to 85°F.

8 Combine the warmed peanut butter with the tempered milk chocolate in a mixing bowl. Stir for 3 minutes by hand, using a paddle, wooden spoon, or rubber spatula.

9 Pour on top of the cooled caramel. Spread to an even layer using an offset palette knife.

10 Allow the gianduja to set until firm, about 1 hour.

11 Remove the entire slab from the pan by inverting and pulling the plastic wrap out of the pan. Leave the plastic wrap on the caramel and turn the slab so that the gianduja is up. Spread a thin layer of the chocolate for enrobing on the gianduja. Allow the chocolate to set.

12 Invert the slab so that the coated gianduja is on the bottom. Peel the plastic wrap off the caramel. Trim all edges of the slab and cut the slab down the middle lengthwise. Cut each half slab into 1-inch bars, yielding bars 1 × 4½ inches.

13 Place the bars gianduja side down on a screen. Pour the tempered milk chocolate over each piece to enrobe.

14 Remove from the screen before the chocolate sets. Place on a piece of parchment paper to set.

15 Garnish with fork marks and a sprinkling of salt. Allow the chocolate to set completely.

Keys to Success

- Add raisins or other dried fruit to the inclusions, if desired.
- Allow the caramel layer to completely cool before making the peanut butter layer.
- If the caramel is very soft when cutting, chill the slab slightly to improve ease of cutting.
- Use an oiled chef's knife for cutting.
- Be sure to remove the bars from the screen before the chocolate sets or they will be hopelessly stuck to the screen!

Marshamels

Two venerable classics in one bar—marshmallow and caramel—make this bar a chewy delight. Add toasted nuts to the caramel layer if you want additional texture.

SKILL LEVEL

CARAMEL

4 oz (½ cup) **Water**

1 lb (2 cups) **Sugar**

1 **Vanilla bean, split and scraped**

1 can (14 oz) **Sweetened condensed milk**

12 oz (1 cup) **Light corn syrup**

6 oz (12 tbsp; 1½ sticks) **Butter, unsalted, soft**

1 tsp **Salt**

MARSHMALLOW

¾ oz (3 tbsp; 3 envelopes) **Gelatin**

4 oz (½ cup) **Cold water**

12 oz (1½ cups) **Sugar**

8 oz (¾ cup) **Light corn syrup**

2 oz (⅓ cup) **Honey**

4 oz (½ cup) **Water**

1 tbsp **Vanilla extract**

ENROBING

2 lb (3 cups) **Dark chocolate, melted, tempered**

---

1 Lightly brush a 9 × 13–inch baking pan with oil and line with plastic wrap (see page 51). Oil the inside of the wrap as well.

2 Combine the water, sugar, vanilla bean, condensed milk, corn syrup, and butter for the caramel in a heavy-bottomed 4-quart saucepan and bring to a boil, stirring constantly.

3 Continue stirring while cooking until the batch reaches 245°F. This is a good estimation of the required tempera-ture. When the thermometer reads 240°F, begin testing the caramels using the spoon technique outlined on page 30. The cooled piece on the spoon should be firm but not hard when the caramel is properly cooked.

4 Remove from the heat and stir in the salt. Pour into the prepared baking pan and carefully remove the vanilla bean using tongs. Set aside to cool while you make the marsh-mallow.

5 To make the marshmallow, stir the gelatin into the cold water in a small stainless-steel bowl. Set aside.

6 Combine the sugar, corn syrup, honey, and water in a 2-quart saucepan. Cook to 250°F using the Standard Sugar Cooking Technique on page 29. Remove from the heat.

7 Pour the hot syrup into the bowl of a 5-quart mixer fitted with a whip attachment. Allow to cool undisturbed until a thermometer reads 210°F, about 15 minutes.

8 While the syrup is cooling, melt the gelatin over a hot water bath.

9 When the syrup reaches 210°F, add the melted gelatin and put the bowl on the mixer.

10 Whip on high speed until very light, about 6 minutes. Whip in the vanilla extract.

11 Remove the marshmallow from the bowl using an oiled rubber spatula and place on top of the caramel. Spread in an even layer with an oiled offset palette knife.

12 Allow to cool completely to room temperature, at least 2 hours.

13 Remove the entire slab from the pan by inverting and pulling the plastic out of the pan. Peel the plastic off the caramel.

14 Spread a thin layer of the chocolate for enrobing on the caramel. Allow the chocolate to set. Tempered chocolate should set within 8 minutes.

15 Invert the slab so that the coated caramel is on the bottom. Trim all edges of the slab and cut the slab down the middle lengthwise. Cut each half slab into 1-inch bars, yielding bars 1 × 4½ inches.

16 Place the bars caramel side down on a screen. Pour the tempered dark chocolate over each piece to enrobe.

17 Remove from the screen before the chocolate sets. Place on a piece of parchment paper to set.

18 Garnish with fork marks, then allow the chocolate to set completely.

Keys to Success

- If the slab is very soft when cutting, chill slightly to improve ease of cutting.

- Use an oiled chef's knife for cutting.

- Be sure to remove the bars from the screen before the chocolate sets or they will be hopelessly stuck to the screen!

Nutty Bars

Sounds like a watering hole for the extremely eccentric, but tastes
like a mature version of a candy bar. Nice combination!

SKILL LEVEL

CARAMEL

2 oz (¼ cup) **Water**

8 oz (1 cup) **Sugar**

½ **Vanilla bean, split and scraped**

7 oz (½ can; ⅔ cup) **Sweetened condensed milk**

6 oz (½ cup) **Light corn syrup**

3 oz (6 tbsp) **Butter, unsalted, soft**

½ tsp **Salt**

10 oz (2 cups) **Toasted whole blanched hazelnuts**

GIANDUJA

12 oz (1¼ cups) **Dark chocolate, melted, tempered**

20 oz (2 cups) **Praline paste**

ENROBING AND GARNISHING

2 lb (3 cups) **Dark chocolate, melted, tempered**

8 oz (104 each; 1¾ cups) **Toasted whole blanched hazelnuts**

---

1 Lightly brush a 9 × 13–inch baking pan with oil and line with plastic wrap (see page 51).

2 Combine the water, sugar, vanilla bean, condensed milk, corn syrup, and butter for the caramel in a heavy-bottomed 4-quart saucepan and bring to a boil, stirring constantly.

3 Continue stirring while cooking until the batch reaches 245°F. This is a good estimation of the required temperature. When the thermometer reads 240°F, begin testing the caramels using the spoon technique outlined on page 30. The cooled piece on the spoon should be firm but not hard when the caramel is properly cooked.

4 Remove from the heat, carefully remove the vanilla bean using tongs, and stir in the salt and hazelnuts. Pour into the prepared baking pan. Allow to cool completely to room temperature, about 1 hour. It is acceptable to leave the caramel covered at room temperature overnight.

5 To make the gianduja, combine the 12 oz tempered dark chocolate with the praline paste in a mixing bowl. Stir for 3 minutes by hand using a paddle, wooden spoon, or rubber spatula.

6 Pour onto the cooled caramel in the pan. Allow to set until firm, at least 1 hour.

7 Remove the entire slab from the pan by inverting and pulling the plastic out of the pan.

8 With the gianduja side up, spread a thin layer of the chocolate for enrobing on the gianduja. Allow to set, about 10 minutes.

9 Invert the slab onto a cutting board. Remove the plastic wrap from the caramel. Trim all edges of the slab and cut the slab down the middle lengthwise. Cut each half slab into 1-inch bars, yielding bars 1 × 4½ inches.

10 Place the bars caramel side up on a screen. Pour the tempered dark chocolate over each piece to enrobe.

11 Remove from the screen before the chocolate sets. Place on a piece of parchment paper to set.

12 Garnish with fork marks and whole toasted hazelnuts. Allow the chocolate to set completely.

Keys to Success

○ If the caramel is very soft when cutting, chill slightly to improve ease of cutting. Do not overchill or the gianduja will become brittle.

○ Use an oiled chef's knife for cutting.

○ Be sure to remove the bars from the screen before the chocolate sets or they will be hopelessly stuck to the screen!

PB&J Bars

Peanut butter and jelly in a candy bar—it is nearly a dream come true. Make different flavor jellies to suit your taste.

SKILL LEVEL

JELLY

1 lb (2 cups) **Raspberry puree**

24 oz (3 cups) **Sugar**

6 oz (2 envelopes; 3 oz each) **Liquid pectin** (see Keys to Success)

½ oz (1 tbsp) **Lemon juice**

GIANDUJA

8 oz (¾ cup) **Peanut butter**

1 lb (1½ cups) **Milk chocolate, melted, tempered**

ENROBING AND GARNISHING

2 lb (3 cups) **Dark chocolate, melted, tempered**

Chopped toasted unsalted peanuts, as needed

---

1 Lightly brush a 9 × 13–inch baking pan with oil and line with plastic wrap (see page 51). Oil the inside of the plastic.

2 To make the jelly, combine the raspberry puree and sugar in a 4-quart saucepan. Cook while stirring constantly to 238°F.

3 Add the pectin, return to a boil while stirring, and boil for 1 minute.

4 Add the lemon juice and remove from the heat. Pour into the prepared pan.

5 Allow to set until completely cool, at least 2 hours or longer. Leaving overnight is acceptable.

6 To make the gianduja, warm the peanut butter over a hot water bath to 85°F.

7 Combine the warmed peanut butter with the tempered milk chocolate in a mixing bowl. Stir for 3 minutes by hand using a paddle, wooden spoon, or rubber spatula.

8 Pour on top of the cooled jelly. Spread in an even layer using an offset palette knife.

9 Allow the gianduja to set until firm, about 1 hour.

10 Remove the entire slab from the pan by inverting and pulling the plastic out of the pan.

11 Leave the plastic wrap on the jelly and turn the slab so that the gianduja is up. Spread a thin layer of the chocolate for enrobing on the gianduja. Allow the chocolate to set.

12 Invert the slab onto a cutting board so that the coated gianduja is on the bottom. Peel the plastic wrap off the jelly. Trim all edges of the slab and cut the slab down the middle lengthwise. Cut each half slab into 1-inch bars, yielding bars 1 × 4½ inches.

13 Place the bars gianduja side down on a screen. Pour the chocolate for enrobing over each piece to enrobe.

14 Remove from the screen before the chocolate sets. Place on a piece of parchment paper to set.

15 Garnish with fork marks and a sprinkle of chopped toasted peanuts. Allow the chocolate to set completely.

Keys to Success

- Sold under brand names such as Certo and Ball, liquid pectin is commonly available in grocery stores.

- Open the envelopes of pectin and have them ready so that they can be added quickly when needed.

- Jellies scorch easily. Moderate the heat during boiling, and keep the bottom of the saucepan clean using a heat-resistant rubber spatula.

- Be sure to have your pan prepared before beginning to cook; the jellies begin to set immediately once they are cooked.

- Allow the jelly to cool completely before making the peanut butter layer.

- Dipping your knife in warm water and drying before each cut will make cutting easier.

- Be sure to remove the bars from the screen before the chocolate sets or they will be hopelessly stuck to the screen!

Peanut Butter Goodness

MAKES 26 BARS

Peanut butter nougat with caramel and peanuts: The name
says it all. This one is for the dedicated peanut fans.

SKILL LEVEL

NOUGAT

1 Large egg white

9 oz (¾ cup) Light corn syrup, divided

1 tbsp Vanilla extract

8 oz (1 cup) Granulated sugar

4 oz (½ cup) Water

3 oz (¼ cup) Molasses

1 oz (½ cup) Milk powder

1 oz (¼ cup) Confectioners' sugar

6 oz (¾ cup) Peanut butter

CARAMEL

4 oz (½ cup) Water

1 lb (2 cups) Granulated sugar

1 Vanilla bean, split and scraped

1 can (14 oz) Sweetened condensed milk

12 oz (1 cup) Light corn syrup

6 oz (12 tbsp, 1½ sticks) Butter, unsalted, soft

1 tsp Salt

12 oz (2 cups) Unsalted toasted whole peanuts

ENROBING AND GARNISHING

2 lb (3 cups) Milk chocolate, melted, tempered

4 oz (¼ cup) Chopped unsalted toasted peanuts

---

1 Lightly brush a 9 × 13–inch baking pan with oil and line
with plastic wrap (see page 51).

2 To make the nougat, combine the egg white with 3 oz/¼
cup of the corn syrup and the vanilla extract in the bowl of
a 5-quart mixer fitted with a whip attachment. Do not begin
whipping yet.

3 Combine the granulated sugar, water, the remaining 6 oz/½ cup corn syrup, and the molasses in a 2-quart saucepan, cover, and bring to a boil without stirring. Remove the lid and insert a thermometer.

4 When the syrup reaches 233°F, begin whipping the egg white mixture on high speed.

5 Continue cooking the syrup until it reaches 255°F. Remove immediately from the heat and pour the hot syrup into the whipping egg white mixture in a constant stream.

6 Continue whipping for 4 minutes after all the syrup has been added.

7 While the egg white mixture whips, sift together the milk powder and confectioners' sugar.

8 Remove the bowl from the mixer and fold in the milk powder mixture by hand using a rubber spatula.

9 Mix in the peanut butter by hand using a rubber spatula.

10 Spread in the prepared baking pan using an offset palette knife.

11 Combine the water, sugar, vanilla bean, condensed milk, corn syrup, and butter for the caramel in a heavy-bottomed 4-quart saucepan and bring to a boil, stirring constantly.

12 Continue stirring while cooking until the batch reaches 245°F. This is a good estimation of the required temperature. When the thermometer reads 240°F, begin testing the caramel using the spoon technique outlined on page 30. The cooled piece on the spoon should be firm but not hard when the caramel is properly cooked.

13 Remove from the heat, stir in the salt, and carefully remove the vanilla bean using tongs. Stir in the peanuts. Pour the caramel on top of the nougat.

14 Allow the slab to cool to room temperature, about 2 hours.

15 Remove the entire slab from the pan by inverting and pulling the plastic wrap out of the pan.

16 Leave the plastic wrap on the nougat and turn the slab so that the caramel is up. Spread a thin layer of the chocolate for enrobing on the caramel. Allow the chocolate to set.

17 Invert the slab so that the coated caramel is on the bottom. Peel the plastic wrap off the nougat. Trim all edges of the slab and cut the slab down the middle lengthwise. Cut each half slab into 1-inch bars, yielding bars 1 × 4½ inches.

18 Place the bars caramel side down on a screen. Pour the chocolate for enrobing over each piece.

19 Remove from the screen before the chocolate sets. Place on a piece of parchment paper to set.

20 Garnish with fork marks and sprinkle with chopped peanuts. Allow the chocolate to set completely.

Keys to Success

- Stream the hot syrup down the inside edge of the mixing bowl so that it goes into the whites and not on the whip or bowl.

- Allow the slab to cool completely before cutting. It is fine to leave it covered overnight at room temperature, as long as it is protected from humidity.

- If the caramel is very soft when cutting, chill slightly to improve ease of cutting.

- Use an oiled chef's knife for cutting.

- Be sure to remove the bars from the screen before the chocolate sets or they will be hopelessly stuck to the screen!

Cocomels

Coconut and caramel team up for a sensational chocolate bar.
Chewy, rich, sweet, and tropical, this one is hard not to love.

SKILL LEVEL

COCONUT

2 oz (¼ cup) Water

6 oz (¾ cup) Sugar

12 oz (1 cup) Light corn syrup

1 lb (4 cups) Sweetened shredded coconut

2 oz (½ cup) Marshmallow creme

1 tsp Vanilla extract

CARAMEL

2 oz (¼ cup) Water

8 oz (1 cup) Sugar

½ Vanilla bean, split and scraped

7 oz (½ can; ⅔ cup) Sweetened condensed milk

6 oz (½ cup) Light corn syrup

3 oz (6 tbsp) Butter, unsalted, soft

½ tsp Salt

ENROBING AND GARNISHING

2 lb (3 cups) Dark chocolate, melted, tempered

Sweetened shredded coconut, as needed

---

1 Lightly brush a 9 × 13–inch baking pan with oil and line with plastic wrap (see page 51).

2 Combine the water, sugar, and corn syrup for the coconut in a 2-quart saucepan and bring to a boil, stirring constantly. Cover the pan and continue boiling for 3 minutes. Remove the lid, insert a thermometer, and continue cooking until the mixture reaches 245°F.

3 Remove from the heat and stir in the coconut using a rubber spatula. Mix in the marshmallow creme.

4 Pour the mixture into the prepared baking pan and spread it evenly with an offset palette knife.

5 Combine the water, sugar, vanilla bean, condensed milk, corn syrup, and butter for the caramel in a heavy-bottomed 4-quart saucepan and bring to a boil, stirring constantly.

6   Continue stirring while cooking until the batch reaches 245°F. This is a good estimation of the required temperature. When the thermometer reads 240°F, begin testing the caramel using the spoon technique outlined on page 30. The cooled piece on the spoon should be firm but not hard when the caramel is properly cooked.

7   Remove from the heat and stir in the salt. Pour into the pan on top of the coconut mixture and carefully remove the vanilla bean using tongs.

8   Allow to cool completely to room temperature, at least 2 hours.

9   Remove the entire slab from the pan by inverting and pulling the plastic out of the pan.

10 Leave the plastic wrap on the coconut and turn the slab so that the caramel is up. Spread a thin layer of the tempered chocolate on the caramel. Allow the chocolate to set.

11 Invert the slab so that the coated caramel is on the bottom. Peel the plastic wrap off the coconut. Trim all edges of the slab and cut the slab down the middle lengthwise. Cut each half slab into 1-inch bars, yielding bars 1 × 4½ inches.

12 Place the bars caramel side down on a screen. Pour the chocolate over each piece to enrobe.

13 Remove from the screen before the chocolate sets. Place on a piece of parchment paper to set.

14 Garnish with fork marks and a few shreds of coconut. Allow the chocolate to set completely.

Keys to Success

○ If the slab is very soft when cutting, chill slightly to improve ease of cutting.

○ Use an oiled chef's knife for cutting.

○ Be sure to remove the bars from the screen before the chocolate sets or they will be hopelessly stuck to the screen!

Glossary

AGAR Binding agent extracted from sea vegetables.

AGITATION Vigorous stirring or working on the table to induce crystallization.

BLOOM (CHOCOLATE) Gray streaks or spots on the surface of chocolate caused by improper handling or storage. *See also* Fat bloom, Sugar bloom.

BLOOM (GELATIN) To hydrate gelatin prior to use by mixing it with water.

CACAO Refers to the tree *Theobroma cacao* and the raw products that come directly from that tree, such as its fruit, the cacao pod, and the beans before fermentation.

CARAMEL Sugar (sucrose) that has turned brown and developed flavor due to exposure to heat. Caramel is brittle and glass-like when at room temperature.

CARAMELS Common name for soft caramels, which contain no caramel at all but develop their color and flavor as a result of Maillard browning.

CENTER Any object that is dipped in, or will be dipped in, chocolate to make a confection.

CHOCOLATE LIQUOR Unsweetened chocolate.

COATING A commonly used shortened name for compound coating.

COCOA Refers to products made from fermented cocoa beans (cocoa powder, cocoa butter, etc.). Also a legally allowable name for cocoa powder.

COCOA BUTTER The fat found in, and extracted from, cocoa beans.

COCOA NIBS Small pieces of the edible portion of the cocoa bean.

COMPOUND COATING A chocolate substitute in which all or most of the cocoa butter has been replaced by another type of hard fat. Compound coatings do not require as meticulous tempering as does chocolate, but they do not have as fine a flavor or mouthfeel.

CONFIT Literally means "preserved." Refers to citrus skins that have been blanched and simmered in heavy syrup to sweeten, tenderize, and preserve them.

COUVERTURE A European term that denotes chocolate meeting the highest standards of ingredients. The term has no legal standing in American standards of identity.

CRIOLLO The variety of cocoa bean that is generally regarded as being of the highest quality.

CRYSTALLIZE To transform from the amorphous state to the crystalline state with a regularly repeating internal arrangement of its atoms. Sugar crystallizes under the proper conditions. Cocoa butter crystallizes when chocolate sets.

DOCTOR An ingredient added to help prevent the crystallization of sugar. Common examples are cream of tartar and corn syrup.

DUTCH PROCESSING Treating cacao with an alkali to reduce its acidity.

ENROBE To cover with chocolate.

EXTRACT A flavoring agent made by extracting the volatile flavor compounds of a substance, such as vanilla, using a solvent.

FAT BLOOM Bloom on chocolate that is caused by improper tempering or by exposure to heat.

FAT-SOLUBLE COLOR A color that will dissolve in fat. Suitable for use when coloring chocolate.

FLAVONOID A type of antioxidant. Cacao is a rich source of flavonoids.

FORASTERO The most prominent commercial variety of cacao grown.

FRAPPE An aerator, similar to meringue, added to some confections.

GANACHE A mixture of chocolate and cream.

GELATIN A binding agent derived from animal collagen.

GIANDUJA Chocolate mixed with finely ground nut paste.

INCLUSION An ingredient added as a garnish that remains discrete in the finished product.

INVERSION Breaking down sucrose into fructose and dextrose. Cooking sugar with an acid inverts some of the sugar.

INVERTASE An enzyme derived from yeast that inverts sugar. It is used to soften or liquefy centers after enrobing.

MAILLARD REACTION (also Maillard browning) A reaction between amino acids found in proteins and certain sugars to create brown color and roasted or caramelized flavors.

MANUFACTURED FLAVOR A flavoring agent that has been manufactured to resemble the fragrance of something. May be labeled "natural" or "artificial" depending on the source of the chemicals used.

MELTAWAY A type of center made by combining chocolate with coconut fat. It is characterized by its rapid melt-in-the-mouth texture.

PECTIN A binding agent extracted from fruit, usually either apples or citrus skins.

PERCENTAGE When listed on a label, percentage indicates the amount of chocolate liquor plus cocoa butter in the chocolate.

PISTOLES Nearly flat pellets of chocolate. A convenient form for buying chocolate because they do not require chopping before melting.

PRALINE A crystalline confection indigenous to the southern United States, traditionally containing brown sugar and pecans.

PRALINÉ European term for a center covered in chocolate. May also be known as bonbons or simply chocolates.

PRALINE PASTE A smooth paste of caramelized sugar and ground nuts, most commonly hazelnuts.

PULL To repeatedly stretch and fold together candy or taffy to incorporate air and lighten the texture and color.

RANCIDITY Degradation of fats due to exposure to heat, light, or oxygen. Rancidity causes off-flavors.

SEED To introduce crystals to promote further crystallization. When tempering chocolate, it is seeded to cause the cocoa butter to crystallize properly.

SHORT TEXTURE Crumbling or breaking easily in the mouth. The opposite of a chewy texture.

SINGLE ORIGIN A chocolate containing cocoa beans from one nation, location, or plantation.

SUGAR BLOOM Bloom on chocolate that is caused by exposure to excessive humidity or other sources of moisture.

SUMMER COATING Another name sometimes used for compound coating (*see* Compound coating).

TEMPER To cool and seed chocolate so that it sets with the desired snap and shine.

TRANSFER SHEET A plastic sheet that is silk-screened with a design of colored cocoa butter. Used to make colorful designs on chocolates.

TRINITARIO A hybrid variety of cocoa bean parented by Forastero and Criollo beans.

TRUFFLE A ganache center that has been shaped to be round and is dipped in chocolate. May be finished with any of a variety of finishes.

WAFER PAPER Thin sheets of edible paper-like material made from starch. Wafer paper is commonly used as a covering for nougat such as torrone.

WATER-SOLUBLE COLOR A color that dissolves in water. Suitable for use in most confectionery applications such as hard candy. Not suitable for use in chocolate.

Resources

Online resources for candy making ingredients and supplies, including molds and packaging.

General supplies: molds, packaging, and flavorings, catering specifically to home confectioners

CANDY LAND CRAFTS
www.candylandcrafts.com

CANDY MOLD CENTRAL
www.CandyMoldCentral.com

CHOCOLATE CANDY SUPPLY
www.ChocolateCandySupply.com

CONFECTIONERY HOUSE
www.confectioneryhouse.com

KITCHEN KRAFTS
www.kitchenkrafts.com

SUGARCRAFT
www.sugarcraft.com

WILTON
www.wilton.com

Professional candy making ingredients, supplies, and equipment

PASTRY CHEF CENTRAL
www.pastrychef.com—carries a wide selection of professional tools and bulk ingredients.

TOMRIC PLASTICS
www.tomric.com—the best online source for chocolate molds of every description, as well as professional tools and bulk chocolate.

Purchasing chocolate

CHOCOSPHERE
www.chocosphere.com—carries a wide range of chocolates from around the world in various size packaging from bars to bulk.

GUITTARD CHOCOLATE
www.guittard.com—carries the full line of Guittard chocolates.

PASTRY CHEF CENTRAL
www.pastrychef.com—carries Cacao Barry chocolates in bulk blocks.

PASTRY CHEF WAREHOUSE
www.pastrychefwarehouse.com—carries Guittard, Schokinag, and Callebaut chocolates in bulk forms.

TOMRIC PLASTICS
www.tomric.com—carries New World Chocolates in bulk packaging of pistoles.

Index

Page numbers in *italics* indicate
illustrations.

A

Acids, in hard candy, 91
Aerated confections. *See* Divinity;
    Marshmallows; Nougat
Agar, 12
Agar jellies, 168–169, 171
Almond(s)
    Amigos (variation), 221
    Dragées, 205, 226–227, *227*
    Marzipan, Cherry-, 212, *217*
    in Nougat Torrone, *182*, 183–184
    Tamari-Sesame (variation), 228
    toasting, 50
Almond Butter
    Amigos, Almond (variation), 221
    Gianduja (variation), 218
    Gianduja, Layered, 219, *220*
Almond Paste
    about, 13
    in gianduja, 198
    in marzipan, 196–197, 211
Althaea officinalis, 157
Amigos, 221
    Almond (variation), 221
    Cashew (variation), 221
    Peanut Butter (variation), 221
Antioxidants, in chocolate, 19
Apples
    Candy-Coated, 110, *111*
    Caramel, 104, *111*, 122
    Caramel, Chocolate-Coated (variation),
        122
    Caramel, with Nuts (variation), 122
Artificial sweeteners, 9

B

Baked goods, inclusions in candy, 8
Baking pans, 4
    lining with plastic wrap, 51
Baking soda
    in brittle, 96
    in caramel, 98, 208
    in sponge candy, 163
Bark, 88
    about, 59–60, *61*
    Peppermint, *86*, 87
    toppings, 88
Barley sugar, 95
Binding agents, 12
Bittersweet chocolate, 21
Black-and-Tan Dipped Confit (variation),
    194
Black Forest Truffles, *66*, 67
Black Pearls, 256
Bloom, on chocolate, 25, 26, 65
Bowls, mixing, 4
Brittle
    about, 96–97
    Cocoa Nibs (variation), 113
    Maillard browning in, 98
    Peanut, *112*, 113
    Pecan (variation), 113
    Sesame (variation), 113
Brown sugar, 9, *10*
Buckeyes, 222, *223*
    about, 200–201
    problems, 210
Butter
    in brittle, 96
    in caramels, soft, 103
    selecting, 11
    in toffee, 99
    in truffle centers, 54
Buttercreams, 249
Buttercrunch, 99
    Pecan, 114

C

Cacao, 20
Cacao percentage, 22–23
Candied Fruit, 14
    in Bark, 88
    garnishing with, 49
    Pineapple, in Marzipan Squares,
        Tropical, 213
    in T'ings, 80, *81*
Candy Bars, Layered
    assembly of, *265*, 265
    centers for, 264
    Cocomels, 283–284, *285*
    finishing techniques, 265–267, *266*
    Kitchen Sink Bars, *268*, 269–270
    Marshamels, 271–272, *273*
    Nutty Bars, *274*, 275–276
    PB&J Bars, 277–278, *279*
    Peanut Butter Goodness, *280*, 281–282
    storage of, 267
Candy Canes, Crushed, in Peppermint
    Bark, *86*, 87
Candy-Coated Fruits, *108*, 109. *See also*
    Caramel Apples
    Apples, 110, *111*
    cherries, in fondant, 129, *130*
    dipping technique, 93–94, *94*
Caramel(s), Soft, 120–121, *121*. *See also*
    Caramel Apples
    about, 103–104
    in Candy Bars
        Cocomels, 283–284, *285*
        Kitchen Sink Bars, *268*, 269–270
        Marshamels, 271–272, *273*
        Nutty Bars, *174*, 275–276
        Peanut Butter Goodness, *280*,
            281–282
    Chocolate (variation), 120
    Coffee (variation), 120
    in dragées, 205–207, *207*
    Fruit (variation), 120
    Maillard browning, 98